Rebellious Cooks and Recipe Writing in Communist Bulgaria

Food in Modern History: Traditions and Innovations

Series Editors
Peter Scholliers
Amy Bentley

This new monograph series pays serious attention to food as a focal point in historical events from the late 18th century to present day.

Employing the lens of technology broadly construed, the series highlights the nutritional, social, political, cultural, and economic transformations of food around the globe. It features new scholarship that considers ever-intensifying and accelerating tensions between tradition and innovation that characterize the modern era. The editors are particularly committed to publishing manuscripts featuring geographical areas currently underrepresented in English-language academic publications, including the Global South, particularly Africa and Asia, as well as monographs featuring indigenous and under-represented groups, and non-western societies.

Forthcoming

Food and Aviation in the Twentieth Century: The Pan American Ideal,
Bryce Evans (2021)

Rebellious Cooks and Recipe Writing in Communist Bulgaria

Albena Shkodrova

BLOOMSBURY ACADEMIC
LONDON • NEW YORK • OXFORD • NEW DELHI • SYDNEY

BLOOMSBURY ACADEMIC
Bloomsbury Publishing Plc
50 Bedford Square, London, WC1B 3DP, UK
1385 Broadway, New York, NY 10018, USA
29 Earlsfort Terrace, Dublin 2, Ireland

BLOOMSBURY, BLOOMSBURY ACADEMIC and the Diana logo are trademarks of
Bloomsbury Publishing Plc

First published in Great Britain 2021
This paperback edition published 2022

Copyright © Albena Shkodrova, 2021

Albena Shkodrova has asserted her right under the Copyright, Designs and Patents Act, 1988, to be identified as Author of this work.

For legal purposes the Acknowledgements on p. x constitute an extension of this copyright page.

Cover image: A page from the old scrapbook of Tamara Ganeva. Photo by Albena Shkodrova
Cover design: Terry Woodley

All rights reserved. No part of this publication may be reproduced or transmitted in any form or by any means, electronic or mechanical, including photocopying, recording, or any information storage or retrieval system, without prior permission in writing from the publishers.

Bloomsbury Publishing Plc does not have any control over, or responsibility for, any third-party websites referred to or in this book. All internet addresses given in this book were correct at the time of going to press. The author and publisher regret any inconvenience caused if addresses have changed or sites have ceased to exist, but can accept no responsibility for any such changes.

A catalogue record for this book is available from the British Library.

Library of Congress Cataloging-in-Publication Data
Names: Shkodrova, Albena, author.
Title: Rebellious cooks and recipe writing in communist Bulgaria / Albena Shkodrova.
Description: London ; New York, NY : Bloomsbury Academic, 2021. | Series: Food in modern history : Traditions and innovations | Includes bibliographical references and index. | Summary: "Albena Shkodrova shows how many women in communist Bulgaria passionately exchanged recipes to build substantial private collections, a borderline contraband activity under a regime where home cooking was considered household slavery and an agent of patriarchalism. Drawing on primary sources, including scrapbook cookbooks, and working from the establishment of cookery classes before communism to their obliteration thereafter, Shkodrova highlights the meaning behind recipe exchange and home cooking for Bulgarian women under the communist regime" – Provided by publisher.
Identifiers: LCCN 2020037975 (print) | LCCN 2020037976 (ebook) | ISBN 9781350132306 (hardback) | ISBN 9781350205444 (paperback) | ISBN 9781350132313 (ebook) | ISBN 9781350132320 (epub)
Subjects: LCSH: Cooking, Bulgarian. | Cooking—Bulgaria.
Classification: LCC TX723.5.B8 S54 2021 (print) | LCC TX723.5.B8 (ebook) | DDC 641.59499—dc23
LC record available at https://lccn.loc.gov/2020037975
LC ebook record available at https://lccn.loc.gov/2020037976

ISBN:	HB:	978-1-3501-3230-6
	PB:	978-1-3502-0544-4
	ePDF:	978-1-3501-3231-3
	ePub:	978-1-3501-3232-0

Typeset by RefineCatch Limited, Bungay, Suffolk

To find out more about our authors and books visit www.bloomsbury.com and sign up for our newsletters.

To Lode Desmet, who brings me coffee in bed every morning and lets me be myself
To Elena Shkodrova, who sometimes started cooking at 4 AM
To Yana, Elena-Mie and Artuur, who kept this book concise

Albena Shkodrova is a historian and a writer. After a career in political journalism, she worked as a travel writer and was for eight years the editor in chief of Bulgaria's food and wine magazine Bacchus. She is the author of the popular book *Communist Gourmet* (2014), a bestseller in Bulgaria, and of popular and academic articles on social history of food and everyday life, published in *Gastronomica, Food, Culture and Society, Food and History*, and *Appetite*. She has been a member of the research groups Social and Cultural History of Food (FOST) and Modernity and Society 1800–2000 (MoSa) in Belgium and is currently a researcher at the Centre for Social Movements in Bochum, Germany.

Contents

List of Figures	viii
Acknowledgements	x
Behind the Communist Kitchens' Steamy Windows	1

Part One. The Context

Cooking Advice in Bulgaria	17
Recipe Manuscripts Take the Lead	47

Part Two. Home Cooking Between Cookbooks and Scrapbooks

Recipe Collection as an Instrument	69

Part Three. The Meanings of Scrapbooks

Navigating the Context	91
Managing Budgets	121
Scrapbooks as Social Capital	133
Entertaining, Indulging and Creating the Self	149

Part Four. What Made Scrapbooks Indispensable

Cookbooks versus Scrapbooks?	167
Communist Foodways as an Act of Resistance	171
References	173
Index	187

Figures

1. The preferences shown in the use of different sources of culinary information in Bulgaria during late communism, as revealed by a national poll, conducted in 2017 for this research. — 6
2. The trends in cookbook publishing in communist Bulgaria, comparing literature addressing professional cooks, with recipe collections for home cooking (new titles). — 23
3. A poster by Simeon Krustev from 1978, reading 'STOP! Not during working hours!' Courtesy: Collection Socmus (*www.socmus.coc*) — 45
4. Domestic trade in foodstuffs in Bulgaria between 1952 and 1988. — 49
5. The table shows the structure of the recipe collections acquired during the research (except for two incomplete copies). — 59
6. Comparison between recipes, taken from the five cookbooks most available to the households in the study group, and recipes in the scrapbooks (according to the type of dish). — 72
7. Comparison between the desserts and dough-based dishes taken from the five cookbooks most available to the households in the study group, and those in their scrapbooks. — 73
8. The diagram on the left (from Zafirka Peneva's scrapbook) shows several designs for cakes. The drawing on the right comes with a recipe for a cake, shaped as a rabbit (from Elisaveta Shkodrova's scrapbook). Drawings were also used to capture the preparation of pâte feuilleté. — 76
9. A recipe, written on a ticket from the Naval Museum in Varna, 1976, from the scrapbook of Elisaveta Shkodrova. — 79
10. A recipe, written on the back of a blood test template, from the collection of Lyubka Georgieva. — 79
11. The cover of *Home Preservation of Meat and Fish* (1959) by Marin Marinov and a dedication, penned by the author to another man, a Dr Zabunov, which reads: 'To use in case of need'. — 98
12. Proportion of recipes for the main categories of dishes in the collections examined for this research. — 151
13. A page of political satire, kept between the pages of Kristin Razsolkova's scrapbook (left) and pages from Tamara Ganeva's cookbook with the

manifesto of the dissident Ecoglasnost (right). The following pages were
   torn out under circumstances which Tamara Ganeva does not remember. 156

14 The diagram reflects some of the ways in which the individual narrators
   remember interacting with their inner and outer social circles, while
   negotiating and shaping their foodways. 165

Acknowledgements

I am deeply beholden for advice and support to Peter Scholliers of the Free University of Brussels and Yves Segers of the KU Leuven. Without their trust in this project, this book would not have been possible.

All across Bulgaria, people generously shared with me their time, life stories, recipes, and often food, for which I am greatly indebted: warm gratitude to Arie Babechka, Bozhurka Velkova, Cathy Ivanova and Neva Mitcheva, Danieka Lyubenova and Lyubka Georgieva, Danya Lam, Dobrinka and Presian Boevi, Ekaterina and Atanaska Terzievi, Elena Salmadzhiyska, Elisaveta Shkodrova, Fatme Ali, Kristin Razsolkova, Lilia and Daniela Denchevi, Mara Tseneva, Maya and Violeta Kaloferovi, Maya and Vasilena Mirchevi, Nedyalka Malcheva and Pepa Peneva, Olga Nikolova, Pepa Mutafchieva, Petya and Yordanka Tsachevi, Silvia and Ivanka Atipovi, Sofia Panayotova-Beneva, Sofia and Veselina Georgievi, Svetoslav Pintev and Vanya Pinteva, Tamara Ganeva, Tsveta Tanovska, Velichka Hristova and Kalina Kechova! I will always perceive the hours, spent with them, as a privilege.

This book has benefitted greatly from the inspiring conversations with, and insightful remarks and encouragement from Martin Kahlrausch, Rayna Gavrilova, Ruth Oldenziel and Paul Erdkamp. I owe much to Iva Rudnikova and Economedia for setting me on the path of investigating the social history of food and supporting for many years my work for *Bacchus* – our encounter so many years ago was one of the happiest happenstances in my life.

Thanks to Nikola Mihov and Nikolay Grigorov of 'Raketa', 'Fabrika Duga' and 'Cosmos' in Sofia for their enthusiastic support of my work on Bulgarian communist food, and for the means and time they invested in supplying visual material for my several projects.

This book would not have materialised without the warm and kind support which my husband Lode Desmet has always given me. I particularly appreciate that despite his many and brilliant film projects, his tight schedules and stressful periods of intense work, he has always found a way to give me space and time to work – and be who I am: so this book is dedicated to him. I also dedicate it to the memory of my mother Elena Shkodrova, who is responsible for my earliest memories of communist cooking and cuisine. To my children Artuur, Elena-Mie and Yana this book owes its conciseness!

Albena Shkodrova

BEHIND THE COMMUNIST KITCHENS' STEAMY WINDOWS

In 2012 a friend put a book in my hands – a kind of book I had never seen before. It was a volume the size of a standard A4 sheet, with hard covers, bound in blue cloth and with faded golden letters that read *Cooking Recipes*. I knew straight away that it was a *samizdat*[1] book: it had the typical appearance that the book-binders in one of the small streets off Klement Gottwald boulevard in Sofia in the 1980s gave to everything from a master's thesis to a collection of valued magazines. But I had never seen a cookbook made this way.

Opening it brought further surprises. Just like a printed book, it had a title page, on which *Gotvarski retsepti* (Cooking Recipes) was typewritten, followed by a dedication in handwriting: '*And don't forget the old saying that 'Love passes through the stomach'*.[2] Then followed a table of contents: fourteen sections, dedicated to generic categories ('starters', 'soups' and 'mains') or more specific groups of dishes ('jellies', 'cookies, biscuits, buns, pastry and others', 'juices', 'cakes, rolls and parfaits'), with several sheets of 'Useful advice' at the end. There were 115 pages, most of which were typewritten and the rest were clippings from the press.

Consumed with curiosity, I arranged a meeting with my friend's mother, Cathy Ivanova. A Sofianite in her 70s, she spoke sophisticated Bulgarian and had the air of modesty and slight insecurity in social interaction typical of her generation – which is also the generation of my mother. Cathy Ivanova told me that she had made three copies of the book for her family. Some of her colleagues also made facsimiles, and as this happened on several occasions, in the end she lost track of how many times her book was reproduced.

To me she gave two folders: one, containing the recipes as they were typed, written, collected through the years, and the other with the laid out pages, which were used as a prototype for all the further copies. They were numbered A4 sheets with typewritten recipes or glued-on clippings.

My acquaintance with this astonishing work came during a broad research project on food under communism (Shkodrova 2014), which later brought me to another avid

---

[1] *Samizdat* was the name for the non-official publishing and distribution of various, often subversive, texts during the communist regimes in 20th century Eastern Europe.
[2] In all cases, when sources or works written in languages other than English are quoted, and unless otherwise indicated, the translation is mine.

collector of recipes, Tamara Ganeva. Slightly younger than Cathy, Tamara had left Bulgaria in the 1990s and had settled in Paris with her husband, the painter Valentin Ganev. In September 2012 I met her in a café in Brussels: she had come to visit one of her daughters, who studied there. Similarly to other Bulgarian immigrant women from her generation, Tamara had fashioned a specific style that combined the homeliness of a Bulgarian housewife, as I knew it from my childhood, with a certain worldliness and elegance. She clearly felt at home in the arty chic of the Brussels café – something that would hardly have been the case for her schoolmates still living in Bulgaria.

Some time into our conversation Tamara opened her bag and took out a sheet of self-adhesive sticker paper, on which she had written a recipe. She explained that she had a personal collection, of which she kept three copies – one for herself and one for each of her daughters, who already lived independently. As she kept adding content to her scrapbook, she also offered it to her children – the sticker paper was aimed to occupy a new page in the scrapbook of her daughter living in Brussels.

We spoke of her family life in communist Bulgaria, where she grew up and married. It was during these reminiscences that Tamara Ganeva told me a story. She and her husband were not quite loyal to the regime – they often criticized it in their closer social circle, just as many other Bulgarians, including my own parents, did. Ganevi had befriended a rebellious, outspoken poet from Burgas. Discovering their close relationship with him, agents of *Durzhavna Sigurnost*, the State Security service, searched their apartment. When in the last months of the regime the Bulgarian dissident movement Ecoglasnost was founded, Gorbachov's *perestroika* seemed to be already breathing liminality into Eastern Europe, but the communist state was still holding its firm grip on politics. Tamara Ganeva felt excited by the news of an emerging dissident movement: she could feel that things were shifting, but also feared she might be wrong. She felt the urge to make things tangible, so she copied the Association act and the list of the founding members of Ecoglasnost. Fearing further searches of her family apartment, she decided to conceal it in her scrapbook with her cooking recipes. 'I thought nobody will think of searching there', she explained.

On the same shelf, among recipes and cookbooks, she hid her copy of *Fascism* by Zhelyu Zhelev. This book by the man who later became the first democratically elected Bulgarian president, was published in 1982. Soon afterwards it was pulled out of the bookstores and destroyed. The state censors thought that while describing fascism, Zhelev's work made subversive references to the Eastern European communist regimes (which it did!).

The stories of Tamara Ganeva and Cathy Ivanova presented me with a puzzle. During my research I had studied the content of the popular women's magazine *Zhenata dnes* (The Woman Today), which has been in continuous publication since 1949. I had also examined numerous cookbooks, released by the state-run publishing houses of the communist state. I had marvelled at the multiple ways in which they had tried to discourage women from cooking – at first with the revolutionary feminist idea of liberating women from their slavery at the stove, later promoting their version of modernity, expressed in appeals to be efficient and spend the minimum amount of time in the kitchen, as well as making use of the available (sometimes only on paper) industrially processed food. I had found that until the middle of the 1980s cookbooks concentrated only on the nutritional value of food, and even when discussing taste, it had been in the light of its faculty for improving digestion. All this had made me wonder how this zealous engagement with home cooking could be interpreted. Was it simply a case of need? Was it the pressure of preserving patriarchal family order in Bulgaria? Or was it a method of self-identification? And if it was part of the role in which women wanted to see themselves, how did it relate to the prevailing ideology, which after all was maintained as a façade of the regime until its very end? Could it be, I asked myself, that the blatant contradiction between their vigorous cooking and the tenets of Marxism-Leninism was a form of incompliance, a kind of insubordination, even resistance?

The 'kitchen dissidence' was a widespread practice under communism, as I can confirm from my own experience at the time. My own family was indulging in it – political discussions which died out as soon as the doorbell rang, and clandestine listening to jammed broadcasts by the forbidden 'Western' Radio Free Europe, Deutsche Welle or the BBC were taking place in our kitchen and bred in me the misconception that I lived in a world where reason reigned. This delusion was promptly dispelled when I reached the age of twelve – a moment in life, when every student in communist Bulgaria underwent an ideological test to join the youth organization KOMSOMOL. Asked to comment on the imposition of martial law in Poland in 1981, I gave the explanation I had overheard from the BBC – an innocent mistake, made only two years after dissident writer Georgi Markov was murdered by the Bulgarian secret services for his BBC broadcasts. I did not join the KOMSOMOL that year, but I learned to distinguish between the things which I think and the things I should say – an early lesson in communist society's hypocrisy and an initiation into its cynicism.

Later I found similar reflections on kitchens as political refuges in the Soviet Union, in Svetlana Alexievich's *Secondhand Time: The Last of the Soviets* (2016). '1960s dissident life is the kitchen life', she wrote. 'Thanks, Khrushchev! He's the one who led us out of the communal apartments: under his rule, we got our own private kitchens where we could criticize the government and, most importantly, not be afraid, because in the kitchen you were always among friends ... We grew up in the kitchens and our children did, too ... we played Vysotsky[3], turned on to illegal BBC broadcasts. We talked about everything: how shitty things were, the meaning of life, whether everyone could all be happy' (Alexievich 2016: 41).

Indeed, to conceptualize the kitchen as a space for some kind of subdued disobedience seemed acceptable – many a researcher has argued that it was an arena of contestation within the cold war (Oldenziel and Zachmann 2009 as one example). To identify resistance in cooking practices, though, seemed problematic. I did remember my mother and many of her friends criticizing the communist state, or ridiculing it. But I never thought of their cooking as if it were sabotage. Yet the stories of Cathy Ivanova and Tamara Ganeva made me wonder.

Eventually a research project, inspired by their stories, brought me to the discovery that recipe exchange was overwhelmingly popular, a social phenomenon, a way to communicate: if in other parts of the world people would chatter about the weather, in Bulgaria women traded cookery advice. This part of their social communication was

[3] Vladimir Vysotsky (1938–1980) was an important Russian songwriter and singer, the Soviet analogue of Bob Dylan, whose lyrics often contained irony and expressed criticism of life in the Soviet Union, hidden behind poetic metaphors.

common, zealous and extensive and many women spoke to me about it as routine. A myriad of uniform replies informed me that women traded recipes 'By all means', 'At any time!', 'Almost daily!', 'Anywhere'. They would launch the exchange 'wherever' they met, they would write recipes on and with 'whatever [was] at hand'.[4]

Most women whom I interviewed, started their collections when they undertook the responsibility to cook – for themselves or for their families. The luckier among them were able to use and build on similar collections from previous generations, but many just began from scratch. Getting married or having children, which created demand for more and versatile cooking, tended to intensify their participation in recipe exchange.

The exchange of recipes occurred typically within the family circle, between friends or at the workplace – the main locations where women spent time. The sources were though not necessarily close contacts. They could be cooks in your workplace canteen, mothers of the children you are teaching, hospital patients whom you are nursing, friends of friends, or people whom you meet at the stop, while waiting forever for the bus. Perhaps the most bizarre experience that the interviewees reported was swapping recipes with random foreign tourists on the beach.

Most often recipes were written down under the dictation of another person, or obtained already written on a piece of paper. Cases in which people wrote straight into their friends' notebooks, like in late 19th-century travellers' memory books, were rare. But one of the striking features of recipes in scrapbooks was their frequent attribution to the person, who had given them: her/his name is very often found next to the name of the dish. Sometimes recipes were dictated over the telephone: students in universities away from their native towns asked their mothers for cooking instructions or friends, seated on their respective couches, were sharing information during long conversations, noting it down on scraps of paper at hand: anything from rough toilet paper to museum tickets. Most recipes were handwritten, but among women who worked in offices recipes, typed on a typewriter and/or copied with a copying machine, were also common.

The bits of paper, amassed in these ways, were commonly copied in a private recipe-scrapbook[5], or kept between its pages. In rare cases they were pasted into collages, or they were simply kept in a pile.

---

[4] The quotes are from the 23 interviews made for this research between 2014 and 2017, and introduced in detail on p. 26.

[5] The private collections of recipes, which are one of the main sources for this research, have been given different names in the scientific literature. Sharpless (2016) named them 'household books', Finn (2011) termed them 'manuscript cookbooks', Theophano (2002) used interchangeably 'cookbooks' and 'manuscripts', Goody (1977) called them 'recipe-books', Pirogovskaya (2017) used interchangeably 'private cookbooks' and 'handwritten cookbooks'. To name them simply 'cookbooks' or 'recipe-books' is confusing when they are being discussed together with the cookbooks printed by printing houses. 'Household books' is technically incorrect, since a few of them contain anything but straightforward recipes. 'Manuscripts' or 'handwritten cookbooks' is also misleading, because the typewriter was much used, and also because the books often contain clippings from magazines. Perhaps the most exact term would be to call them 'cookery scrapbooks' or 'scrapbooks with recipes'. For convenience I simply refer to them throughout the text as 'scrapbooks', as no other types of scrapbooks are discussed in this work. This term reflects best the multiplicity of the bits and pieces of papers, the different handwritings, the collections of clippings, the inserted pages of the collections, which the documents contain. Finally, I use the term 'cookbooks' to indicate the printed cookery manuals released by the exclusively state-owned publishing houses.

Cathy Ivanova's book proved to be quite exceptional as I never found another collection that had been transformed into such a resemblance of a professionally printed cookbook. However many other scrapbooks revealed extraordinary investments of energy and thought. Some women's collections extended to several volumes, which were not always simply chronological. Some have divided their recipes between different notebooks, so that they maintained separate records on soups, main dishes, preserves and desserts – as if in specialized cookbooks.

The collections were quite often started by the generations who formed households in the 1940s and 1950s, or even before 1944, when many city girls attended the 'Household economy schools' or evening cooking classes, organized across the country. In this way the collections spread over an entire century, covering three to four generations.

Most women believed that recipes are to be shared and participated in the exchange regardless of their interest in cooking. In this regard Cathy Ivanova and Tamara Ganeva were two contrasting examples – the first of them sharing Socrates' thought *I eat to live not live to eat*, and the second defining herself as a gourmand. But even women who did not cook at all were involved in the activity, which had a significant place in their everyday life.

Once a woman acquired a recipe, she almost always tried it, adapted it gradually to her own skills and taste and then shared it again. In this last stage the giver presented either her own version of the recipe, or offered the original, elaborating on her experience with it and her improvements.

The interviews made it clear that trading of recipes was widespread in communist Bulgaria. Still the limited number of individuals that I was able to reach for qualitative in-depth research were not enough to allow me to draw conclusions as to the scale of the phenomenon. Moreover, because I spoke only to a group of women who maintained scrapbooks, their impressions of how widespread recipe exchange was might have been influenced by their specific interests and their social circles.

To obtain a less biased idea of the importance of recipe exchange, at the beginning of 2017 I included several questions in a national sociological poll, which was carried out by the Bulgarian polling agency Alpha Research[6]. The results, based on a representative sample of 1,025 interviews, showed that 90 per cent of the Bulgarian households before 1989 used handwritten recipes, while 80 per cent used cookbooks. More strikingly, the answers revealed that the self-collected recipes were by far the most popular written source of culinary information. While 58 per cent of the female respondents said they used it 'often' or 'very often', only 25 per cent gave the same answer regarding the next popular choice, the cookbooks. Thirty-two per cent used

---

[6] The questions asked within the poll were designed to provide information in four areas: 1. How many people used (i.e. possessed) a collection of exchanged, collected written recipes? 2. What was the number of cookbooks owned by a Bulgarian household before 1989? 3. How did people rank the different sources of culinary information? 4. What made people cook: was it an obligation or a preference, and what feelings did they remember experiencing while cooking?

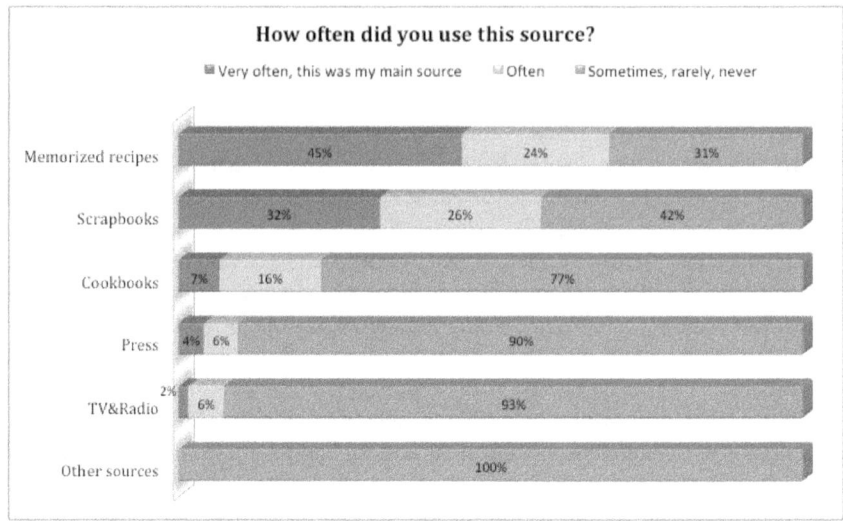

Figure 1 *The preferences shown in the use of different sources of culinary information in Bulgaria during late communism, as revealed by a national poll, conducted in 2017 for this research.*

exclusively exchanged recipes as a source, compared to 7 per cent, who used exclusively cookbooks (Figure 1).

A similar survey, made in the early 1990s in the UK, helps to add some international perspective to the data collected in Bulgaria. A poll on a smaller scale – among fifty people in the area of Edinburgh, showed that cookbooks were the most used source, followed by recipes from friends and neighbours, magazine articles, food labels and food manufacturers' leaflets (McKie and Wood 1992). This survey suggested that the two most popular sources came in reverse order, compared to Bulgaria.

To someone who is familiar with Bulgarian communist cookbooks and their distribution before the end of the regime in 1989, this might not come as a surprise. The publishing of culinary advice after 1945 was quite limited both in variety and in the total number of copies of the cookbooks that were released, so that simply not having access to cookbooks must have been one of the reasons for their lesser importance in households. About 20 per cent of the female respondents said they did not have a cookbook at home before 1989. Even so, the percentage of those who preferred to use handwritten recipes is significantly higher.

What made women persist in recipe exchange?

The kitchen, as Oldenziel and Zachmann argued, is a 'techno-political knot', connecting state, market and family, a 'historical juncture when the feminist movement, socialist[7] ideology, and war emergencies had fundamentally challenged conventional women's roles' (Oldenziel and Zachmann 2009: 3). Within the aggressive, prescriptive ideological framework of Eastern European communism, how did women negotiate their roles in the household and how did they imagine their modernity, where such a prominent place was left for recipe writing and home cooking?

The very foundation of all these questions is how the meanings of that most basic human practice, the daily preparation of food, are being shaped. The scientific interest in this topic dates from the late 1980s. The Armenian–US anthropologist Avakian was probably the first to acknowledge that women, tending to forge spaces for themselves within oppression, find in cooking 'a vehicle for artistic expression, a source of sensual pleasure, an opportunity for resistance and even power' (Avakian 1997).

As home cooking has been historically mostly women's responsibility, it has been particularly interesting to gender studies. Many a sociologist, social historian and anthropologist have tried to crack the secret of what seems to be the resilient attachment of women to cooking. Putting aside the truism that this connection is socially constructed, numerous puzzles seem to remain. Legerski and Cornwall (2010) wondered, for example, why in couples in which the men lost jobs and remained unemployed, there was no serious 'undoing' of gender: women continued to assume most of the cooking obligations in the family. They explained it with the reinforcement of the traditional and the lack of new family ideology, which would 'support the equal participation of men in household labour'. But in a way, this was more a description of the situation than an explanation: why were traditional roles reinforced, and why did new family ideology not materialize? Indeed many researchers observed ambivalence among women regarding home cooking, which was both craved and overwhelming. Counihan (1999) studied attitudes among women in modernizing Florence and discovered how emancipation evoked contradictory feelings regarding their role as food providers in their families. Risman (2004), conceptualizing gender as a social structure, pointed out that men and women are not only 'coerced into differential social roles; they often choose their gendered paths.' She sought explanation in the structural theory of action of Burt (1982), which says that 'actors choose the best alternatives without presuming they have either

---

[7] The three terms are used interchangeably in historiography, and the slight confusion originates from the use of the words by the regimes themselves – the one in Bulgaria promoted itself as communist consistently in the first decades of its rule, and later started describing the state as socialist. The main ruling party, though, kept the name Bulgarian Communist Party until 1990, when it was renamed the Bulgarian Socialist Party. Nowadays in Bulgaria current members of the Socialist Party raise objections against calling the former regime communist. I chose to use the term 'communist' because it is internationally accepted (according to the Oxford Encyclopaedia of the Modern World), and it puts terminological distance between Western-European socialism and the Eastern-European authoritarian governments, which historically exploited socialist ideas to impose oppressive regimes of government, maintained by means of the military, state security, and other mechanisms, as opposed to the rule of law. To refer to the former regime, I use the term socialism/socialist here only when it was used in the original text of direct or paraphrased quotes.

enough information to do it well or the options available to make choices that effectively serve their own interests.' Married women, for example, would do much more than their share of certain chores, if they do not believe that their partners will do their part, providing care/work that the women would consider to be of reasonable quality.

Gvion's research (2015) provides evidence that contradicts the importance of cultural inertia and perhaps endorses the role that striving for quality played as a driver in the women's choice to cook at home. She studied the second generation of women in the Israeli kibbutz, who, after their mothers had arranged for the cooking to be taken care of on a communal level, practically fought to get it back. Having been raised and fed by the commune instead of by their mothers, the women from the second generation opted in their adult life to return to the traditional gendered roles in the households. One of the limitations of Gvion's study is that she does not present a broader context of the process. It remains unclear how the interviewed kibbutz women appropriated the traditional gender model, considering that in their personal stories a role model of a mother as a family nurturer was absent. Yet Gvion's work offers a unique parallel and is very helpful in making sense of the women's experience in communist Bulgaria. It allows us to compare two groups, subjected to the pressures of similarly aggressive feministic ideologies in very different cultural contexts. What kept women attached to cooking within a prescriptive framework, which tried to keep them away from the kitchens? Could the scrapbooks offer an answer to such question?

Women's connection to food has certainly been one of the themes of another significant body of research, the recently expanding investigations into cookbooks – historical documents whose value in this field of study has been seriously underestimated until recently, and which are seen both as empowering their authors or the communities which created them, and as conveying various, sometimes oppressive ideologies. The value of these documents had been overlooked in the past, but lately the realization that they were a blessing in disguise is spreading: in fact they have proved to be so obviously rich a source, that the earlier neglect has become somewhat of an embarrassment to historical science.

The interest in cookbooks has been growing since the 1980s, when they started bringing multiple, often unexpected insights into history 'from below'. Groundbreaking in this respect have been the studies examining the agency of cookbooks (and their authors) in forging national identities, like Appadurai's study of the consolidation of Indian cuisine (Appadurai 1888), or Ferguson's investigation into the construction of modern French identity in Antoine Carême's culinary writing (Ferguson 2004). Cookbooks have also been utilized to gain understanding of social order, tensions and transformations: some early examples are the research of Kirschenblatt-Gimblett (1987) on how Jewish women bridged the religious canon with the imperatives of modernity, as transpiring from their recipes, or Zlotnik's study of how British women participated in building the complex relationship between colonizers and colonized, evident from the history of curry in Victorian cookbooks (Zlotnick 1996). Both works showed the agency of women in the specific framework and revealed the lack of critical nuance in earlier interpretations of the discussed historical periods.

As historical research advanced, the understanding of the political nature of food expanded and so did the studies on how cookbooks transmit ideologies. Researchers addressed the presence of explicit, politics-related ideologies, gradually proving that many oppressive regimes saw cookery literature as an opportunity to manage people's everyday life. Notaker (2008) was the first to demonstrate this, by studying how the ideological beliefs and political interests of the Nazi regime in Germany in the 1930s influenced the content of the cookbooks from the period. His research *Cookery and Ideology in the Third Reich,* more descriptive than analytical, illustrated how ideas of 'correct nutrition', of protectionism of local, German production, and on the role of the woman in the family were reflected in the pages of the cookery manuals. After Notaker, a new line of research opened that investigates the ideology in cookbooks published in various communist regimes. Their prescriptive doctrines, intended to dominate every sphere of public and private life, brought about volumes of cookery advice, dripping with ideology.

Analysing different editions of the popular cookbook of Nitza Villapol in Castro's Cuba, Fleites-Lear (2012) searched to identify the redefinition of the ideal woman under the pressure of ideology. Many works have been dedicated to the multiple editions of the principal cookbook of the Soviet Union, *Kniga o vkusnoy i zdorovoy pishche* (The Book of Tasty and Healthy Food) (1939), the influence of which could be traced across 20th-century Eastern Europe. Gronow and Zhuravlev interpreted it as a politically-grounded attempt at establishing Soviet *haute cuisine*, a clearly propagandist act of the political leadership (Gronow and Zhuravlev 2011). Geist saw it as a unique example of Socialist Realism, an 'aestheticisation of reality in order to facilitate the reconstruction of Soviet existence' (Geist 2012: 296). In other countries from the communist bloc Keating (2018), Nilgen (2020) and my own research (Shkodrova 2018a) showed how cookbooks reflected the dominant ideologies of domesticity, gender and nutrition, trying to shape, but also being shaped by, everyday life. These studies revealed many parallels between the Nazi and the communist domestic and gender ideology: from treating women as a female body mass and workforce to use and control, to assigning public roles to domestic life (the Nazi gender ideology in Italy was described in these terms by De Grazia 1996). The research on communist cookbooks showed that in spite of the evolution in the discourses throughout the communist period and a certain polyphony that they gained towards the end, oppressive regimes in the 20th century retained the wish to control and the ability to mobilize propagandist resources for this purpose.

However many insights cookbooks as a historical source may deliver, they have one great limitation: they tell us what has been 'coded' into them, what they are meant to convey. But they cannot tell us how they were read and used. Gronow and Zhuravlev (2011: 25) pointed out, as one reason for that, the impossibility of really reconstructing in 'any comprehensive manner' such information about the past. But perhaps the investigation of a recent period like communism, which is still alive in the memory of contemporaries in Bulgaria, could be made? Perhaps women could be asked how they read their cookbooks, and how did they negotiate their decisions to use them or not? Moreover, if they maintained scrapbooks of recipes, which they had exchanged, they must have – consciously or not – negotiated daily their choice as to which source of recipe to use? Would an inquiry about their motives for maintaining scrapbooks not tell us how they read the commercial cookbooks which they had in their households?

Contemporary scrapbooks, and women's practice and motivation for maintaining them, remain one of the least explored areas in the study of cookbooks and in cultural food studies in general. Things stand differently when it comes to older cookery manuscripts. Those, predating the rise of cookbook publishing, have been analyzed as unique historical sources for everyday life in different epochs. One illuminating example, relevant to the present volume, is Pennell's study of recipe manuscripts from Early Modern England, where she ponders over the possible motivation of women for collecting recipes (Pennell 2004). But the spread of cookbooks seems to have successfully obscured the manuscripts' potential to bring insights about contemporary history, and studies of contemporary manuscripts remain extremely rare. Among the very few researchers who studied scrapbooks, are Theophano (2002), Supski (2013), Weiskopf-Ball (2013) and Davis et al. (2014).

That scrapbooks were very popular under communism in Europe is certain. In a work on socialist everyday life, the Bulgarian historian Nenov (2001) mentioned them as widespread. He used a collective cookbook, developed by the personnel of a communist bird farm, to discuss sexual life under socialism (Nenov 2013) – the scrapbook, which is part of the History museum in Rousse, contains multiple jokes, many of which feature sex and sexuality. It is possible that these familial documents had similar importance across the communist bloc.

Three recent publications, which have appeared in the period between the completion and the publication of this book, made an important contribution by putting the communist-era scrapbooks in the limelight. Pirogovskaya (2017) and Lakhtikova (2017, 2019) shed light on recipe exchange practice and scrapbooks in Soviet Russia. They asserted that there was a surge in the popularity of scrapbooks in the 1960s, in reaction to 'the public campaign for the new domesticity of the Khrushchev Thaw' (Pirogovskaya 2017: 339) and that scrapbooks became 'a ubiquitous cultural phenomenon' across the Soviet republics (Lakhtikova 2017: 113). Fine-grained and insightful, the two analyses interpreted scrapbooks as documents of trust and solidarity, as strategies for coping with economic difficulties and as instruments for constructing identity. They confirmed in many instances the research of Theophano (2002), whose focus was also on solidarity and female networks.

With Soviet reality in mind, these works also went further to establish that scrapbooks were perceived as contrasting with the officially published cookbooks. While cookbooks were 'notoriously unrealistic', scrapbooks were engaged with reality in 'the most direct manner', wrote Lakhtikova (2019: 109). Pirogovskaya (2017: 337) added that official cookbooks had 'little credibility', while scrapbooks embodied women's trust in their social circles of recipe exchange.

Despite this important research on the USSR, many aspects of the recipe exchange remain unaddressed – aspects, that are critical to understand the social practice in its entirety and complexity. Issues such as the economic use of scrapbooks and their emotional value remain undiscussed. Most importantly, the extant research, both on communist and non-communist cookery manuscripts, lacks the discussion on how women negotiated their choice with the dominant ideological discourses: when composing their scrapbooks, or when choosing between the different types of advice (in other words, how they read the communist cookbooks). Lakhtikova (2017: 112) asserted that scrapbooks are 'one of the most politically unbiased' sources of information about Soviet everyday life, leaving out the innate political nature of human food choices and the increased probability of conscious political connotations in such matters within an oppressive regime that wished to control everyday life. Pirogovskaya made insightful observations as to how the 'official' was regarded with mistrust but did not go into an enquiry about how this translated into choices, preferences, and actions, and how it related to recipes and cooking. Were the two sources perceived as a dichotomy in all cases? In which ways? And when were they not?

Precisely because cooking seems so trivial, it has the potential to contribute to one of the most heated debates in recent years, namely how to conceptualize everyday life under communism – or in any oppressive regime[8]. Interest in the experience of living under communism emerged in the 1990s with the poetic book of Svetlana Boym *Common Places. Mythologies of everyday life in Russia* (1994). Her intimate descriptions of life in *communalki*, the typical shared apartments in the Soviet cities, and her attention to what she named 'the inner workings of the culture' – attitudes towards 'ordinary life, home, material objects' – revealed the potential of this perspective to offer a nuanced understanding of social life under communism and to escape some of the limitations of earlier, cold war-influenced studies. It paved the way for an entire, booming subfield of studies into communist everyday life.

Thousands of articles on a broad range of topics have been published in this domain since then, but three themes seem important to mention here, as they are also central to this book. One of them is communist consumption, which was quickly recognized as an excellent way to access one innate contradiction of the socialist regimes: their existential need to simultaneously reject bourgeois consumption, and assert their ability to provide it. This ambivalent attitude has been discussed in many studies, perhaps most notably by Gronow's research into Stalin's luxury politics (Gronow 2003), Reid's investigation into the effect of the 'Thaw' on consumption (Reid 2002) or Reid and Crowly's exploration of pleasures under socialism (Reid and Crowley 2010). The 'controlled' consumerism in Bulgaria and the efforts to endorse the notion of a 'correct' – i.e. restrained and science-informed communist consumer – was surveyed by Mineva (2003).

Early on in the post-communist research of communist everyday life the argument was introduced that within the oppressive regimes people were still allowed to have their agency. One of the first to claim this, and in particular with regard to Bulgaria, was Gerald Creed. His important *Domesticating Revolution* (1998) demonstrated the somewhat fluid character of the system, which both created needs and tried to a certain extent to accommodate them, even if only for the main purpose of survival. The understanding of

---

[8] The use of the word 'regime' to indicate the authoritarian communist rule in Eastern Europe has been objected to by Yurchak (2005), who argued that 'the widespread use of phrases such as "the Soviet regime" are part of the terminology that manifests the common assumptions that "socialism" was "bad" and "immoral" or had been experienced as such by Soviet people'. However, the concept of 'regime' indicates simply any system of government or administration (The Concise Oxford Dictionary of Politics 2009). Thus I have accepted and used the term. Whenever I wanted to emphasise the exercised authoritarian governing methods, I termed it 'authoritarian regime'.

the individual agency in the late communist period quickly became central and was convincingly demonstrated by many. However its interpretation has been somewhat different. Reid spoke of the communist consumer as not only 'a passive object of central planning, market research, representation, and discipline, but as an active agent who, through her consumption choices, or refusal to consume, may or may not have had an impact on the way policy and ideology were shaped' (Reid 2002: 214).' However, she explicitly emphasized the lack of liberalization in the period she researched (Reid 2002).

Another angle of interpretation was assumed by researchers like Scarboro, and Klumbyte and Sharafutdinova, who, behind the scant possibility for individual agency, saw what they termed 'communist humanism' (Scarboro 2012) and 'liberal individuals', able to live 'free, and happy lives' (Klumbyte and Sharafutdinova 2013: 10). Such interpretations drew to a great extent on the influential arguments of Yurchak. His *Everything Was Forever, Until It Was No More* (2006) marked an important shift in post-communist studies, as it criticized the interpretations of communist everyday life within dichotomies. Yurchak's objections were formulated against 'the use of binary categories to describe Soviet reality such as oppression and resistance, repression and freedom, the state and the people, official economy and second economy[9] (...) morality and corruption and so on.' (Yurchak 2006: 5). He dismissed all those as emanations of cold war ideologies and appealed to scholars to 'rehumanize Soviet socialist life'.

Also taking a stand against the previously used dichotomies were Bren and Neuberger (Bren and Neuburger 2012: 6). One of their landmark observations was that 'the history of the region should not be defined by "Western" narratives of the consumer experience'.

To many people from my generation, who have lived under communism, these assertions would seem contraintuitive. It has been often argued that this is the working of the cold war doctrines on the researchers (and presumably on any common person, who had experienced life under communism). The widespread practice of home cooking and recipe exchange might be an excellent area in which to probe these assertions. If there is any way to see politically-based dichotomies dissolved, it must be in a field that very few people think of as political. Home cooking and scrapbooks seem to be just such a field.

Most of all, this book tries to answer the question of how widespread was recipe exchange in communist Bulgaria, what motivated women to engage with it, and were there any political currents underlying this practice? US anthropologist Gregory Bateson argued that social phenomena are best studied from several perspectives simultaneously: structural, social, economic and affective. Applied here, it means to investigate **how recipe collections related to communist modernity, which forcefully took women out of their households to employ them in the state economy. Was there resistance in their actions – conscious or not, and of what kind?**

---

[9] Under this term Yurchak understands the communist grey economy, realised via 'secondary' networks. The concept is developed by Ledeneva (1998), Lomnitz (1988) Deyanov (2003, 2006) among others.

How did the recipe collection make sense within the communist economy, and in which ways did scrapbooks support food practices? How did scrapbooks relate to women's social needs and interactions, and, finally, to their emotional needs?

Another group of questions, related to ongoing scientific discussions are whether an investigation into recipe scrapbooks could offer more insights into how cookbooks are used? Will understanding how women negotiated between different sources of culinary information teach us something about how written culinary advice works and how ideologies, coded in cookbooks, are perceived by their users?

Finally, will we find dichotomies – between official and unofficial, between state and private, East and West, communist and anticommunist? They are increasingly criticized as cold war indoctrination, but were they indeed absent from this layer of communist everyday life? This discussion is not simply a contest for the interpretation of the communist history of Eastern Europe, since it both reflects and influences the shaping of present, post-communist discourses. Moral categories and moral judgement may not belong to social sciences, but it is always a good idea when they are grounded in it.

The importance of this research also goes beyond societies under oppressive rule. An analysis of how points of tension in everyday life are resolved on different levels can be instrumental in easing social frictions in general. As Ore pointed out, the understanding of how everyday actions are also political practices can help our comprehension of how such actions 'bring about broader social change' (Ore 2011: 694).

This book is composed of three parts

The first outlines the context in which scrapbooks became popular and flourished in Bulgaria. It looks at how early communist ideology planned to reform the national foodways and gender roles, and how this affected culinary advice and education. It also follows the evolution in the everyday ideologies through the decades of communist rule, and outlines specific aspects of the communist reality, such as the peculiar value of time and money and the flourishing of social entertainment in domestic settings. Against this background is explained the advent of scrapbooks as a popular familial document. Finally this part explains the sources and the methodology of the research, presented in this book.

The second part is a discussion of the scrapbooks as an instrument in cooking and as a medium for transmission and preservation of cookery information. It highlights different aspects of the recipe collections, which the interviewed women identified as important, when choosing a source of culinary information in their domestic cooking practices.

The third part of the book considers four different clusters of meanings, which women invested in their scrapbooks: structural, economic, social and affective. They are brought together and analysed in their complexity in the concluding section 'What made scrapbooks indispensable'. There I go back to my initial question if indeed there was some sort of rebellion in domestic cooking. I also suggest a more nuanced understanding of the ways in which various types of cookery advice are situated in the individual cook's hierarchies, and how such hierarchies are influenced by ideologies.

PART ONE

THE CONTEXT

COOKING ADVICE IN BULGARIA

'Stealing with the eyes', the traditional method of learning through observation, was as good as the only way to master cooking in Bulgaria until well into the 19th century. In other parts of Europe a tradition of household manuscripts had developed since the 14th century and cookbooks were printed for commercial distribution since the 17th century (Notaker 2012: 135). The first Bulgarian cookbooks though only appeared in 1870s (Slaveykov 1870, Smrikarov 1874), and not much happened in the following decades. Little further culinary advice was released until the end of the 19th century, as Bulgaria, along with other emerging states in the Balkans, consolidated from fragments of the crumbling Ottoman Empire and struggled to construct a state. My research identified only eleven cookbooks, published between 1870 and 1900, and seventeen in the first two decades of the 20th century[1], the growth probably impeded by the First World War.

The actual rise of commercially printed cookbooks occurred between the two world wars. Women's magazines, agricultural societies, cookery schools and private individuals joined forces and released at least thirty-two new titles in the 1920s and seventy-nine in the 1930s, to which numerous additional print runs of earlier books were added. However puzzling it may seem, the 1930s turned out to be the golden age of the 20th-century cookbooks' publication in Bulgaria – the abundance of new advice, which this decade saw, was not achieved again until the 1990s.

Several key circumstances came together to provide for this success, and one of them was the growing literacy among the female population. Lagging behind some economically developed countries like Great Britain or France, Bulgaria entered the 20th century with literacy levels similar to Italy's,[2] somewhere above 53 per cent, which was the percentage of children attending primary school. By 1925 though this proportion was already at 84.2 and it reached nearly 100 in the 1950s (Bulgaria XX Vek 1999: 618).

The system of schools expanded and in 1909 a reform in education directly interfered in women's patterns of learning to cook: the state introduced a four-year education cycle for girls to level it with that of boys, and added as an obligatory subject 'home economy, science of education and needlework'. High schools were still not

---

[1] These numbers include only the new titles and not the further editions of already published ones.
[2] According to Our World In Data, a publication of the University of Oxford, Italy and Argentina had a literacy rate of about 50 percent by 1900. https://ourworldindata.org/literacy/, visited last on 12-11-2016

accessible to everyone – by 1930 71 per cent of the children in the country attended secondary education and in 1940 it was 80 per cent. Girls attended less than boys (Bulgaria 20th Century: 622). Still the growing attendance of home economy courses – in or outside schools, must have rapidly boosted the number of women, confronted with written cooking advice.

As a result of parallel efforts to encourage sophistication in cooking a significant network of women's societies were created, which were thriving across the country in the 1930s and early 1940s. These influential organizations used their membership fees and volunteer work to arrange charitable opportunities for the education of young girls, preparing for married life or work as household servants. Archive materials of these societies suggest that they cooperated with local chambers of agriculture, schools, and between each other, developing vast networks and ensuring good media exposure.[3] Examples of their enterprises were exhibitions, educative events and publications, which travelled across the country. Women were taught how to cook potatoes, how to prepare healthy and cheap food, how to be practical, or adopt nature-friendly practices and similar (Tsoncheva 1941: 3).

The growing school attendance among girls not only offered access to an alternative source of knowledge, but changed women's lifestyle, particularly in rural families. Many sources confirm that girls in pre-modern Bulgaria learned to cook by practising, assuming part of their mothers' cooking obligations, while the other family members were spending long days working on the farm or in the fields[4]. School attendance, though, took them out of their parents' households at least during daytime and changed the family routine for many (Gavrilova 1999: 350). They learned to read and to cook independently from their families, and for purposes different from maintaining their parents' household: many of them hoped to find jobs in other people's homes, or to be prepared to run their own household.

The critical contribution of the cooking classes was that they combined practice with reading and writing of recipes, thus combining the traditional method of learning through observation with the habit of acquiring knowledge through written text. It is very likely that the joint efforts of home economy classes in schools and cooking classes and lectures by various societies and organizations laid the foundations of written recipe culture in Bulgaria, and also of many collections of recipes in that country. During my research I encountered three sets of notes from courses, followed in the 1920s and 1930s, which were inherited and treasured by the succeeding generations. A similar connection was established elsewhere, for example according to Knezy (2003: 144) recipe writing in Hungary became popular in the 1930s, when girls were able to attend similar cooking classes. Also Goody (1977: 141–142) observed a connection between the mobility of young women, the time they spent in school and away from their familial houses and gardens, and their tendency to 'learn cooking indirectly from books'. Indeed, the other effect of cooking classes on women in Bulgaria was to make them users of cookbooks.

---

[3] These findings are based on materials in the State archive, dating from the late 1930s and early 1940s: the archive of the Society for domestic culture 'Bulgarian Home', CSA 8-1-14.

[4] A wealth of information on this is offered in the People's Memory Archive, which contains 90 biographical interviews or autobiographical writings, collected by sociologist Galya Misheva at the Critical Social Studies Institute at the Paisiy Hilyandarsky University in Plovdiv, Bulgaria.

The rich variation of advice, provided in the Bulgarian cookbooks by the end of the 1920s and throughout the 1930s, must have served domestic cooks' expanding interests. There was a giant leap between the food culture that transpired from the late 19th-century introduction into absolute basics (Slaveykov 1870, Smrikarov 1874) and the lamentation over the lack of basic skills and taste in the Bulgarian kitchen (Domashna gotvarska kniga 1895), and the culinary cosmopolitanism in the cookbooks from the 1930s, which brought together Middle Eastern, Central and Western European, Russian and American cuisines, quoted Escoffier, the Danish minister of health or Greta Garbo and had developed the notion of 'Bulgarian cuisine'. If in the first half a century of its existence political life in modern Bulgaria did not exactly flourish, one could reasonably state that its food practices did.

The arrival of communism though was to reboot the process.

SETTING UP THE COMMUNIST ARENA

The communist state in Bulgaria was made possible on 8 September 1944, when the week-old national government declared war on Nazi Germany. This was an attempt to escape the alliance with Hitler, concluded four administrations earlier – but as it turned out, one that came just too late. Trapped by a sequence of strategic miscalculations and brought into an impermeable international isolation, later the same day Bulgaria was invaded by the Soviet army. On the following morning a Soviet-supported coup, dubbed 'an uprising' by the communist historiography, ousted prime minister Muraviev. It brought to power a coalition with the participation of the Communist Party. Thus started a process, which led to 45 years of communist rule and profoundly influenced the 20th-century modernization and everyday life in the country.

Between 1944 and 1947 the Communist Party was consolidating and asserting its power. Transformed overnight from an illegal group of 2,500 members into an official political organization, it formed a national militia and launched the pursuit and executions of enemies: politicians, monarchists, the military elite, the upper-middle class, industrialists or intellectuals. According to a recent investigation by Lilkov and Hristov an estimated 26,000 Bulgarians perished in the initial purges, some of them through executions, staged to spread terror. Entire villages were exterminated, after being robbed. A communist militia, led by then still unknown Todor Zhivkov, was formed from criminals released from the prisons at the height of the coup, and many were also killed in criminal acts or in resolving personal feuds (Lilkov and Hristov 2017: 28). Rape, extortions and mass graves asserted the ultimate power, which scared some and attracted others, providing for a fast swelling membership of the Communist Party.

The process profoundly repositioned layers of the society in a way that was very similar to the Soviet October Revolution. Entire social groups were obliterated as 'former people', as they were literally called by the communist State Security, the infamous *Durzhavna sigurnost* (Lilkov and Hristov 2017). Among them were also socialists, who were thought to disagree with the methods of the new vanguard. These too were airbrushed from history as if they had never existed, suffering the same fate as the early Czech communist Clementis, described by Kundera (1983: 3).

The new leadership developed along the lines of the ideological orthodoxy of Joseph Stalin and with the support of his close aide, the Bulgarian communist leader Georgi Dimitrov, who returned from Moscow to lead the transformations and the country, to falsify the people's support for the regime's actions, and to ensure its subordination (Znepolski ed. 2011: 77–78, Deyanova 2003: 202–203).

In this context the early communist idea of the role of women in the kitchen in Bulgaria was shaped, repeating the radical ideas of Clara Zetkin and the October revolution. Clearly articulated – and particularly pronounced in the post-war Stalinist years, when the communist industry was forced into life – was the intention to replace home cooking with affordable public catering on a national scale. It had to open the way to employing the female population in the state economy (Shkodrova 2014: 236–237, 2018a: 472).

Even if the idea of reforming women's role in food preparation was one of the ideological pillars of the new rulers, the cookery advice did not change overnight. One reason was that it remained in private hands and its publishers, even if investing effort to align with the new power's ideology, did not fully grasp the implications that ideology had for home cooking, or on lifestyle in general. One such example was the *Obedineni Domakinski Spisania* (United Household Magazines), a pre-war consortium of several women's magazines, which continued its regular releases after 1944. Its post-war issues tried to convey support and collaboration with the new state: they featured women with 'masculine' jobs and texts in support of the government's agenda. One of its last issues, in the spring of 1947 urged women to participate in the 'shared enthusiasm' to fulfil the two-year economic plan. 'No woman should assume that since many others work to accomplish the [state economic] plan, she can avoid making a contribution. On the contrary, each woman should realize that precisely her input is needed to achieve the goals,' advised an editorial article. The magazine though continued many earlier content lines: reporting on fashion shows from Paris, occupying pages with knitting or embroidering advice, or offering a recipe for 'Swiss soup' when cultural references to the West were becoming increasingly dangerous (Obedineni domakinski spisania 1947: 3–5).

In 1948, which marked the end of the liminal period and the establishment of the Communist Party in power, *United Household Magazines* were attacked in the central party's newspaper Rabotnichesko delo (Workers' Affairs) as reactionary (Rabotnichesko delo 1948, as quoted by Deyanova 2005: 14 of 26). Blamed for 'irresponsibly' featuring texts about women's charms, 'cheesy short stories', and 'not a line about the new woman–hero: brigadier and super-performer', the magazine was soon shut down. At that time a government decision assigned monopoly to the state over publishing activities of any kind.

The only women's magazine that survived was *Zhenata dnes*. Established in 1945, it was published by the Demokratichen Suyuz na Zhenite (Democratic Women's Union), a communist women's organization formed by the new political elite. Even if a brain child of the new regime, this magazine allowed for a certain continuity: it was founded with the support of Hristo and Penka Cholchevi, the publishers of the previously influential *Vestnik za zhenata* (Newspaper for the Women). The couple's publishing activities made them part of the intellectual elite of the country before 1944. Different sources suggest they were quite reticent in regard to the new order. Their children later recalled that Cholcheva never addressed anyone with the standard communist *drugar* (comrade) (Malinova et al. 2015: 8), which was considered a stark sign of political disloyalty. It was probably the experience, connections and rationality of the couple that saw them through. It seems that they deemed the collaborating with the regime unavoidable. Cholchev was known to say: 'It is neither socialism, nor communism, but it is our future' (Milanova et al. 2015: 7).

The commitment to adapt is clearly visible in Cholcheva's work. A comparison between two editions of a cookbook – the first from 1947, released by Cholchev's publishing house, and the second from 1952 by a state publisher – offers a good illustration of the (self?)-censoring process of the early communist years. The striking change is in the direct references to Western countries/cuisines: from thirty-three in 1947, they are reduced to four in 1952 (Cholcheva 1947, 1952). Cholcheva's winning strategy was to keep her cookery advice simple and accessible. The first editions paid attention to the hardship in Bulgaria and advised women to restrain from follies: 'Do not buy anything you don't need, or one day you will have to part with what you need', she wrote, quoting a popular Bulgarian saying (Cholcheva 1947: 330). She admonished Bulgarian housewives for being wasteful with soap, water or energy, and fashioned new style rhetoric arguing that parsimony is beneficial not only to private budgets, but to the people's republic's economy (Cholcheva 1947: 334). 'We need to shed everything old and make space for the new'. In this way the first communist cookbooks already participated in the construction of what Utehin (2001) called 'culture of poverty'.

Hristo Cholchev was not able to keep his leading position in *Zhenata dnes*, but his wife preserved her page of cooking advice in the magazine, published on and off in the following years. In 1949 *Zhenata dnes* released her new cookbook, which praised the new regime for overcoming the shortages, caused by the fascist period, the war and the drought. If the market is still tight, it is because the prices are now low and production, while booming, cannot satisfy the growing demand, explained Cholcheva, somewhat contradicting the earlier statement that the market was no longer tight (1949: 3).

EARLY COMMUNIST COOKING ADVICE

Cholcheva was as good as the only author who published cookbooks for domestic use between 1948 and 1955, adapting her earlier work. There were a couple of exceptions – a book on cooking for children (Trifonova 1954) and a cookery guide intended for both domestic and professional use in the state canteens (Maleev and Stanchev 1948) – but it could be reasonably argued that the first cookbooks to embody the spirit of the communist period arrived only in 1955–1956: the compendiums *Our Cuisine* (Naydenov and Chortanova 1955) and *The Housewife's Book* (Cholcheva and Ruseva eds. 1956).

The cookbooks of the 1950s were in the first place very few: the number of titles was radically smaller than before 1944 (Shkodrova 2018a: 471). They also came with the end of the Stalinist period, but were created in it and displayed the most rigid form of the early domestic ideologies of communism.

The complex ways in which state ideologies tend to penetrate cookbooks – in oppressive regimes or not – need yet to be studied. It is certain that their path is not a straight top-down one: ideological discourses are formed on many levels, through differently motivated individual interpretations and as a result of internal tensions and struggles (some examples are given by Glushchenko 2010; Geist 2012; Scott 2012). But what seems certain is that the culinary literature in oppressive regimes not only reflected 'the structure of domestic ideologies' (Appadurai 1988: 3), but was routinely subjected to purposeful interference from different levels and authorities to adapt to ideological and other state interests. This is evident from Notaker's research, which revealed how the relevant national guild of professionals was issued with printed instructions on the production of cookbooks, that would support the governing plans of the Third Reich (Notaker 2008: 68). Multiple works reveal that the same approach was applied in Eastern European communist states, where the supply of culinary information came to be regulated on a long-term basis and in a prescriptive manner, in accordance with the requirements of official communist ideology (Petranova 2003: 177, Franc 2003: 82; Elenkov 2011: 140). As a very rough generalization, the way the communist states influenced cookbooks was by setting the directions of the ideological discourses from above: through leadership decisions or statements, and relying on administrative and social hierarchies and networks, created to reasonably interpret the guidelines, when expressing them in more specific strategies or applying them in practice. Totalitarian states had greater powers to ensure such submissive, compliant interpretations: if not throughout their populations, at least on many levels inaccessible to a democratic state. This rough design naturally functioned far from flawlessly within the complex social structures. It could not avoid contestations and deviating interpretations, it could only try to suppress them, which it did in different periods with varying harshness. But in general it resulted in much greater uniformity of opinions, maintaining the perception of a single meta-discourse with significant success.

As far as cookery advice is concerned, the reduced polyphony provided for the uncontested dominance of nutritionism. This term was coined by Scrinis to describe the reductive understanding of food solely in terms of nutrients (Scrinis 2008: 39)[5]. Nutritionism became probably the most prominent feature of communist culinary literature. This was not surprising as such – after all this reductionist view became 'the dominant paradigm' in the professional and government-endorsed dietary advice in the USA and came to dominate, undermine, and replace 'other ways of engaging with food and of contextualising the relationship between food and the body' across the developed world (Scrinis 2008: 39). By 1944 it was not new to the Bulgarian user of cookbooks either – the nourishing faculties of food have been in the limelight since the beginning of the 20th century. The trend, which occurred across Europe and the USA (Scholliers 2013: 18, Dantec-Lowry 2008: 108), echoed also in Bulgaria, where *Food of the Future* by R.H. Wheldon was released, staging biochemistry as the basics of

---

[5] Under 'nutritionism', Scrinis understands the ideology 'to think about foods in terms of their nutrient composition, to make the connection between particular nutrients and bodily health, and to construct 'nutritionally balanced' diets on this basis.' (Scrinis 2008: 39).

nutrition (Wheldon 1914), and mainstream cookbooks included sections on nutrients (for example Kassurova 1933, Hristova 1937).

But before 1944 this approach was paired with parallel literature, which took into account that food also gives pleasure and entertains. Early communist cooking advice on the other hand ignored social aspects of cooking and eating (Shkodrova 2018a: 473). Both *Our Cuisine* (Naydenov and Chortanova 1955) and *The Housewife's Book* (Cholcheva and Ruseva eds, 1956) dedicated extensive chapters on nutrients and their impact on human vigour and the nation's work potential. The latter complicated women's responsibilities in the kitchen and justified political interferences in the domestic world: to feed a hard-working nation was discussed as a serious matter of state concern.

In this spirit home cooking was routinely viewed as inferior to public catering and industrial food, as it contained potential dangers of diminishing the nutritious qualities of food (Bulev 1951: 3) and wasting foodstuffs (Naydenov and Chortanova 1955, 11). To live up to such responsibilities, domestic cooks were called upon to apply scientific methods and professional approaches (Cholcheva 1949, Naydenov and Chortanova 1955, Cholcheva and Ruseva 1956).

The emphasis on scientific methods provided for (and resulted from) a fundamental change in the ways in which cookbooks were written: they were no longer authored by domestic practitioners, but by collectives of scientists. The model was established with the first two compendiums and reproduced throughout the following decades.

Understanding domestic cooking as a bad version of industrial/professional preparation of food, cookbook authors at times tried to merge the two readerships. *Our Cuisine* was in fact a book, released two years earlier under the name *Manual for Public Catering* (Naydenov and Chortanova 1953). Many manuals for domestic cooking, published in the following years, employed measures, techniques, equipment or language that only made sense in professional kitchens. The attention to professional cooking in the communist state is well illustrated by the statistics of cookbooks published throughout the period. The following figure shows how the titles, addressing professional cooks, in the late 1940s equalled those for home cooking and stayed at the same levels until the 1980s.

Figure 2 *The trends in cookbook publishing in communist Bulgaria, comparing literature addressing professional cooks, with recipe collections for home cooking (new titles).*

In this context, in which the entire society was seen as a machine, consuming and digesting in order to fulfil the state economy plan and cooking was no more than 'the first phase of digestion' (Cholcheva 1947: 337, Bulev 1951: 7), the sense of taste was reduced to a prerequisite for digestion (Shkodrova 2018: 473–474).

These radical attitudes were well pronounced in the strategies of what was considered to be an alternative to home cooking: the industrial preparation of ingredients and meals. Authors of cookery advice often rendered home cooking as wasteful and even dangerous, foretelling its dying out (Naydenov and Chortanova 1955: 11, Hadzhinikolov 1983: 9).

Zhenata dnes, which until 1959 remained the only women's magazine and had become the second largest print medium in the country – second only to the central communist newspaper *Rabotnichesko delo* (Workers' Matter) (Dimova 2005; Shkodrova 2014), perpetuated the same early discourses. Women were presented exclusively in professional roles and the cooking advice was kept basic and minimal.

The hardships of the post-war period and of the radical reorientation of the economy, combined with political, Stalin-backed terror and the difficulties in reorganizing agriculture shaped the spartan character of the earlier communist years. But more importantly the radical nature of the views on everyday life was defined by the novelty of the experiment. Having stated its far-reaching discourses, the new power had to transform them into actual social mechanisms and that, as the example of the October revolution showed, was a challenge of a different scale.

REFORMING NATIONAL FOODWAYS

Principal elements of the modernization, with which the communist state planned to make possible the liberation of women from their obligations in the kitchen, was the creation of a solid network of canteens and restaurants and of advanced food industry and agriculture, supplying households with processed products (Shkodrova 2014: 236–237).

The canteens came first chronologically, and were developed by the communist authorities with significant consistency. Their network steadily expanded from 2,340 canteens in 1947 (Hadzhinikolov 1983: 15) to over 6,500 in 1986 (State Statistics Yearbook 1989). They covered economic enterprises, institutes, schools, universities, hospitals, state institutions, agricultural cooperatives. The rationale behind these efforts was that canteens would save time from chores such as daily purchasing of products and domestic cooking and washing, and would thus liberate women 'to participate in the socially-organised labour' (Hadzhinikolov 1983: 7). They were meant to provide nutritious and healthy meals, prepared by professionals with the greatest efficiency: with no waste and all nutrients preserved.

Putting great hopes in canteens, in 1956 the state lowered the prices of their services via subsidies[6] and put pressure on to increase the quality of food. It also extended the

---

[6] Hadzhinikolov stated that by 1968 in 95.9 per cent of the restaurants in Bulgaria the added value did not exceed 35 percent, which was significantly lower than in the other communist countries. He also claimed that the subsidizing of canteen food was greatest in Bulgaria (Hadzhinikolov, 1970: 7).

access to any institutional canteen to the entire families of the employed personnel (Hadzhinikolov 1983: 16). The strategic plan was to provide, by 1990, canteen food for 90 per cent of the students and 70 per cent of the workers (Hadzhinikolov 1970: 27, Shkodrova 2014: 237).

These expectations were never met and canteens never came close to replacing home cooking. A survey from 1969 claimed that barely 8.5 per cent of families used canteens for lunch and 3 per cent for dinner (CSA, 1969), and that people 'stubbornly' refused to use the service more (Dinkova 1980: 46). Later, canteen users even diminished – by more than 10 per cent by 1981, in comparison to 1965 (Hadzhinikolov 1983: 17).

Even if centrally organized, the canteen system was not of even quality and a certain hierarchy was in place: the more elite the enterprise or institution, the better the food and the service. The simple ones had cement floors, bare tables, used metal plates, often smelled of old grease and disinfectant and offered bland food and despicable service. The best ones resembled good restaurants. The population, especially in the bigger cities, was aware of these variations. While many places were frowned upon, access to some was considered a privilege. However the attitudes towards canteen food were often hostile: there were cases where parents forbade their children to eat in the school canteen (Shkodrova 2014: 238–240, 242).

The other form of public catering, the **restaurants**, enjoyed higher esteem. But they were fewer – by 1988 there were 767,113 places for visitors in canteens and 437,227 in restaurants (Yearly Statistics Book 1989). They were also pricier and access to them often depended on connections. To most of the urban middle class they were accessible only on special occasions (Popova, 1984: 4, Shkodrova 2014: 147–192).

Another source of ready-made meals for households were the **culinary shops**. First created in the mid-60s, they sold food, cooked in professional kitchens, on central urban locations in the bigger cities. Their number though remained marginal: according to an expert survey there were nine such shops in Sofia, while the smaller towns had only one or none (State and Trends, 1971). Moreover, the culinary shops were criticized in the press for their narrow choice of dishes. A 1971 article stated that 70 per cent of customers found dishes containing meat infrequently, if at all. On offer were mostly desserts, as if 'the culinary shop competes with the pastry shops' (Dimitrov 1971). Another article from 1984 announced that the number of culinary shops in the country had grown to 281, but according to the Ministry of Domestic Trade and Services even in Sofia their services remained 'only a promise' (Metodieva 1984). A control body report, claimed the article, established the food choice in the culinary shops to be at the bare minimum.

Another similar initiative failed in the middle of the 1960s: the **public kitchens** for takeaway food. They were meant to function like canteens, but were situated in residential areas and sold mainly takeaway food. They never picked up, judging by their number: nine in the middle of the 1960s and eleven at the end of the 1970s (State Statistics Yearbook 1979: 330).

In any case the concern with the culinary shops and public kitchens was minor compared to the **industrial production of processed foods**, which was a much larger-scale project. In 1947 the communist regime expropriated all factories with the intention of building a sweeping state industry. But its history of resetting and expanding food production was hardly as successful as hoped: like all communist food industries in Eastern Europe, the Bulgarian one became notorious with its shortages of food products – processed or raw. One of the main reasons was that the consumer industry never became a real priority to the regime, which, instigated by Stalin, prioritized the development of heavy industry.

Perhaps the greatest and fastest success was the industrialization of bread production, which started in 1949 and in the cities was completed in the 1950s (Shkodrova 2014: 24). Pasteurized milk, cheeses and yogurt, cured meats and pastry, which were widely available in the urban zones before the communist revolution, gradually spread towards rural zones and escaped further the traditional seasonal cycles.

Apart from these early developments, an advance marked the canning industry, which was constituted by consolidating already existing private factories and building new ones. In 1948 the communist state opened what it claimed to be the largest canning factory on the Balkan peninsula, *Vitamina*. Having 'collectivized' (i.e. consolidated) most of the available agricultural land and having nationalized it by the end of the 1950s, the regime held the industrial supplies in its hands. A traditionally agricultural country with a benign climate, Bulgaria was gradually regaining and then increasing its capacity for food production and rising quantities of fruits and vegetables were processed by the industry.

However it is arguable how big was the difference that the canning industry made to Bulgarian housewives. From the mid-1950s exports grew: mostly of vegetables and fruits, processed and fresh, to the USSR and the rest of the Eastern bloc. The state also used any opportunity to sell agricultural produce to Western Europe, which was a primary source of much-needed foreign currency (Znepolski ed. 2011: 290–305). By the 1970s Bulgarian authorities were praising themselves over the scale of production and export of agricultural, fresh and processed foods. A book, celebrating the advance of the communist economy announced in the 1980s that 'due to the rich assortment and the high quality of the produce, 70 per cent of it is gladly welcomed in many countries – from USA and Canada to Japan'. The authors informed their readers that by the 1980s the percentage of exports reached 80 per cent of the total production (Petrov et al., 1983: 97–99).

The exported volumes of food did not indicate abundance in the country. On the contrary, they were often causing deficits. Foreign markets were prioritized over the domestic due to state debts and currency crises, which followed one after the other. In the meantime the home market, despite the triumphalist rhetoric, suffered shortages. Even when the Communist Party had the best of intentions of giving priority to the people's consumption in 1975, its commitments only lasted a few months until the next economic crisis (Ivanov 2011: 246). Data of the Food and Culture Organisation of the United Nations (FAOSTAT) confirm this as well: between 1971 and 1981 the supply of the domestic market with fruits and vegetables in Bulgaria marked a stagnation, or even a drop in quantities, but exports reached a peak[7].

---

[7] The data in the databank of FAOSTAT (http://www.fao.org) on the export of agricultural products from Bulgaria between 1960–1981 shows that the export of most vegetables, fruits and wine reached an absolute peak somewhere between 1965 and 1980, after which it rapidly dropped. For example the export of vegetables from 100,000 tonnes in 1960 reached 340,000 tones in 1975 and fell back to 120,000 towards 1988.

To cover the gaps in the failing food industry, in the 1970s the government tried to change course and make space for certain private economic activities. Allowing for some (strictly controlled) liberalization of the agrarian sector, it tried to arrange the regions' and then the local communities' self-sustainability in terms of food production. But in ten years this delivered little success. By 1980 persisting economic failures brought to the point where the population was consuming only half of the recommended quantities of fruits and vegetables, with the consumption of all types of food except dairy products and sugar/sweets staying way below the UN norm (Ivanov 2011: 247).

The other side of the problem was that the consumers' trust in industrial food was low. In her study of post-communist attitudes to industrially canned food, anthropologist Jung described the strongly negative reactions of some Bulgarians to the produce of the communist factories (Jung 2009: 42). The success story of the industry was in any case not convincing enough to change the enduring practice of producing home preserves in nearly industrial quantities by most households. Preserves were so central to Bulgarians' yearly menu, that US anthropologist Smollett named the phenomenon 'the economy of jars' (1989: 126) – also due to the ability of canned food to circulate within social networks as a token of care and affection.

The triumphant rhetoric, which glorified the state industrialization, was compromised by various state-validated actions, like for example the courses, organized to teach people that 'home canning makes savings to the people's economy by making use of the fruits and vegetables during the harvest season, without which they would have been wasted and lost to the economy' (Petrov et al. 1983; Shkodrova 2014: 329). In a country where even onion, vinegar and sugar were at times difficult to procure, the notion of a ready-made meal bought from the shop was very problematic. In reality, Bulgarian housewives began to enjoy products like industrially made mayonnaise or sour cream only in the late 1970s, and frozen chicken was not available until well into the 1980s.

The continuous efforts to pursue economic advance of an industrial type on the one hand, and the limitations of the centralized planned economy on the other, created specific dynamics, which pushed towards diverging manifestations of the meta-discourse. The political elite and the social structure, created to reproduce the main ideological lines in the field of food practices, felt both compelled to exaggerate the success of modernization and industrialization, and to teach the population how to handle the realities outside this imagined world. The situation was no more than a new stage of the irreconcilable controversy in the very foundation of state socialism, which was built on the denial of the petit-bourgeois lifestyle only to be able to build a version of it for everyone. While the forced frugality of the early communist years was blurring this innate conflict, the advance of modernization only raised the tension, exposing the idea of a 'correct communist attitude' to the material world as utopian.

LEGITIMIZING CONSUMPTION

The death of Stalin in 1953 made space for 'the Thaw' of Khrushchev. The official denouncement of the former Soviet leader in 1956 echoed across the Eastern bloc, softening the regimes somewhat and focusing their rhetoric towards the nations' wellbeing. In Bulgaria, where the war-time food rationing system ended in 1953, the events in Moscow marked the end of the open repressions and declarative asceticism, and in 1956 gave way to the subtler authoritarianism of Todor Zhivkov and his 'care for the man' (also known as 'the April line' in Bulgaria). Some post-communist researchers defined the policy of the following decades as a policy of 'bribing' the society into a consensus to sustain the imitation of communism by the regime (Ivanov, 2011; Znepolski, ed., 2011). Others went as far as calling it a 'communist humanism' (Scarboro, 2012). At least in words, the improvement of the living standard became the priority of the political establishment in the following three decades (Ivanov 2011: 242; Dichev 2005: 76-77; Mineva 2003: 143-145). In this process erstwhile luxury was 'normalized' as a key motor of modernity, argued Crowley and Reid, but leisure and luxury in communism were 'at once accommodated and marginalized within a conceptual apparatus that excludes state socialism from modernity' (Crowley and Reid 2010: 20,11).

Long before the Bulgarian communist ideologists faced their limits in delivering the material modernization for the lifestyle they promoted, Lenin had identified with concern the difficulty in providing 'the material conditions for ending women's historic household-bondage' (Vogel 2013: 126). These material conditions were one of the most challenging hurdles the communist states faced, and not only because they were difficult to achieve on a practical level, but because they contained in their core the oxymoronic contradiction of the communist modernization project, which both rejected the consumer's comfort and tried to democratize it.

This problem was not experienced exclusively by the communist regimes. De Grazia argued that the rise of mass consumption challenged the ideology of any nation-state, and its sovereignty: if the mass media offered new opportunities to organize the nation, mass production encouraged individualization through goods (De Grazia 1996: 338). But the issue was particularly painful within the communist states, which experienced an authority crisis because of the ways in which they were established, and the particular mismatch between what they publicly aimed at and what they delivered. It was precisely this side of the modernization that made a significant difference in everyday life, and where the Eastern European regimes seemed to stand so badly in comparison with the alternative Western model.

In their illuminating book on consumption in communism, Bren and Neuberger (2012: 7) argued that 'the history of the region should not be defined by "Western" narratives of the consumer experience ... or by a 'modernisation theory' that assumes all societies develop along the lines of a familiar American consumerist model.' They had a point that the nations of Eastern Europe had their own mode of modernizing, their own scale to measure the process. But the development in Eastern Europe was conceived and conceptualized as an alternative to the Western capitalist model and through the years the regimes continuously negotiated their politics against the developments in the West, while struggling to reconcile the individualist humanism of their consumption goals with the collectivism of their ideology.

Not the Western model as such – with which the general public remained unfamiliar – but the repeated vows of the communist elites to reach and surpass the West in levels of consumption created a lasting sense of failure in a competition. This failure was further boosted by the fact that to most people in the East, the West was inaccessible and its material world was widely fantasized about in individual and collective imaginations (as Yurchak for example argued, 2006: 158–159).

The concern with the material wellbeing of the communist peoples was not invented in late communism, as already Stalin's efforts to offer luxury to the masses are well documented and researched (Gronow 2003). Still scholars agree that in the 1950s the idea of adequately satisfying the consumer needs of the citizens became prominent in the ruling parties' rhetoric (Reid 2002, Gronow 2003, Crowley and Reid 2010 on the USSR, Bren 2010a, b, on Czechoslovakia, Elenkov 2008 and Stanoeva 2015 on Bulgaria). In Bulgaria the trend started as early as in 1954, when the Stalinist-style leader Vulko Chervenkov spoke of the role of trade as a means 'to better satisfy the growing needs of the working population' (BCP 1954: 30, Stanoeva 2015: 115).

The communist regimes resolved to pursue an ideal that was essentially petit-bourgeois; as Buck-Morss (2002: 7) argued in more general terms, the two divided by the Iron Curtain systems were competing 'to excel in producing the same utopian forms'. Thus it is not so surprising that there were similarities in the desires (and needs!) of women as consumers on both sides of the Iron Curtain. In the last years researchers point at more similarities in the societies of the two 'camps' of the cold war, than was usually (pre)supposed. Not only were the desires of women similar, but their 'will to consume' was treated similarly 'as a potent political force' (Reid 2002: 222).

Consequently, 'the consumption and gradual redefinition of luxury, along with access to particular forms of leisure, not only by a privileged few but increasingly by the masses', brought a significant change. By the 1950s they started a process, which in the following decades transformed the Eastern European societies into mass consumer societies (Crowley and Reid 2010: 11).

EVOLUTION IN FOOD DISCOURSES

With the advance of the modernization, which was exposing the controversy at the very core of the communist project, the discourses in the culinary advice became less uniform. Both a tendency to exaggerate the advance and an urge to cope with the limitations of it transpire from articles, introductions and recipes. While some of the authors continued to reproduce the original discourses, others sought ways to reconcile them with the reality, or at least showed ambivalence.

The promotion of the public catering system continued: it was endorsed by *Zhenata dnes* (for example Koleva 1958) and in the cookbooks, where professional nutritionists and food technologists continued professing the gradual replacement of home cooking by organized public catering (Chortanova and Dzhelepov 1977: 49) and even stated that the dying out of home cooking was inevitable and beyond human control (Petrov and Dzhelepov 1978).

But since it became increasingly impossible to ignore the delay of the modernization, which would have reduced the women's kitchen labour, authors resorted to focusing on prescribing discipline and professionalism. Instead of pursuing the presentation of home cooking as risky and erroneous, the authorities in nutritionism embarked on greater efforts in educating women how to cook correctly and efficiently (some examples are Cholcheva, Angelova, and Kalenderova 1967; Kanturski 1968). In a way, this was helping them in their oxymoronic task to write instructions for a practice which they felt compelled to denounce.

The projection of home cooking as a responsibility to feed a working nation also remained very visible in the cookbooks from the 1960s. Cholcheva defined cuisine as 'public necessity' (Cholcheva 1964: 8). Naydenov and Chortanova emphasized that domestic cooking is after all important for the labour and combat potential of the nation (Naydenov and Chortanova 1967: 4).

Thus it was women's duty to cook 'correctly': based on efficient, science-informed cooking practices, which would preserve the nutritious qualities of the ingredients and save time, allowing women to pursue another part of their duties: to fully participate in the communist society and raise children as proper communists (Naydenov and Chortanova 1967, Cholcheva et al. 1967; Kanturski 1968 among others). It is in the hands of women to solve their issues by applying greater rationality, argued Konstantinova and Vasilev from the pages of *Zhenata dnes* (Konstantinova 1958, Vasilev 1966). 'We are obliged to be better housewives, better mothers, more cultured than our mothers and the previous generations', wrote Ignatova (1971) in the magazine.

Addressing housewives in technical language and equipping them with detailed tables of nutrients, calories and temperatures, cookbooks insisted on professionalizing home cooking. This was taken to extremes in the introductory parts of many cookbooks, where discussions of nutrition included the movement of bowels, the rhythm of the digestive glands' functions and similar. Food was always treated in the first place as a biological necessity (Shkodrova 2018a: 479).

Domestic cooks were stirred towards responsible cooking, just like communist consumers were directed towards responsible consumption. Just like all across the communist world, in Bulgaria the early talk of improved consumption was dominated by appeals for 'a most-stern regime of frugality' (BCP 1954: 58). 'Overconsumption was perceived not only as an economic problem, but as an act of political sabotage,' stated Stanoeva (2015: 16), quoting further communist food strategies specialist Hadzhinikolov (1954: 18): 'wasting public property is a form of enemy action against the people's power'.

Calling for 'rational consumption', distinguishing between 'false' and 'real' needs (Castillo 2009), was a way to legitimize consumption without losing (the ideological) face of communist modernity. The state assumed the task of predicting and managing popular desires, stated Reid (2002: 218), who also warned against the common misconception of the 'Thaw' period as liberalization: consumption under communism was not seen as a private matter and was subjected at all times to ideological directions (Reid 2002: 249).

In a certain sense such 'ruling over people's desires', as Fischler has branded it, took place also in the US, where the Committee on Food Habits, composed of social scientists, tried to 'get people to want what they need' (Fischler 1988: 276). As Auslander wrote, if 'capitalism encouraged women's individuation through goods, the state needed women to subordinate those needs to the needs of the nation' (Auslander 1996: 104). The difference though was that while this stirring in the capitalist world led to adaptations in both consumers' demand and the industry's supply (or failed both), in the communist world it led consumers towards expectations, which the industry was unable to meet.

The intention of the communist regimes to customize and control consumerism proved to be a difficult task, and the following decades were spent in a laborious and only partially successful search for equilibrium and renegotiations of the limits of acceptable consumption. Reid (2002: 218) argued that most regimes' increasing concessions were driven by several consumer demands-based uprisings across the bloc. Bren made a similar interpretation of the Prague events of 1968 (Bren 2010a: 181). Even if Bulgarian society did not stir towards revolution, the authorities followed suit and vowed to improve the daily life of their citizens. The meta-message to be delivered was of the supremacy of the communist economy before the capitalist one (Stanoeva 2015: 116). In the process an 'ideologically acceptable social stratification' was legitimized (Elenkov 2008: 276). More importantly for this study, the pursuit of wellbeing was validated.

This is precisely where the other line in the adjustment of the food discourses eventually led: the one which both unrealistically praised and criticised the country's modernization and industrialization advance.

EQUIPPING AND INDUSTRIALIZING DOMESTIC COOKING

The confusion which reigned over how to reproduce the inconsistent elements of the meta-discourse on home cooking transpires well from the discussions of kitchen equipment, in particular on the pages of *Zhenata dnes*. Acknowledged as a necessity to the modern household ever since the Kitchen Debate[8], cooking equipment also legitimized the activity of home cooking. One of the specific qualities of kitchen appliances is that they are essential both to those who don't want to spend much time in the kitchen, and to those who do. This allowed for their introduction as a tool to achieve 'correct consumption', and then for their exploitation in destroying the credibility of the ideology, denouncing home cooking.

The theme was introduced cautiously by *Zhenata dnes*, where news on kitchen technological innovations came at first along with an immediate denouncement of home cooking practice. An article from April 1959, which advertised two early models of electric stove and electric grill, also promoted 'tens of different ready-made or semi-prepared foods', stating that 'it was scientifically proved that industrially prepared meals are more nutritious than home-made ones. For example, the proteins of cooked

---

[8] The Kitchen Debate is the name for a historical conversation between Nikita Khrushchev and Richard Nixon, then a vice-president, which took place in July 1959 against the background of an Electrolux Kitchen, exhibited by the United States at the American National Exhibition in Moscow. The exchange, in which the two politicians argued about whether capitalism or communism provided better material comfort, is sometimes interpreted as the first internationally visible sign of the 'Thaw'. It has been also been seen as a turning point, when the technological competition between East and West in the cold war has arguably moved from space and nuclear energy to consumer goods (Oldenziel and Zachmann 2009).

meat, prepared in a home kitchen, are absorbed by the body at barely 83 per cent, while for those of industrially cooked meat the rate is over 96 per cent.' (*Zhenata dnes*, April 1959).

By the 1970s the views had evolved and the magazine presented the electric grill as 'a necessity in the modern household', but one serving to cook in a healthier manner, with less fat and salt (*Zhenata dnes* 1975/4). The kitchen mixer another couple of years later was no longer discussed in such terms. Instead, its value in saving time was emphasized (*Zhenata dnes* 1977/1).

Another time-saver, which was central to the communist discourses of food modernization, was the industrialization of the cooking process. Many cookbooks of the period emphasized the impact of the food industry on domestic foodways. Authors praised the diversity on the market and reduced home cooking to the task of just 'perfecting the convenience food into culinary dishes' (Sotirov 1959: 1). Cooking with semi-prepared products only takes minutes and 'does not require any special knowledge', argued Chortanova and Dzhelepov (1977: 51).

This advice did not stem from the actual situation on the market – towards the 1960s even the official press had begun to criticize the lack of advance in providing prepared or semi-prepared meals or at least processed ingredients. Overstating the achievements of the industry was a common trope of the official rhetoric, assumed not only by the political elite, but by state officials on various levels. In his study of the material culture of everyday life, Bulgarian historian Elenkov (2011: 138) observed that 'images, based on simulated factuality, reproduce the fundamental ideological norms of the 1960s basic and frame positively the entire message regarding the future,' oblivious of the chronic deficits of consumption goods. Such simulative representation was typical of the cookbooks and of articles in *Zhenata dnes*, which overstated the richness and the variety of the food market and denied the market's shortages, seasonality or territorial contrasts to imply wealth. They heralded an increase in the diversity of cans in the shops (Voynov 1957) using phrases like 'rich assortment of industrially semi-prepared foods' (Sotirov 1959), or the 'enormous richness' of available ready-made pastry (Enderlein 1968).

But this declarative praise was paired with certain efforts to shape home cooking in line with the possibilities of the industry and the available ingredients. One example was the influx of recipes using pork meat, which was the easiest to produce industrially and most used to replace the pre-communist consumption of veal, beef, mutton and lamb. An increased application of minced meat in recipes allowed for the use of lesser quality cuts. Cooking recipes, featuring simply 'meat' reflected the unreliability of the market.

Meat was central to the communist idea of healthy nutrition and the regime found it important to reiterate its increased consumption as evidence of achieved national wellbeing (Franc 2003: 52–53 observed the same trend in Czechoslovakia). In the span of only two years, 1958 to 1959, the Bulgarian state publishers released four cookbooks, specifically dedicated to domestic meat preparation. This prolific publishing activity was a leap after the six titles published in the entire preceding decade, three of which were on diets and hygiene.

It is difficult to judge to what extent and in which instances cookbooks reflected the market, or tried to stir the demand in a direction favourable to the industry, since they certainly engaged in both. Clearly traceable in the cookbooks is the campaign for fish consumption from 1965 to 1968, when Bulgaria was developing its ocean fishery and the state gradually saw it as a resource of much-needed proteins for the population. The 'first and broadest advertisement campaign', as its strategists dubbed it, involved several key institutions: the Bulgarian Academy of Sciences, the Health Education Institute at the Ministry of Health, and the Ministry of Trade (Lesichkov 1970, as quoted by Elenkov 2011: 140). The special state department *Reklama* (Marketing) released two recipe leaflets: *51* and *101 Recipes for Home Cooking of Fish,* and distributed recipes for fish through the media. A few years later, in 1974, the leaflet expanded into a small booklet with 202 recipes, preceded by a foreword on the importance of fish to human health (*202 Recipes*, 1974). The campaign was also supported by the introduction of two culinary programmes on national television, where chef Popinski promoted fish as an ingredient (Elenkov 2011: 140), and is visible in cookbooks, where the sections featuring fish were expanded.

Just like in other fields of consumption, in modernizing food and cooking technologies communist ideology faced the same challenge: to prove the success of the non-capitalist model of legitimized consumption. This tension pushed the consumption discourses to evolve closer to those dominant in capitalist societies. The legitimization of consumption had allowed for open criticism against the failures of the communist state to deliver the consumer goods it promised. Officially published texts started reassessing the situation. Over 80 per cent of Bulgarian women of active age were employed by 1970 in the state economy (Dinkova 1980), but the industrial and trade infrastructure, which was supposed to be part of their employed lifestyle, was not materializing. 'It is estimated that the purchase of products and the preparation of food takes two to three hours, and often 50 per cent of all the free time of women. This is far too much!', wrote Chortanova and Dzhelepov (1977: 51). 'The contemporary woman obtained the right to participate in the building of a new life on equal grounds, but this undoubted achievement did not relieve her from her domestic obligations', stated a cookbook from 1967 (Cholcheva, Angelova, and Kalenderova 1967: 34).

The diverging discourses are particularly visible on the pages of *Zhenata dnes,* which spent the last fifteen years of communist rule both exaggerating the achievements of the communist state and fretting over their insubstantiality. The magazine published open and articulated criticism of producers, who five years after the adoption of the official economic agenda to produce more consumer goods were only beginning to consider the task (Vulcheva 1981).

When the perception of these failed promises developed, as Crowley and Reid (2010: 16) observed, 'by the late 1980s, these same citizens had come to understand themselves as frustrated consumers unable to command goods and services to which they had a right'.

These alterations in the formally perpetuated discourses directly affected culinary advice. They brought the idea that everyday life, and the home kitchen and table in particular, should express and reflect the wellbeing of the communist nation. This idea advanced at a low speed and cautiously, leaping forward in the 1960s and slowing down in the 1970s. But eventually its development in the 1980s undid the early communist home cooking ideology in Bulgaria and allowed for the return of indulgence in cooking.

TAKING PLEASURE IN FOOD

After having discussed cooking solely as a duty for decades, the possibility of enjoying it was mentioned for the first time in 1968, in the foreword to a translated East-German cookbook (Enderlein 1968). Authored by the Bulgarian publishers, the brief introduction was an evident attempt to secure the correct communist approach to home baking: 'The assortment of desserts in bakeries and pastry shops is enormous. We, the women, involved in production, greet this fact with satisfaction, as it lessens our domestic chores. However, most women are always interested in recipes for home desserts, as their preparation gives them joy', stated the foreword (Enderlein 1968: 5). It implied that even if a folly, home baking was an admissible manifestation of the good life in the industrialized communist society.

Such a perspective though soon proved to be an outlier, as in the course of another entire decade no other cookbook repeated the idea. While seeking to imply that life was good in the country, the authors were careful not to break away from the ideological prescriptions of the earlier decades.

With its twelve issues per year, *Zhenata dnes* reflects well the fluctuation of the ideological moods in the 1960s and in the 1970s. A separate section with recipes, usually on half to one page, had appeared in almost every issue until 1961, but afterwards recipes were featured only occasionally: seven times in 1961, twice in 1962 and 1963, once in 1964, five to seven times in the following decade. The magazine published instead educative articles on nutrition, appliances, industrial products, and, once in a while, on table and party etiquette. One event relevant to this research was the appearance in June 1967 of a new chapter, 'From the reader to the reader'. Taking half to one page, it was written not by the usual food professionals, but, as the title suggested, by home cooks. The idea of inviting women to share their recipes on the pages of the magazine involved *Zhenata dnes* on a practical level in the widely popular process of recipe exchange: instead of reprimanding it, like it did in previous years (for example Paneva 1958: 17), it facilitated it.

This novelty was not to last: the rubric appeared only seven times in a period of about three years and was abandoned. In the 1970s the entire magazine seemed to be undergoing an identity crisis, publishing on one cover the most popular female pop-singer sailing a yacht in shorts, and on the next – a woman in a headscarf, riding a tractor (*Zhenata dnes* 1973/7,8). The front and the back covers of the magazine also sometimes differed strikingly, as if the front was made to fit the 'culture of poverty' and the back – to defy it. While the recipes increasingly suggested leisure as an element of the lifestyle and cooking as part of it, other articles in the magazine continued to speak of the kitchen as a 'dictator' and to discuss 'women's liberation from kitchen slavery' (Spasovska 1974).

In 1975 the recipes regained their monthly presence in the magazine. By then they already contained signs of the advancing modernization of households, and some very early steps towards liberation from nutritionism, and towards a more colourful cuisine, aiming to please and not only to nourish the body. The reader was introduced to the concept of the cold buffet, the names of the recipes were occasionally changed from entirely descriptive to more imaginative (e.g. Pirate's goulash, Labrador's cuts in

Zhenata dnes 1975/6, Sailor's Borscht, *Zhenata dnes* 1977/1) and tiny articles on history of food appeared a few times. Some foreign cuisines were featured, such as the Viennese (*Zhenata dnes* 1970/12), Arabian (*Zhenata dnes* 1975/10), or Italian (*Zhenata dnes* 1977/10). In the years, leading to the end of the regime in 1989, the fluctuation continued, with cooking advice expanding on the pages or vanishing altogether, the magazine's team clearly quite unable to decide how to approach it.

The expansion and transformation of the idea of communist consumption reached the cookbooks firmly in the 1980s. The most striking development was the retreat of excessive nutritionism. A book, translated from Czech, announced boldly that some of the dishes it featured 'mostly for technological reasons' did not 'satisfy entirely the requirements of healthy food' (Fialova 1984: 5). Another, by a Bulgarian author, announced that the matters of nutrition should remain a concern of science (i.e. implicitly not of the authors of cookbooks) (Saraliev 1984: 7), and even the authors of the most nutrition-obsessed cookery literature from the previous decades Chortanova and Dzhelepov conceded that the home cook does not need to know the chemical formulas of the nutrients (Chortanova and Dzhelepov 1983: 3, Shkodrova 2018a: 481). Where considerations of 'healthy' were concerned, 'tasty' regained authority for the first time in cookbooks such as T*he Gourmand Kitchen* (Fialova 1984), *We cook well* (1984), *Seasonal cuisine* (1988), *Culinary Spectrum* (Ilieva 1983).

The evolution described here is only a general outline of the dominant 'official' views, with which the women negotiated their own conceptualization of routine food practices. Evidently these views were neither uniform, nor necessarily acknowledged by each woman. They must have also been of varying importance and possibly moving up and down within individual hierarchies. But before examining the perception and the reasoning of the interviewed women, it is important to outline a few more elements, without which the discursive structure they inhabited would not have been complete.

COMMUNIST COMMENSALITY

The central role of food in fostering social bonds has been discussed at length since Lévi-Strauss (1969) and food studies have considered it a central theme (Young 1971, Khare 1976, Weiner 1976, Douglas 1997). Anthropologists, historians and sociologists have remarked on the particular aptness of food to express ideas about relationships and to consolidate and demarcate social groups (Meigs 1997: 104, Bourdieu 2003: 70).

The central place of food in social construction and the ability of food practices to reinforce 'a coherent ideology of the family throughout the social structure' has led to conceptualizing the family meal as an epitome of 'social relations of power and subordination' within the family, a social order, defining generations' and gender roles (Charles and Kerr 1988: 17). Campbell (1995: 107) argued that modern commensality has taken over the central role in ensuring cohesion of the traditional family, a role which was previously played by the shared participation of families in production.

Various cultures fill the social institution of the family meal with different content, but the meal's function of keeping up the familial cohesion seems to remain constant.

Bulgarian society before communism had foodways that generally fell into the common European pattern: no tradition of family breakfast (which was a peculiarity in the European context); secondary in importance came lunch meals and dinners, which functioned as family meals; and a more elaborate Sunday lunch (Gavrilova 1999: 111). At the end of the 19th century the urban lifestyle evolved to divide family time from working time (Daly 2001: 284) and enforced 'independent day-time trajectories of family members' (Gavrilova 2016: 295), increasingly deviating from the rural way of life. The concept of free time formed among urban upper classes and family meals gained structure, shifting their focus from satisfying biological needs to serving social functions. Commodity food was introduced and meals outside the household became more common, changing the idea of ideal practices of family coherence (Gavrilova 2016: 320). By 1944 food culture and practices had divided Bulgarian society between an emancipated and cosmopolitan culinary urban lifestyle, and an early modern rural lifestyle.

In this sense communism brought at first a certain regression, as the political and social turbulence after 1944 worked against the developing urban culture. It did so by deliberately destroying the lifestyle of the upper classes on the one hand, denouncing it as retrograde and antagonistic to the communist ideology, and on the other by bringing rural population into the cities and empowering it to redefine overnight the modern lifestyle – a phenomenon, quite eloquently named 'rurbanisation' by Roth (1997: 30). The tendency of the communist state to regulate private lives and its notion of collectivism additionally disrupted the establishment of the pre-war style of commensality.

However communism also had a certain modernizing effect over the population in general, and in particular over the inhabitants of rural areas, still more numerous at the time. In the post-war years the communist leadership was committed to 'civilizing' the rural population and initiating it in modern food practices[9]. As one example, sociologist Bilyana Raeva researched documents from one of the major voluntary post-war projects, the brigade to construct a new utopian city of Dimitrovgrad, and pointed out that nutritionists were attached to the units of brigade workers to ensure diverse, healthy food, and the participants were led into a pattern of four meals a day (Shkodrova 2014: 79, 304). From the archive of the communist-led mass organization *Otechestven front*[10] (Fatherland Front) it transpires that a long-term programme to educate the countryside population in modern communist lifestyle, foodways included, took place in the 1960s and 1970s (CSA 417-4-42 1957, 1968, also Brunnbauer 2008, Nikolova and Ghodsee 2015).

---

[9] Lebow (2013: 167) wrote of the paternalism that was ingrained in the communist ideology. Believing in their superiority over 'common people', communist intellectual strategists assumed it as their mission to treat people well, but also to 'civilise' them, i.e. educate them on all matters, ranging from political consciousness and education to everyday life and hygiene.

[10] *Otechestven Front* (OF) [Fatherland Front, FF] was established during the Second World War by the Bulgarian Communist Party as an anti-fascist organization and for a period of time united parties from a broad political spectrum. But in 1948 it lost its multi-party character and became a puppet-organization, which streamlined the political agenda of the ruling Communist Party into simulated grass-roots activity: membership was as good as compulsory and encompassed more than half of the population (i.e. an overwhelming majority of Bulgarians of active age) (Detrez 2015: 198).

Thus early communist ideology on the one hand transferred commensality from the private to the collective table of the canteen. On the other hand it never explicitly attached attention to the social side of the canteen ritual, as the focus was kept on nutrition and the instrumentality of meals, rather than on their social and hedonistic values.

Late communism marked a change in this regard. It modified the idea of modernity by developing further the idea of free time, and by half allowing back onto the family stage a (somewhat adapted) version of the old 'petit-bourgeois' rituals of familial socializing around food. After the culture of austerity and poverty had ruled over the discourses on Bulgaria's everyday life until the 1960s, the theme of meeting guests at home surfaced in *Zhenata dnes*, and then in cookbooks, framing the housewife as an entertainer at social gatherings. The advice on home entertainment evolved from relatively modest and matter-of-fact tips regarding a surprise afternoon visit by a friend, into prescriptive articles on how to impress guests as a host of elaborate dinners.

To align this with the ideology, which was built on negation of the old lifestyle, the earliest article in the magazine justified the reintroduction of the theme by placing it in the discourse of national pride. 'Guests have always been welcome in the Bulgarian family,' reads the opening – 'Also nowadays, a guest won't be allowed to leave without a treat, not before being offered the best that there is in the house. This Bulgarian hospitality is renowned far beyond the borders of the country' (Aleksandrova, 1962). This 'nationalisation' of women exceeded their treatment as national resource, which De Grazia identified in Nazi Italy (De Grazia 1996). It was more like the situation in 19th-century France, when women were expected to represent the nation and to consolidate the national identity through everyday actions and lifestyle (Auslander 1996).

At first, in the 1960s, the housewife was described as a dutiful and professionally efficient servant, who knows how to serve without too much ado that would tire her and irritate the guests (Aleksandrova 1962). The woman was entrusted with a growing list of new tasks, and was required to perform them effortlessly: one and the same article would advise her to organize an effort-sparing New Year party, adding in passing that 'washing the windows, sweeping the carpets and putting the cupboards and the wardrobes in order, if needed – washing the curtains and the tablecloths will give the house a pleasant, fresh-air look' (Dimova 1964). The same article explicitly warned that 'an exhausted housewife with her tired look can spoil the good spirits of the guests and make them leave much earlier than intended'.

If this early heralding of the returning petit-bourgeois world was not focused on the woman's own delight and amusement, but rather on her role of hostess, the discourse gradually developed and by 1969 *Zhenata dnes* wrote of the 'privacy and intimacy' of home celebrations (*Zhenata dnes*, October 1969). The instructions indeed remained highly prescriptive. Private life remained a not-entirely-private matter. The roles were distributed in detail: the children sitting on a small table apart from the parents, the oldest among them urged to mind the behaviour of the rest; the removal of furniture before the party – the unnecessary items inventoried piece by piece. Even the presents for each of the family members were specified as in the American game-song 'The Twelve Days of Christmas': 'to cheer up granny with a pair of warm winter slippers, to please grandpa with a warm scarf, the husband with a favourite book, a pair of good socks or gloves, your friends with a bottle of eau de cologne, a brooch, a handkerchief or something else' (Dimova 1964). Central in this game was the task of keeping up appearances: 'It is less important what we will cook, than how we will prepare the food and present it to the guests. If we follow this priority, we can be sure of coming across as good hosts' (*Zhenata dnes* 1967/12, 1970/2, 1972/9). With the passage of years the advice on how to decorate a festive table appeared with greater regularity around New Year and became increasingly opulent (although in some years it was also entirely absent).

Such changes of attitudes were less visible in the cookbooks of the period, which were after all not too numerous in the 1960s and in the 1970s: nineteen and twelve titles for domestic cooking respectively, a number of which were dedicated to specific diets, conservation technologies and similar. Still by the end of the 1960s the published cookery literature showed a tendency to portray certain modern-style commensality. The very act of publication of advice on how to prepare cocktails (Hubenov 1968) or how to make and serve soft drinks at home (Bakurdzhiev et al. 1968) presented a claim that the Bulgarian society of the epoch was keeping up with the times. The cookery compendiums contained modest, but expanding, sections on how to arrange the table or organize a party, although in some of them these addressed professional rather than domestic cooks (for example the section on official receptions in *Our Cuisine*, Naydenov and Chortanova 1971). Still the advice grew towards wealthier (and unrealistic to most), complex menus, including rarely available products.

At the end of the 1970s individualism, centred on private health, diet, and wellbeing emerged as a more prominent theme. Weight, good teeth and good health became more discussed in the food-related articles than pleasing guests. By 1978 the very concept of having guests was reconsidered and simplicity ruled. The advice to the housewife was to serve sandwiches and beer instead of tiring herself, as the communication during the evening was 'what brings friends together' (Stoyanova 1978).

REARRANGING GENDER ROLES IN THE KITCHEN

The gender paradox of Eastern European communism was that it arrived with a revolutionary ideology for equality of sexes, but, in certain ways, deepened the inequality between them. On the surface of it, changes were made to align women's rights with those of men. Women received the same education as men. They were told that they were given the same right to work. This 'right' was however an obligation, and as women sharing men's work in industry did not mean men sharing women's work at home, the change broadened the gap in the workload between genders. As anthropologist Victor Buchli observed, 'it was the woman/housewife who was the pathologised object of reform' (Buchli 2000: 154). Men remained 'conspicuously absent from this discourse on consumption and domesticity' (Reid 2002: 250). Researchers of 20th-century European communism, well familiar with this situation, have dubbed it a 'double burden' (Corrin 1992, Ghodsee 2014), or even a 'triple burden', accounting for the high levels of social and political activity expected from women (Einhorn 1993: 23).

Looking retrospectively one can clearly see the exploitative aspects in the application of the communist ideology for equality of genders. In Bulgaria the communist government, which came to power with the support of the Soviet Union and through terror in the aftermath of the Second World War, worked to rapidly industrialize and urbanize the country. Large masses of people moved from rural areas into fast developing towns and cities. The entire active female population was obliged to participate in the state-run economy, working full-time six days a week. At the same time women were encouraged, and also found themselves forced, to run, alone, households of pre-industrial character: with little access to technologies, industrial goods or childcare, all of which were promised, and essential to make the full-time employment supportable[11]. Thus an entire generation was raised on the shoulders solely of working women, before actual feminism started to emerge and the sharing of domestic-life chores with men was discussed.

This situation was not entirely intentional. It was rather a result of circumstances. The effect of the stumbling communist-style modernization was amplified by the low priority which the new women's issues held in the hierarchy of the ruling class well into the period. There were internal contradictions in the ideology, which sought solutions to the women's problems not in equalizing the roles of the sexes in the household, but in introducing technologies and public catering, combined with the strong, residual patriarchal models of power relations.

The ruling class acknowledged the inequality, which the new urban lifestyle perpetuated, and in the following decades tried to address it with fluctuating intensity and understanding. Especially after the 1960s, when the first results of the communist modernization started taking effect and the general levels of wealth allowed the country to leave behind the extreme scarcities and poverty of the war period, the care of the state leadership was verbalized more explicitly. But the intended practical measures lagged behind, sometimes failed altogether, and while the idea of gender equality broadened, it only forced a discussion on the roles in the household onwards to the 1980s.

As a result, the history of the communist decades is one of difficult, continuous renegotiation of the female gender role, and central in it is the domestic preparation of food: an object of particular attention within the communist modernization project.

While building an ideologically-driven society, the Bulgarian communist regime, like many other authoritarian systems, sought to control private life. It went as far as to interfere in sexual life (Popova 2016: 67) and seek 'the birth of healthy children, which would ensure the reproduction of the communist society' (Engels 1975: 69, Stoykova 2005: 111). Among all the everyday-life activities, home cooking had particular importance: it was regularly discussed as occupying women's time and as potentially obstructive to the state's intention to use them as a work force.

---

[11] Cowan argued that if home technologies in the West did not really reduce the time which women spent on household chores, they at least reduced the drudgery of housework and allowed the woman to do a 'double day without destroying her health, to work full-time and still sustain herself and her family at a reasonably comfortable level' (Cowan 1987: 6). Communist women had to look elsewhere for resources to reduce the burden to feasible levels.

The recognition of women's rights to participate in the labour market, combined with preserved traditional gender segregation was common for the Communist bloc (Sacks 1977 in the Soviet Union, Corrin 1992, Einhorn 1993, Nuss 1980 for Central and Eastern Europe, Massey, Hahn and Sekulić 1995 for Former Yugoslavia, and Petrova 1993, Kotseva and Todorova 1994 specifically for Bulgaria, to name a few of the works which demonstrated it). Miroiu (2007: 198) even insisted that communist feminism is a contradiction in terms, arguing that 'there were unofficial islands of feminism in communism', but 'it is hard to admit that something like *communist feminism* ever existed'.

After all indeed the upholders of the official discourses in the women's magazine *Zhenata dnes* and in cookbooks described the social expectations of women as not so different from what Dantec-Lowry wrote of the United States in the 1950s, where in suburbia 'once again, the woman's role (...) was to be a homemaker keeping her house in ship-shape order, nurturing her children, and providing comfortable space for her husband away from the rat race'. But while Dantec-Lowry describes the researched phenomenon in the United States as a return of 'the cult of true womanhood' and saw the women being 'once again put on the domestic pedestal' (Dantec-Lowry 2008: 108), it is difficult to evaluate the situation of the women emancipated by Bulgarian communism in the same way.

Echoing the general idea that 'the socialist order creates a new man – exemplary not only in his work, but also in his culture and daily life' (Kovacheva 1966: 3), woman was seen as a construction project – in political and social terms – by the political establishment. The earliest representations, which deprived her of femininity and portrayed her as a workaholic amazon, lasted well until the 1960s, when *The Housewife's Book* (Cholcheva and Ruseva eds. 1962: 12–17) instructed that besides being perfect housewives, the women needed to be employed, active participants in social, cultural and political life, pleasantly dressed and clean. 'The mother needs to ensure the general hygiene in the house – an important prerequisite to everyone's health,' reads the introductory chapter on the role of the woman in the communist society, authored by people's teacher Mara Puhovska. She further states that women are responsible for the clothing, the friendly relations within the family, for raising their children diligently and educating them in appreciation of the arts. Among other things, they are expected to put 'great care into their family's food'. They are supposed to supply fresh and nutritious food daily 'together with her husbands', but in the end the cooking is left for them alone.

Towards the end of the 1960s this view evolved, incorporating more complexity and *Zhenata dnes* advocated (with the voice of a male author) 'the creation of such a type of woman, which will correspond to the requirements of contemporary society': to all the previous obligations, the author Vassilev (1966) added the duty of women to please their men.

With its typical inconsistency, *Zhenata dnes* had published some appeals to men already in the late 1950s. 'There is no such thing as female and male work', argued one article (*Zhenata dnes* 1958/6), others routinely assigned obligations in the house to the woman. This was paired with another, already mentioned fluctuation in the attitudes to cookery information as essential, and to home cooking as an activity which does not befit the modern woman.

Towards the end of the 1960s the magazine became increasingly a champion of the criticism against the work overload of Bulgarian women. Ghodsee (2014) asserted that the magazine, whose editor-in-chief was the wife of a prominent communist leader, at the time put significant pressure on the state leadership to deal with women's problems. A survey, commissioned by the editors, established that women worked on the average fourteen and a half hours a day, including eight hours on the job and on the average one and a half hours a day cooking and washing dishes, while men spent eight minutes daily on household work (Pesheva 1962, Shkodrova 2014).

The results of this survey were picked up by the communist leader Zhivkov in person and incorporated in his rhetoric. In 1971 he spoke at the 10th Party Congress of women's overload, highlighting its negative effect on 'labour efficiency in public production'. This coupling of women's burden at home and their efficiency at work recurred in Zhivkov's speeches, closely resembling Göring's idea of the importance of feeding people well, 'so that they can work' to the best of their ability (quoted by Notaker 2008: 71). By repeating the promises to lessen the burden on women by building more canteens, producing convenience food and similar, Zhivkov also confirmed the insufficiency of the measures already in place (Directives of the 10th congress of BCP in 1972, BCP 1973).

By then cookbooks were openly pointing out the uneven distribution of the household tasks, although they did not call on men to assume their share (Cholcheva et al. 1967: 34). But throughout the 1970s and 1980s *Zhenata dnes* initiated on its pages an actual debate on men's role in the family.

The 1980s marked a significant shift of mood and the first cookbooks not addressed exclusively to women were published: *What to Cook When Mum Isn't Home* (Kondova 1984) targeted the children; *What to Cook in No Time* (Dimcheva 1983) suggested that also 'other members of the family' could sometimes prepare a quick and easy meal. Most importantly, *A Cookbook for Men* was released, in which the author assured his male readers that it is not shameful for a man to cook (Saraliev 1984). The book was far from a straightforward appeal for gender equality: it identified its readership to be single men, students, or men whose wives worked on shifts, implying that in all other cases it was the woman who would be cooking. Besides, stated Saraliev, 'all around the world chefs of famous restaurants are men. In addition to this, gastronomy is more popular amongst men' (Saraliev 1984: 5).

Besides a possibly honest controversy, these contradicting views may have been the author's deliberate policy to get his book published. Reiterating the official political line was often a way to get away with expressing non-conformist views around it (Ghodsee, 2014: 549). A *Cookbook for Men*'s foreword was revolutionary in many ways (Shkodrova 2018a: 468) and might have needed to sound as if it was at least to some extent aligned with the orthodoxy.

Thus contradictory discourses on gender roles were coexisting, intertwined, and sometimes impossible to separate. Evidently the development of emancipatory ideas in time manifested syncopation: while the liberation of women from household chores had been targeted in communist propaganda since 1944, the idea of gender equality within households only really started to be tentatively acknowledged in the 1980s.

Gender consciousness is crucial for achieving egalitarian relations, as sociologist Oriel Sullivan has established in her illuminating research on how professional lives affect gender roles in the family (Sullivan 2004). Bulgarian women's idea of their own role, though, was mostly very far from what Lenin or Marx taught. The communist regime granted them rights that for most women were not even an issue: in the first place because when it came to the 'right' to be employed, it was only a new form of the earlier set-up, within which, according to the statistics, they did not stand far behind men. A census from 1934 established that 44.6 per cent of women and 55.4 per cent of men were economically active (Kotseva and Todorova 1993: 17).

The communist state pushed them into a new framework. In time it gave them greater economic freedom, broadened their social contacts outside the household, and perspectives for professional realization in the contemporary sense opened up similarly to the developments in non-communist Europe (Kotseva and Todorova 1993: 17–19). In this new framework people were expected to lead a lifestyle typical of an industrialized society, but were not provided with the relevant material or social structure to fulfil these expectations. Moreover the partial refocusing 'on the domestic domain helped anchor a traditional gender hierarchy at the very historical juncture when the feminist movement, socialist ideology, and war emergencies had fundamentally challenged conventional women's roles,' as Ruth Oldenziel argued (Oldenziel 2009: 3).

VALUE OF TIME AND MONEY

Many contemporary scholars share the notion that communist economy should be best described not as an economy of shortages, which functioned on the level of top players such as state, party, market or society, but as an *arbitrage* economy, active on the level of several interconnected networks (Hristov, T. 2015; Deyanov 2003, 2006; Bundzhulov, 2003; Nikolova, 2001). To compensate for the permanent shortages, the society produced informal networks of interaction – *vruzki* (Bulgarian for 'connections'). They had a complex infrastructure and served to exchange objects (goods) and statuses (Ledeneva 1998, Lomnitz 1988, Tchalakov 2003, and Deyanov 2003, 2006). In the late communist years some of them connected people who had access to crucial state resources and exploited them privately. These advanced networks were involved in production, aiming at profit and challenging the monopoly of the political establishment over the political capital (Tchalakov 2003: 112–116).

The operation of these networks affected communist everyday life in a number of ways, and were deemed by many to be unavoidable. 'Every living being in our country who has an instinct for self-preservation swims in the muddy waters of the connections practice,' wrote the dissident Georgi Markov in the 1970s (1980: 101). Many households were employing their *vruzki* to secure access to better cuts of meat, to the delivery of items hidden behind the counter such as exotic fruits, strawberries or lamb, which were exported for dollars and of which there was never enough on the internal market, and so on. To use the words of Lomnitz (1988: 42), networks served as social security systems.

The active operation of *vruzki* throughout the communist decades suggests that at least in some cases, the research of low and medium levels of interaction may be more illuminating of communist everyday life than the research of ideology and government. An increasing number of researchers believe that economy under communism should be thought of not in the sense of the usual monetary exchange, but as a system in motion, which 'operates by intertwining different markets'. As Hristov (2015: 93) generalized the principle of communist economy, 'in order to acquire something, it was not enough to pay its price'.

The direct consequence of this was the devaluation of money – not of its value on the international markets, but of its role in the exchange of valuables. 'The problem of the common people was that the strength of money melted before their eyes, that the share of the social capital grew and that this way of participating in the economy was becoming increasingly demanding in consuming time and energy', wrote Možny (2003: 71, as quoted by Deyanov 2003: 78). Developing this argument further, Deyanov pointed out that the shortages in communist economies were precisely a result of this shortage of money power (Deyanov 2003: 82).

Related and consequential to that was the specific value of time. Anthropologists have accepted that the perception of time is a cultural variable, which changes with social order (Claude-Lévy Strauss 1962; Gell 1992 among many). Influential in the study of time under communism is Verdery's (1996) analysis of Ceausescu's Romania, where communist regimes subjected time to 'etatization' (lit. nationalization) – i.e. were seizing it 'from the purposes' which individuals wished to pursue. She highlighted the different ways in which the state tried to regulate private time: 'rituals, calendars, decrees (such as curfews), workday schedules' (Verdery 1996: 40). Appropriation of private time by party and state occurred in Bulgaria along the same pattern: apart from their employment obligations, people were forcefully assigned participation in party meetings and initiatives, parades, brigades, military training, working days for the maintenance of public areas and similar (Shkodrova 2014: 69).

Until 1974 the working week in the People's Republic of Bulgaria consisted of six days, and when the state reduced it to five, the population quickly started perceiving the liberated Saturdays as private time. The very act endorsed the broadening of the idea of private time and privacy. But contrary to these changing perceptions, Saturdays were regularly claimed back by the multiple state-related organizations, which scheduled working activities. If accepted by some who trusted the regime, these interferences in private time were building pressure for many others. Verdery identified three options for behaviour in such situations: complying with the imposed obligations; engaging in them formally, while disagreeing with the concept and content; or resisting. She concluded that many Romanians chose the second and the third option: they 'preferred to use their bodies in time toward reproducing households and local relations rather than toward promoting the power of the Romanian state and its ruling Communist Party.'

Also, in communist Russia people developed numerous tactics to slow down or customize, or 'reinterpret' time according to personal tastes or needs, engaging in 'shifting the temporality of state socialism' (Yurchak 2005: 151–2). Yurchak pointed out the increasingly popular practice in late communism of taking undemanding jobs with multiple sickness leaves, bonus days off and so on, and above all to shift 'the parameters of temporality altogether by engaging in temporally 'distant' activities such as pursuing ancient history or engaging in archaeological expeditions and trips into remote, 'timeless' areas of the state' (Yurchak 2005: 155).

Demotivated, pro-forma working was a typical feature of late communism in Bulgaria as well. It affected many social circles, and those of white-collar workers in particular. There are many evidences of such a climate prevailing in the country in the 1970s and in the 1980s: multiple publications in the press and archive documents offer glimpses into the habitual personalization of time, 'abducted' by the state. Taking time for coffee or queueing for a rare catch on the market during working hours, long private telephone conversations, endless lunches were all habitual practices. One article in the magazine *Sofia* from the 1980s gives an idea of the spread of such practices, with the author asking rhetorically: 'Of course you find the saleswoman sluggish (You work in an office, right? So when YOU act sluggish, it is just less evident, no?). Besides you find her too talkative (and how many coffees did YOU have today?).' (Mircheva 1983).

The main folkloric genre of the period, political and social jokes, also discussed the issue extensively. A popular gag listed the wonders of communism, playing with the contrasts between the declarative and actual faces of daily life, between the social orders as assigned and as used:

The Wonders of Communism:

1. *Everybody has a job.*
2. *Everybody has a job, but nobody works.*
3. *Nobody works, but the production targets are met 100 per cent.*
4. *The production targets are met 100 per cent, but there is nothing in the shops.*
5. *There is nothing in the shops, but everyone has everything he needs.*
6. *Everyone has everything he needs, but everybody steals.*
7. *Everybody steals, but there is still enough for everyone.*
8. *There is enough for everyone, but everybody complains.*
9. *Everybody complains, but everybody votes in support.*

Even today multiple blogs with memories, found online, elaborate on the habitual *skatavane* – the slang word for truancy, absenteeism.[12] The lack of working zeal was structurally encouraged – in the specific order of the labour market a career was not made by working hard, but by party loyalties and connections, and professional goals could not be set beyond the limits of the restrictive ideology. Individual accounts of the communist working day, especially among people with more intellectual professions, testify of experiencing pools of free time – which did not necessarily evoke nostalgia: some related the experience with dead-end professional paths, typically framed by political pressures (Shkodrova, 2014: 199).

Yurchak called these pools 'utopian amounts of time', and Boym wrote that 'the excess of time for conversations and reflection was a perverse outcome of a socialist

---

[12] Several examples are http://milom.blog.bg/biznes/2011/12/08/za-hubostite-na-socializma.863354, http://www.diaskop-comics.com/article.aspx?id=478, http://komitata.blogspot.be/2009/11/blog-post_13.html.

Figure 3 *A poster by Simeon Krustev from 1978, reading* 'STOP! Not during working hours!' Courtesy: Collection Socmus (www.socmus.com)

economy: time was not a precious commodity …'. She even thought that 'the slow rhythm of reflective time made possible the dream of freedom' (Boym 2001:XV).

Not all professions allowed workers equally to practise procrastination or absenteeism. The more the opportunity to shift temporality was valued, the more the value of those jobs that accommodated it better increased – even if they were unattractive financially or in terms of social status. Yurchak, who wrote of this trend in Soviet Russia, argued that this practice of shifting temporality should not be seen as resistance because it was not exceptional, it was what everybody did, it was accepted and in a way was the norm (Yurchak 2005: 151). To add to that, – and perhaps to add a question mark to Yurchak's interpretation – the talent to practise *skatavane* in Bulgaria in the 1980s was considered by many a virtue. It connected to the idea that work is done not out of actual professional interests, but 'for them', i.e. for the state, albeit malfunctioning and careless about its citizens.

In this sense communist-era statistics of the hours which women spent at work and at home were not entirely indicative of how women used their time. They were much more an indication of the tension between the expectations from women to work full days and at the same time to complete alone most of the laborious domestic chores.

Zhenata dnes' statistics, already quoted, showed that in 1969 women spent on the average 480 minutes a day at work, travelled between 60 and 120 minutes, spent 41 minutes on shopping and 93 minutes on cooking and washing the dishes (the time for the two is combined in the survey) (Pesheva 1962). Another 124 minutes were spent on cleaning, washing of clothes and ironing. Queues, lack of foodstuffs, shortage of cooking equipment, absence of variety of industrial products and semi-prepared or prepared food in the shops, forced them to find significant slots of time for food procuring and cooking. Many of the elements of kitchen work which they had to perform were still similar to those in a pre-industrial household: plucking birds, washing dried mud off (purchased) vegetables, producing condiments due to lack of commercial alternatives, hand-beating, grinding, kneading, peeling with a kitchen knife, using unreliable heating devices for thermal food processing – providing food required significant resources of time.

However tight a women's schedule was in the hours after work though, many of them, especially white-collar workers in urban areas, found reserves of time during their working hours. As Verdery and Yurchak highlighted, they were using their 'seized' time for purposes, other than those they were assigned. Many women had 480 minutes from which to pull pockets of time, available for personal reinterpretation. Some were more successful or better placed than others to do so, or were more eager to use the opportunity. But generally it was a widespread social practice. Moreover it was a social practice, created by the tension which occurred between the assigned and the possible. What the regime and society expected from women, combined with the difficulties they encountered in effectively performing each of their expected obligations, contradicted the natural laws of temporality: the fixed amount of minutes in a day. This forced women into alternative arrangements.

RECIPE MANUSCRIPTS TAKE THE LEAD

The pre-war-style education for girls, which had paved the way to the use of written culinary advice in Bulgaria, ceased to exist in 1948, when the communist government fundamentally reformed the secondary schools (Virtual Museum of PHAF). But in the meantime many other processes had started, which influenced the need for written recipes and the ways in which cookery knowledge was transmitted.

Undertaking a centrally planned industrialization campaign, the new communist state boosted migration of population to the cities. While until 1946 the rural population of Bulgaria was steadily growing, since that year it had begun to rapidly diminish: the urban population made up 19.8 per cent in 1900, 24.7 per cent in 1946, and then grew at a rate of over 10 per cent per decade, reaching 58 per cent in 1975 and 64.8 per cent in 1985 (Yearly Statistics Book 1993: 47). This large-scale migration separated families, in particularly generations, and reduced the opportunities for transmission of culinary knowledge by observation and participation.

Urban markets, on the other hand, offered some unfamiliar ingredients – even if this challenge was limited within the poor communist market, – and opened needs for new skills. The urban lifestyle also introduced into the lives of migrating women the concept of free time, opening up space for the use of cooking for entertainment. Historical sources and research suggest that such an attitude to food was hardly popular in the traditional Bulgarian society of the 18th and 19th centuries, when the meaning of food was mostly limited to 'filling up the stomach with rich, healthy food', while any 'luxury and variation' was considered just 'folly' (Gavrilova 1999: 69). Gavrilova argued that 'Bulgarians, who were raised in eastern-orthodox rigour and respect of fasting, did not possess the Mediterranean reverence towards good food and wine, towards epicureanism and gastronomy' and invested their creative energy elsewhere.

The attitude observed in the urban zones must have slowly started to change in the first decades of the 20th century, judging by the character of the printed culinary literature. From an initially basic approach at the start of the century, cookbooks increasingly suggested a degree of modern wealth, offering elaborate recipes, calling for imported ingredients and for equipment that was advanced for the period. The focus turned towards diets, and fashions and recipes were borrowed from an increasing range of foreign cuisines. One of the illustrations of the dramatic change in attitudes is the publication in 1932 of a cookbook, containing what the editor Teodora Peykova claims to be 'favourite recipes of [Hollywood] cinema stars' (Peykova 1932: 3). Other cookbooks from the 1930s featured elegant tables, arranged with fine cutlery in Art

Nouveau designed living spaces. The upper-middle classes of Bulgarian cities seemed to be opening up to the pleasures of a cosmopolitan culinary culture.

A good window into the actual cuisine of the middle and upper-middle classes of the period is given in a 1938 cookbook, compiled from the cookery scrapbooks of charitable housewives from Burgas, on the Black Sea coast (*250 Tried and Tested Recipes* 1938). The recipes, which are relatively complex and refined, contain many references to other European cuisines – from Sweden to France or Russia – and foreign ingredients – from various citrus fruits to tapioca.

Early communism greatly limited this trend, which was labelled pejoratively as 'bourgeois', especially at the end of the 1940s and in the 1950s. Indeed the cut on imports, the reforms in industrial production, and the economic difficulties of the centrally planned economy dramatically reduced the choice of ingredients on the urban market – a phenomenon which could also be clearly followed by the changing content of cookbooks (Shkodrova 2014: 313–319). The weakness of trade forced many of the newly settled city dwellers to count on their relations with their native villages. In this way a significant part of the new urban population continued to consume overwhelmingly the ingredients known from their previous rural life. This was particularly valid for the earlier decades, when despite the nationalization of the agricultural land, the rural population in Bulgaria continued to rely mostly on their own production, as the shops in the villages remained exceptionally poorly stocked (the same was observed in communist Hungary (Knezy 2003: 147) and Czechoslovakia (Dillnbergerova 2003: 278).

Still, the gradual industrialization began to play an increasingly important transformative role. Previously seasonal dairy products became all-year-around commodities (Atanasov and Masharov 1981) and the consumption of all basic foodstuffs greatly increased. Figure 4 shows the plummeting trade in rice; trade in haricot beans and fish grew until the 1960s; and trade in meat, milk and dairy products, and eggs also grew throughout the period, marking a nearly ten-fold increase in 35 years. The quantity of fresh vegetables sold was doubled in the period, and that of fresh fruits almost tripled.

These statistics might suggest a significant increase in wellbeing and stability of consumption. However such judgement is incomplete without taking into account the decrease in private production in the course of the urbanization, for which there is no data. In any case the consumption in the cities, even if beset by shortages, was generally stable in the late communist period and sufficient for the nutrition of the population. Communist industry – even if to a lesser degree than its capitalist analogues – was also able to increase the accessibility of meat (pork), fish, dairy products and alcohol. Its relative ascent turned into a descent in the 1980s and abruptly stopped with the end of communism, when most of the state industries crashed during the transition to the liberalized market.

The rapid urbanization underway in the early communist decades dramatically changed the lifestyle of the traditional city dwellers, of the newly migrated population and also of those who remained living in the villages. Besides sending great numbers of people to cities, it also imported urban lifestyle elements into the daily life of rural communities (Nenov 2001: 49–51; 2013: 145). In the pre-communist period it was the school teachers who were often associated with progress and innovation in the village.

		1952	1960	1968	1975	1980	1988
Rice	kg	1,6	3,3	3,8	3,6	3,6	3,8
Haricot beans (dry)	kg	0,3	2,4	2,8	2,5	2,4	1,6
Meat	kg	4,4	8,5	11,7	20,1	20,9	27,5
Meat products	kg	0,4	1,4	3,5	3,2	3,8	3,7
Fish	kg	0,4	1,4	3,5	3,2	3,8	3,7
Milk and yogurt	ltr	6,3	16,8	31,7	45,5	50,7	59,4
Cheese	kg	1,8	5,4	5,1	7,7	8,6	11,8
Eggs	pcs	17,4	21,2	30,5	51,6	60,0	93,8
Fresh fruits	kg	7,3	13,0	18,5	17,5	15,8	15,2
Fresh vegetables	kg	23,0	30,7	38,9	43,5	42,3	33,2
Canned fruits	kg	1,7	4,8	4,0	4,4	3,6	3,2
Canned vegetables	kg	1,0	3,8	4,6	5,7	6,0	6,7

Source: Statistical Yearbooks of Republic of Bulgaria, 1959, 1969, 1979, 1989.

Figure 4 *Domestic trade in foodstuffs in Bulgaria per capita between 1952 and 1988.*

In the communist years the presence of intellectuals in rural areas was increased by a peculiar set-up, which sent certain types of professionals: physicians, veterinarians, dentists, engineers, on obligatory internships in the countryside. Many women had such periods in their family history due to their partners' or their own '*razpredelenie*', as these assignments were called. This type of migration from urban to rural, although significantly more limited (and in most cases temporary) to the movement of millions from villages to towns, had an impact on diffusion of culinary practices and was transformative to rural foodways.

Another shift of importance was the increasingly common commuting from villages to towns, which provided for a regular flow of ingredients from the urban market to rural areas. Exploring the consequences of urbanization in communist Slovakia (as part of Czechoslovakia), Dillnbergerova observed that 'villages were no longer providing food for the towns but vice versa, since a woman did her shopping in the town and brought food home to the village' (Dillnbergerova 2003: 278). Unlike the *razpredelenie,* this process was not specific to the communist states.

This trend was additionally boosted by the reform in agriculture in the 1960s, which transformed most farmers into employees of cooperatives. Their lifestyle became similar to that of white-collar workers with regulated working hours and free time/holidays. The ways of communication also changed: both in cities and villages women met in their workplaces, which became important arenas for socializing. There they engaged in intensive communication, which, in a way similar to traditional domestic forms of socializing, often unfolded around food. As the importance of the workplace in women's lives grew, so did its influence over domestic cooking. Women started exchanging food, experience and innovations in their workplaces, turning them into a ground for trading skills and social capital and of social power contestations.

Thus social changes between 1900 and 1950 brought together by the middle of the 20th century several crucial circumstances. Women still had the daily obligation to cook from scratch. They also could write, and they had time. At home they had acquired the chance to cook for pleasure, and being at work together, they could discuss their experiences with it and exchange knowledge about it.

It was under these circumstances that, by the mid-1950s, the communist state had begun to establish its methods for disseminating cookery skills, wrapped safely in the correct ideological interpretation.

One way to do this was through the publishing of state cookbooks and women's magazines, as already discussed, which in the period between the 1950s and late 1970s released a limited number of titles. The high numbers of printed copies had a limited beneficial effect on the availability of cookbooks, which remained insufficient to cover the demand, at least until the mid-1980s. During the field study I interviewed three village women, who said that they had never used or owned a cookbook, nor even handwritten recipes, in their lives. Two of them, in the village of Ribnik next to Sandanski in South Bulgaria, said that they had never held a cookbook in their hands. However I also encountered evidence that written sources started spreading in rural areas at least from the beginning of the 20th century and their role gradually increased.

Besides cookbooks, two Bulgarian women's magazines: *Zhenata dnes* (1945–) and *Lada* (1960–1992) published recipes on and off, with significant fluctuation throughout the years.

Another form of disseminating culinary knowledge were the cookery courses, organized by the Committee of Bulgarian Women (CBW): the communist women's organization, which monopolized the women's social movement, and by the *Otechestven Front* (Fatherland Front, FF), a mass political organization, which worked under the guidance of the leadership of the Communist Party to ensure 'Marxist-Leninist views amongst the working people, their socialist and patriotic attitudes, to overcome the influence of the bourgeois ideology and to expose the ideological sabotage of imperialism' (CSA 417-4-42 1968: 46). The two organizations joined forces in nation-wide campaigns to define the new Bulgarian housewife. Their activities are well documented by the preserved archives and in the 1970s were streamlined within the *Movement for New Socialist Material and Cultural Life*.

The history of this Movement shows the complexity of the communist state's machine for social engineering. Numerous organizations were engaged on different levels to implement the framework programme, which was developed into regular educative events. With access to state property and financing, and having at their disposal experts and state-controlled media, CBW and FF unfolded their undertaking on a scale only achievable in a centrally run state. Food-related educative events were organized regularly across the country within the set of other activities, including also fashion and sewing courses or lectures on sexual life, family relations, raising children and similar.

The aim of the Movement was to teach women to cook or sew in a correct communist way: the activities were dressed in layers of prescriptive ideology and were based on an articulated understanding of their manipulative power. 'The material lifestyle is an important factor in people's cultivation. Through it we can influence their mentality, educate their tastes, change their views, to direct and rule their psychology. Therefore the efforts for its improvement, for its continuous update is one of the goals of our party and government,' stated a chairwoman of a regional women's city council participating in the organization (CSA 417-4-36 1973: 5).

To accomplish this goal, the cooking lessons came along with lectures on rational nutrition, planning of daily intake according to norms, the 'correct' composition of a menu. They spread the idea that women needed to be freed from their chores in the kitchen by public catering services, so as to spend their time on 'other, more meaningful and useful material needs, cultured entertainment and similar' (CSA 417-4-91 1969: 51). Part of the efforts were reportedly dedicated also to the obliteration of old (often religious) festivities, and the introduction of new, communist celebrations (CSA 417-4-91 1969: 12). The activities also included tastings, exhibitions of semi-prepared foods, and ready-made meals for children. The actual courses provided theoretical information on cooking methods and recipes for main dishes, desserts and preserves (CSA 417-4-91 1969: 104). In fact the organizers also pursued state interests on the level of actual recipes: several reports mentioned courses, specifically aiming at teaching women to cook fish, which coincided with the national campaign to promote fish, mentioned earlier (CSA 417-4-91 1969: 36). Among all the activities, cooking courses were reported to be the most difficult to organize. Problems with finding suitable places, cutlery or experts resurface in the statements of the regional representatives.

These courses were often initiated from below and, as Nikolova and Ghodsee argued, were probably a way both to serve the interests of women, and to educate them (Nikolova and Ghodsee 2015: 336). However it is highly unlikely that any grassroots voices or desires that differed from the Women's Organization's goal of educating 'correct communist women', had a chance to be heard. One reason is that the local organizations, which often initiated the courses, perceived themselves as promoters of the official discourses, which is clearly visible from the meeting protocols in the archive of the organization. As Nikolova and Ghodsee themselves pointed out, the organization worried that the courses only reached people who were already convinced communists and not those who 'needed them most' (and were possibly not so convinced of the regime's teaching). Another source of doubt is the clear (and sometimes plainly arrogant) propagandist intentions, which clearly stood behind the cookery courses.

Particularly controversial as an example of this are the Fatherland Front-run activities that focused on 'civilizing' the minorities. Many reports by regional representatives and organizers of events concentrated mainly on these aspects of the programme. Criticizing the Turkish and the Roma minorities as conservative and uneducated, especially among the older generations, the regional representatives spoke of efforts to modernize their clothing, underwear, and sexual life, which meant abandoning their taste for colourful fabrics, or their habit of wearing particular types of traditional clothes (CSA 417-4-36 1973: 65–67). In the domain of food this policy was expressed in encouraging Turks to abandon their religious taboo on eating pork. Such policy is never mentioned explicitly in the reports from FF activities across the country, but it transpires from a lecture in 1976 by the chairman of the regional women's council in Razgrad, where a significant Turkish minority lives. In her speech she reported that the Turks in her region had 'not only consume[d]' pork for a long time already, but had 'begun to farm pigs', supporting the completion of the regional economic plan. 'This, comrades, is an actual revolution, to make a Turkish family breed pigs, in a Turkish home. This is a defeat of their prejudices (...) it was far from easy for us, because at the beginning we encountered a lot of resistance' (CSA 417-5-440 1976: 13–14).

Whether these civilizing intentions originated from the central organization or from its grassroots cells, this would not change the oppressive nature of the ideas with which such courses were initiated. While it is in theory possible to interpret the emphasized ideological value of these events as a cover for their actual intention to answer local women's interest in cooking, it is also possible to see the courses as using women's interest in cooking to advance ideological ideas – which seems more probable, considering the circumstances already mentioned, and some other research (see for example Brunnbauer 2008).

Considering the communist state mechanisms of planning, accomplishing and reporting, it is impossible to say how successful or useful these cookery courses were to the targeted participants. During the research I encountered one person who participated in such a course, and two others who said they had heard of such courses. But I did not find any reference to them in their or other scrapbooks.

Against all these state-managed efforts to educate the Bulgarian woman as a modern cook scrapbooks flourished. Considering the situation in Russia, Pirogovskaya (2017: 334) wrote that private cooking manuscripts were popular in the 19th century, but then marginalized by printed sources – to enjoy another Renaissance in the Soviet Union after the 1930s. While printed cookbooks might have indeed limited the practice of maintaining manuscripts, it seems that their impact served more to curb the growth of the trend, rather than to reduce the absolute number of manuscripts: after all, with the rise of printed cookbooks since the end of the 19th century, literacy among women also rose. If cookery manuscripts were a privilege of the upper classes in the past, they became an accessible means of storing cookery information for growing layers of societies across the world. In this sense it is perhaps more just to see the 1930s not as a renaissance, but as a transformation, a popularization of this medium, actually parallel to the evolution we have observed for printed cookbooks.

As the poll in my research suggested, cookery manuscripts were preferred by far to all the other sources which the state-controlled networks offered. They provided for a circulation of recipes along separate, autonomous circuits, in endless modifications; their constant reconnection to everyday realities, practices or desires made them common heritage, an object of shared culture much like what until recently was referred to as 'national folklore'.

The authorship was very rarely assigned to a fixed, or possibly original source. Instead, the giver of the last version, possibly an author of recent adjustments, was credited.

In her work on cookbooks as resources for rural research, Sharpless (2016: 203) asserted that the attribution of creation or gift reminds the reader that recipes may be considered intellectual property. My research, though, reveals that at least in the case of the Bulgarian scrapbooks, this would be an overstatement. Apart from using the crediting mostly for convenience, the belief that a recipe was actually authored by the giver was very rare, if existent at all. The cookery instructions carried the giver's endorsement of their quality, rather than implied acknowledgement of authorship.

The exchange was an important element of the recipes' existence, it was the public arena, where their life unfolded and where they evolved, being continuously renegotiated with the market and the users of culinary advice. Even women who did not cook at home participated in the process, providing in this way an extension of this social arena and taking part in the survival of recipes and their influence. But it was those, who applied the recipes and passed them over with the added weight of their own experience, that created the credibility of the recipes and defined their 'exchange life'. In a way, identical to Pennell's observation regarding early modern English cookery manuscripts, it was 'the continual practice, rather than the circulation' that was the 'primary means of knowledge authorisation' (Pennell 2012: 252).

In his survey of a scrapbook found on a poultry farm near Rousse in Northern Bulgaria, Nenov (2013: 146) suggested that the document could be treated as an expression of the specific contemporary urban common heritage. His reasoning was that the examined scrapbook contained two parts, one of which – recipes, addresses, songs – was used primarily at home, while the other, containing erotic jokes, must have been used at the workplace. Pointing to the characters and plots inherited from the oral tradition that were used in the jokes, and the exploitation of slang and dialects, Nenov concluded that the collection could be classified in such terms.

Theophano (2002) sought to express a similar idea, arguing that 'individual women created their cookbooks from a common cultural template' and indeed most recipes, arriving from a variety of sources, circulated as a common pool of knowledge. Besides, as Theophano noted, the scrapbooks reflect the authors' idea of how a recipe should look, how should it be structured, what language it should use. Each individual work was a personal interpretation of this common idea, sometimes a simpler, at other times a more elaborate variation of it.

The recipes as a shared body of culture, though, were defined in many ways by the existence, however marginal it might have been to some, of printed culinary works. The scrapbooks were effectively a hybrid form of knowledge: one which was passed by word of mouth, but was written down by its literate recipients to facilitate its use. The form, in which the recipes were written down was often influenced by the printed sources.

Hanging in a limbo between the pressures to switch to modern food practices and the lack of infrastructure to enable them to do so, Bulgarian women also faced the shortage of both traditional and modern sources of cooking information. Their creative answer to this was the hybrid form of written culinary common heritage: the scrapbooks with recipes.

HOW THIS RESEARCH WAS DONE

When I began my research for this book, I was not familiar with Gronow and Zhuravlev's judgement that it 'would be almost impossible to reconstruct ... in any comprehensive manner after so many decades' (2011: 25) how cookbooks are read.

Standing in my own shoes, trained in investigative journalism and qualitative research methods, I did not see the inquiry ahead of me as particularly challenging.

I was not so much after 'facts' about everyday life under communism; I wanted rather to know how people reasoned about it. And the best way to find out 'not just what people did, but what they wanted to do, what they believed they were doing, and what they now think they did,' to use the words of Portelli (1997: 67), was to ask them. Oral history offered the greatest heuristic potential to answer my questions. Its specific value as a method was one reason for that. But also, one peculiarity of the communist period made the interviews irreplaceable: widespread censorship and self-censorship had muted many informal discourses. Accessing them retrospectively was sometimes the only option.

The interviews

As the generation of people born in the 1940s and running households since the 1960s, were around and eager to recall their youth, their narratives became one of the principal sources for my research. The stories of Tamara Ganeva and Cathy Ivanova shaped my initial idea of how to select narrators. Even if I perceived their two examples as exceptional and comparable, I realized that their different backgrounds and attitude to food provided for contrasting accounts of their food experiences.

Intrigued by these differences, I looked for a group of people who had run households before 1989, had exchanged recipes, and were willing to give access to their collections. They also had to come from different backgrounds. Urban-rural seemed the most obvious difference to look for. I expected contrasts in the type of cuisine, the culinary culture, and in their access to industrially produced/processed foodstuffs. Not only had the rural population more access to gardening and animal farming, but they were forced to make greater use of their land by the state policy of supplying the less populated areas in the country with a smaller assortment of goods (Shkodrova 2014: 122).

I also looked for narrators with varying political affiliations, which I expected to affect their interpretation of the past. The political debates in the post-communist years had revealed that the society remains deeply divided in individuals' evaluation of their experience of this historical period.

I gradually came to realize that the type of employment might also have played a role, affecting women's free time, financial possibilities and their social network. All the women I interviewed had worked full time throughout their adult lives at least until 1989, as did almost all women of active age in Bulgaria. But their narratives suggested that those employed on administrative or intellectual work positions have had more time and energy to invest in recipes and home cooking than those involved in production or in trade.

I found the people I interviewed through my formal and informal networks, making occasional use of what anthropologists call 'the snowball method'. Refining twice in the process my search criteria, I composed a sufficiently diverse group of women. I was unable to find men who have participated in the recipe exchange and owned collections of recipes, although the data from my poll showed that they existed, in very small numbers. The interviews took place in October 2015, March 2016, July 2016 and

September 2016, and I stopped at 23, when I realized that a point of saturation was reached and the conversations had stopped delivering new information.

I grouped my questions in six clusters[1] and at first I was committed to keeping the conversations within the developed questionnaire. It was not an easy task: many of my narrators were women older than seventy. Arriving at their homes, I was usually seated in front of coffee and cake and first began with small talk, which tended to soon naturally unfold into an interview. The women opened their scrapbooks as if they were brightly illustrated chronicles of their lives, out of which the years of their youth, communist or not, flowed, fragrant and tempting. Hurried everyday cooking or festive meals, efforts and indulgences, tastes, relations, places that no longer existed – all rushed into the narratives, often in chaos and with great emotion. Covering questions that were still unasked or returning to a story already told, I soon realized that trying to streamline the interactions was not working: it interrupted the natural chain of thoughts and associations of the women, which I grew to appreciate as particularly insightful.

Instead of limiting the free narration, I started to encourage it. Instead of trying to lead the women through the memories of their experiences, I decided to follow them there. This method brought me to places where I wouldn't have gone myself, as I did not know that they existed. So I asked the questions in the order in which they came naturally as the conversation unfolded, only checking now and then what remained to be covered. Whenever possible, I tried to use the 'zooming in' and 'zooming out' technique of Kurtz (2014), to encourage the narrator to lead me through a well-remembered detail, but also to give me her general view.

The material which came out in the narratives is certainly not a simple and straightforward window into the past. 'As any history, oral history also never coincides with the past, but is rather a story about the past', as Bleyen and Van Molle wrote (2012: 14). This story is a complex creation, which is formed on the one hand by the life experiences and accumulated reflections from different perspectives of the person who tells her story, and on the other by the interview interaction.

The theory of oral history as a method has reached great sophistication and yet remains somewhat open to discussion. The pro- and contra- arguments always hit the bottom line of the big dispute in science: the one between positivists and constructivists. While some scholars religiously keep believing in the possibility of objectivity, others deem it plainly unachievable and see the claims of objectivity as unreasonable denial. In this discussion I tend to stand on the side of the second group. Instead of repudiating her impact on her sources, I believe a historian needs to be reflective on the disadvantages of subjectivity and make use of its advantages.

While advancing with this research, I grew to understand the interviews not only as interactions between two inevitably subjective persons, influencing each other, but as

---

[1] In the first I asked the narrators to describe the process of recipe exchange and their participation in it. The second part of the questions was examining the meanings which they attributed to the recipes. The third was dedicated to the alternatives of home cooking: were there any and how were they used? The fourth investigated the alternatives of recipe writing: if and how women used cookbooks and other sources of cookery advice. One set of questions examined the scope of the recipe exchange as to the narrator's knowledge. And finally, the concluding questions were inquiring about the women's sensitivity towards state propaganda and social pressure, as well as, optionally, their political affiliations.

an intersubjective exchange. An interaction, that draws on our acts and presumptions and on the circumstances in which it unfolds but in which it acquires autonomy. Such understanding of the human interaction was developed by cognitive philosophers Hanne De Jaegher and Ezequiel di Paolo, who called it 'participative sense-making' (De Jaegher and Di Paolo, 2007). It has not been incorporated so far in oral history theory, but it is the theory which I found best for capturing the dynamics of the interview interaction. Differently from all the previous theoretical models, it accommodates the often experienced interview situation, when the communication unfolds with its own dynamic, independent of the individual intentions of the persons involved. The interaction modulates the behaviour of the participants, just as they try to take control/make sense of it: through ongoing instances of renegotiation.

The interviewed women brought in their memories and views, their moods, tasks in the back of their minds, their understanding of what I expected from them, and so did I. But when each of us stepped into the conversation, our exchange took its own path, transforming on the way our intentions, our preconceived ideas what to do or say next, none of us being in full control of what was happening, each of us participating in creating together what would become my research source. The participatory sense-making theory, which so well connected to my interview experiences, added a new dimension to my understanding of the collective quality of individual memory (Halbwachs 1976). An oral historian not only needs to be aware that the recollections of his narrator are shaped and renegotiated with collective discourses, that they have passed through the collective strainer, sorted into 'mainstream' and 'marginal'. She is also facing her own contribution into the 'collective' nature of the source, once more sifted in the process of interaction. In other words, the memories of the individual are not only grounded in and resulting from social interaction, but they are also often collective in the sense, that they are produced within groups, which define repertoires of representations of the past. As Schachtel observed, 'the memories of the majority of people come to resemble increasingly the stereotyped answers to a questionnaire' (Schachtel 1982: 193–194).

On the surface of it, this characteristic of memories might render them an untrustworthy source: a person retells not her personal experience, but a sequence of modules, with which such experiences are memorized within the social group. But in fact these elements in the narratives capture group identities. 'By concentrating on identities of groups, we could understand the personal stories as part of shared experiences. In this way the unique stops being so unique . . .', argued Bleyen and Van Molle (2012: 91). As Schudson (1995: 347) pointed out, 'As soon as you recognise how collective memory, and even individual memory, is inextricable from social and historical processes, the notion of 'distortion' [of reality] becomes problematic'.

The time distance was certainly one of the challenges before me. One immediate practical problem was that the interviewed women often failed to distinguish between different periods (decades, or before or after the end of the regime). It made them speak of the communist period 'in bulk', while other sources reveal important evolution of many relevant ideological discourses through the decades. Some of the interviewed were also unable to date their recipe exchange practices, or even to identify which parts of their scrapbooks were filled in after communism ended. As households did not change overnight, twenty years later many women found it difficult to remember clearly how and when their foodways evolved and changed.

Some of these problems were partially solved by specific references in the scrapbooks, for example to TV cooking shows, or magazines that were only available after 1989. Sometimes timelines were reconstructed later and clarified during follow-up conversations.

While this peculiarity of mundane memories – their detachment from the immediate political events – could cause a certain confusion, it also has advantages. It might have diminished what Schudson calls the 'distortions' of memory: the instrumentalization, narrativization, and conventionalization of the stories (Schudson 1995: 348). Daily routines are sometimes less subjected to the usual 'distortions of memory', as most people do not expect to be asked about such matters and do not have prepared narratives on them (Abrams 2010; Bisschop 2014a,b; De Caigny 2010). Indeed questions, concerning the practice and importance of recipe collection, seemed at times to leave the interviewees at a loss. They often needed time to gather their memories and compose a narrative. There were also moments, especially when it came to discussing the involvement of ideology, when the needed vocabulary to express their idea seemed to be more at their fingertips.

Another challenge I faced was to estimate my influence on the interviews. Not only were the women's recollections filtered by the quality of memory to be selective, and by the strainer of public discourses, but they were once more reformulated to match what my interlocutors presumed to be my expectations and personality. This was a particularly difficult point, as some months earlier my book *Communist Gourmet* had been published and became widely known, the media presenting me as a critic of the communist regime. The 'self' being ambiguous and unstable (Abrams 2010), the women chose roles, which they adapted to my presumed ideological 'self'. I detected such influence several times, and in particular once, when one of the narrators interrupted her answer to my question and suddenly made a reference to my book, pointing to one of my statements as expressing her own opinion well.

My means to deal with this was to stay alert regarding the possibility of such references and remain reflective upon their role. During the interviews I left more freedom to the narrators. I encouraged them to follow their own chain of thoughts as much as reasonably possible. I also invited them to tell stories rather than to make evaluations. Also during the interpretation, while contemplating on the meanings, which surfaced in the narratives, I was weighing their importance in the scale of the narrator. I analysed the narratives attentive to their consistency and looking for potential outliers. Such inconsistencies are taken into account in the analysis. They were considered in a cross-analysis with the two main written sources of information: their scrapbooks, and the cookbooks which they owned before 1989.

The scrapbooks

Access to personal recipe collections was one of the requirements I put forward when looking for interviewees. But the collections of recipes which I used were, at the end fewer, than the narrators. When looking to cover the division line urban/rural, I visited a secluded mountainous place, populated with Pomaks[2]. When I arrived there, I realized that the recipe book which I was promised belonged to a child and was started a few years ago. The interviews, which I made in the neighbourhood, and also in another, non-Pomak village in the region proved that scrapbooks were more an urban phenomenon, and so were cookbooks.

I was able to obtain copies of twenty familial recipe collections. When arranging the interviews, I always asked to see the scrapbooks just as they were kept in the narrators' homes. But many of them said they would find this embarrassing, as if letting me into a disorderly home. Before presenting their collections, they combed them for loose papers, pictures, unrelated documents. Fortunately most of the collections were so rich of these insertions, that I almost always found many inside anyway. Some women were also less worried and gave me their notebooks just as they were. But I believe that I was allowed to see less than many women actually had, or at least used to have: some of the collections were clearly continuations of earlier work, which might have been lost, or just considered of lesser quality and unfit to be shown.

This attitude of the women testified that my request to look at their recipes in most cases found them unprepared. Even if they were previously informed of my intentions and conceded to them, their actions showed that they didn't think of their documents as 'representative', they made their scrapbooks for 'their eyes only'. There were some exceptions, but mostly the women were not 'objectively' proud of their collections. Some found them important for themselves or for their families, but most thought of them as messy and unworthy of strangers' attention, simple mundane instruments to use in the kitchen. In many ways their attitude showed that as documents, their scrapbooks were not meant to serve ideological purposes of self-presentation (which was not necessarily valid for their cooking).

The aforementioned lack of clear division between recipes before and after 1989 was a limitation of the source. If the records followed chronologically, the problem was relatively small: indications like dates or reference to brands or sources created in the post-communist years, helped to chart a rough timeline. But some women had completely rewritten their scrapbooks, mixing up all the recipes – and without a clear memory as to when that could have happened.

I used the scrapbooks by applying a combination of techniques, between which I shifted depending on my numerous purposes. I found it very useful to make a quantitative summary of the documents and of their content, which outlined the proportions of different types of dishes and gave an overview of the scale of such documents in a household. Figure 5 is a breakdown of the content of each collection of recipes into types of dishes.

The table also reflects the number of 'clippings': i.e. cutouts from magazines, leaflets or similar, as part of the collection. The numbers themselves though do not reflect the use of magazines from the communist period as sources. First, many of the clippings were from before 1944. There is an easy and trustworthy way to establish this, because

---

[2] A group of ethnic Bulgarian muslims, formed during the Ottoman empire and maintaining identity as a separate group.

	Tamara Ganeva	Cathy Ivanova	Lilia Dencheva	Violeta Kaloferova	Tsveta Tanovska	Maya Mircheva	Sofia Georgieva	Kinche Angelova	Atanaska Terzieva	Ivanka Atipova	N. Malcheva	Dani Tsacheva	Dobrinka Boeva	Vanya Pinteva	Kalina Kechova	Kristin Razsolkova	E. Shkodrova	E. Salmadzhiyska	Total
Number of books	3	1	1	4	7	1	2	1	1	1	1	3	1	2	0	1	1	1	32
Number of pages	145	115	103	383	407	145	314	118	81	49	170	249	90	146	153	397	199	76	3340
Salads	1	14	0	14	15	3	2	0	0	0	1	2	2	3	1	1	1	1	61
Sandwiches	1	1	0	0	0	0	0	4	0	0	0	1	0	1	0	0	1	0	9
Other starters	0	13	1	1	15	5	8	0	0	0	0	0	0	1	0	7	6	1	58
Soups	1	22	1	14	14	4	2	0	1	1	0	0	1	4	0	0	0	0	65
Souces	0	17	3	2	17	2	0	1	0	0	0	0	2	16	0	5	1	0	66
Main dishes without meat	11	45	9	60	26	12	5	1	1	1	5	3	27	8	11	9	5	0	239
Main dishes red meats	3	57	6	38	41	22	5	1	2	2	0	7	4	12	7	10	8	3	228
Main dishes game meat	0	7	0	0	0	0	0	0	1	1	0	0	6	2	0	0	0	0	17
Main dishes cured meats	1	6	1	3	3	1	1	0	0	0	0	0	1	0	0	0	0	0	17
Main dishes chicken, birds	6	9	0	5	13	13	5	0	0	2	0	0	4	3	1	0	5	1	67
Main dishes with fish	3	13	1	8	3	2	0	0	1	1	1	1	1	1	1	0	4	0	40
Side dishes, garnishes	0	0	0	1	6	0	0	1	0	0	1	3	0	1	0	4	0	0	17
Dough - based:																			638
Breads	3	9	4	6	9	4	8	11	2	0	11	15	3	7	5	4	6	1	108
Salty banitsa	2	7	3	13	9	2	8	0	2	4	3	3	4	2	4	7	3	0	76
Solenki	4	9	4	8	17	14	11	13	2	1	4	12	3	5	1	25	8	1	142
Buhti mekitsi, pancakes	3	21	12	9	8	2	3	13	3	0	6	13	3	5	0	13	3	2	119
Pizza	0	8	2	4	1	5	0	4	0	0	0	5	1	1	2	3	0	0	36
Other salty bread-based	0	2	4	10	12	24	12	6	2	0	4	12	1	7	4	11	5	0	116
Buns	1	5	0	2	7	3	1	2	4	1	0	6	0	1	1	2	4	1	41
Desserts:																			2434
Kozunak	2	1	2	1	3	0	0	1	1	1	5	2	7	1	0	7	1	2	37
Cakes	23	47	18	47	71	29	78	36	20	15	50	77	13	12	24	90	25	8	683
Layered cakes	11	34	8	21	67	16	37	23	11	10	17	53	4	7	13	61	22	7	422
Cookies	9	44	8	25	94	12	48	54	17	0	50	97	8	8	21	52	26	8	581
Other sweet preparations	7	16	6	20	69	14	27	27	6	7	37	39	9	9	13	42	21	8	377
Bonbons	2	0	1	1	5	0	1	1	0	0	0	1	0	0	0	0	1	0	13
Sweet banitsas	1	6	0	1	3	0	0	2	1	0	0	2	0	2	1	2	1	2	24
Syruped sweets	0	8	2	5	15	4	2	3	3	1	7	18	8	3	1	19	3	1	103
Puddings and custards	6	11	4	3	33	7	10	7	1	0	11	15	0	3	1	26	11	3	152
Ice Cream	0	1	1	0	2	1	3	5	0	0	0	3	0	0	1	24	0	1	42
Preserves:																			444
Vegetables	0	35	2	9	71	21	0	25	18	3	19	29	21	22	8	39	35	7	364
Meat/fish	0	0	0	0	0	0	1	0	1	0	3	4	0	6	1	2	1	0	19
Jams and marmalades	0	18	0	3	22	0	0	1	0	0	1	0	1	0	0	4	1	5	57
Herbs, spices	0	0	0	0	2	1	0	0	0	0	0	0	0	0	1	0	0	0	4
Drinks	5	15	1	1	16	0	13	15	1	0	3	16	4	0	0	48	22	1	161
Non-alimentary:																			122
Medicinal preparations	2	5	0	0	6	17	0	0	0	1	1	59	1	1	2	0	0	3	98
Cosmetic preparations	0	6	0	7	0	0	4	0	0	3	0	3	1	0	0	0	0	0	24
Total number of recipes	108	512	104	342	695	241	294	257	101	55	239	502	138	156	124	518	230	67	4683
Out of them - clippings	18	300	0	0	39	9	0	14	7	0	0	1	32	1	0	0	27	1	489

Figure 5 *The table shows the recipe collections acquired during the research, and their structure (except for two incomplete copies).*

in 1944 Bulgaria underwent a transliteration reform, which was immediately reflected in virtually all printed materials. Secondly, there were some cutouts from Western magazines (like Burda). There were also many clippings from the period after 1989 (also often clearly identifiable because of the colour of the paper, the references on the clippings and other signs). All in all the clippings and their origin show that magazines were a quite marginal and exceptional source of recipes for the scrapbooks – at least in the form of direct copying/clipping.

Quantitative analysis on several occasions supported the qualitative enquiries, micro- and content analysis, to verify claims such as contrasting precision of the recipes, employment of deficit ingredients and similar. The scrapbooks are treated in this research as resulting from women's efforts to gather their own collection of recipes for private use. With their very creation in a context where commercial culinary literature existed, scrapbooks constituted a form of dialogue with it. My goal was to explore the nature of this dialogue, of how women negotiated their choice between the various available sources of recipes. In this sense I used the scrapbooks as a counterpoint to the interviews, and also in juxtaposition with the commercial culinary literature.

The cookbooks

The cookbooks, produced within the communist state system of controlled publishing, were printed in great numbers of copies (Shkodrova 2018a). Sometimes republished six to seven times, some of them were released in over 200,000 copies (the top record, in the 1980s, exceeded half a million copies). The centrally planned economy however was notorious for breaking up the connection between demand and supply. On the one hand, it left large gaps of unsatisfied demand and on the other people often ended up purchasing not what they wished, but what they were able to put their hands on. Considering this, I decided not to use the available information of print runs, but to concentrate on the books, that were actually available in the households of the interviewed women before 1989. Several of the interviewees had a small library of culinary books, but most owned one to three or four titles. The national representative opinion poll showed this to be the common situation: only 12–13 per cent of the households in bigger towns and cities, and below 8 per cent in the smaller towns and villages, had more than five cookbooks before 1989.

I narrowed my focus down to the cookbooks, which were owned by at least three narrators. These were seven titles: *The Housewife's Book* (Cholcheva and Ruseva eds. 1956), *Bulgarian National Cuisine* (Petrov et al. 1978), *Contemporary Domestic Cooking: 2000 Bulgarian and Foreign Recipes* (Cholcheva and Kalaydzhieva 1969), *Our Cuisine* (Naydenov and Chortanova 1967), *Contemporary Cookbook* (Cholcheva 1964); *What to Cook in No Time* (Dimcheva 1983) and *The Art of Pastry-Making* (Smolnitska 1983).

The first five cookbooks share the quality of encyclopaedic, all-encompassing manuals and were considered as essential, even 'generic'. The 'generic cookbook' is a phenomenon which I observed during my field study among people of different generations. Many of them live today with the idea that there was only one, single cookbook under socialism, or at least one that was dominant. They usually have difficulties recalling its name and on many occasions interviewees asked for time to check, in order to evoke it – even if they might have used it all their lives. They referred to it simply as 'the book', or as 'the big book' (i.e. the voluminous one), and recalled the colour of the cover or the author (if indicated). Even in households that had more than one book, the rest, which were often from the 1980s, were somehow ignored. But what various people perceive as 'the book' turned out to be one of the dozen universal cooking manuals, published between 1956 and the late 1970s.

The first five cookbooks on my list were all part of the 'generic cookbook illusion' phenomenon. The last two, published only in the beginning of the *perestroika* years, were far less defining of the women's experience during the years of communism (three of the narrators denounced them explicitly and several others implicitly – some remembered about these books only after our interviews). For this reason these books were less taken into consideration here.

Our Cuisine (Naydenov and Chortanova 1955) was the first cookbook for home cooking that was both written and published in the communist years[3]. It was reprinted six times, probably in about a hundred thousand[4] copies in total. Three of the households I studied owned a copy. The book gave explicit expression to the early communist ideology, which aimed at taking the woman out of the kitchen and making her join the work force of the country. Endorsing industrial food and warning of the traps of domestic cooking, it instructed women to be professional in the kitchen, spending as little time there as possible. The book was authored by food technologist Sonya Chortanova, who prior to 1944 was teaching cookery classes for women in Sofia and authored a cookbook for professionals, and Ivan Naydenov, one of the first and leading nutritionists of the period. The cookbook gave an overwhelming priority to nutrition: prescriptive advice on the 'correct' diet in communist society occupies one third of the book, and is also found in the instructions to each section of recipes. Written in the spirit of a scientific work, it ends with a bibliography, manifesting strong Soviet influence. More than half of the quoted titles are from Soviet authors, many in Russian, and feature medical literature and research in nutrition, military hygiene, chemistry, biology, physiology and similar.

The Housewife's Book (Cholcheva and Ruseva eds.1956) was available in seven of the twenty-three households. It was given six reprints between 1956 and 1966, reaching a total of 72,500 copies. *The Housewife's Book* was a household manual – the first one of the communist period. It presented an elaborate guide to communist domestic ideology and thus constructed implicitly a detailed image of the ideal modern woman. The introduction, written by 'the people's teacher' Mara Puhovska, cast the communist female model as a committed worker in the state economy, bearing with heroic silence and resilience all the responsibilities of a traditional housewife: from sewing clothes and curtains to raising children to be well behaved and knowledgeable in art, literature and communist ideology. The book outlined the ideas of a modern household – both urban and rural, and also opened the cookery advice section with information on nutrition.

Authored by Cholcheva, the recipes in *The Housewife's Book* are in general simple, generic, having shed off many of the problematic references to Western cuisines in Cholcheva's earlier (and also later) publications – presumably in an effort to comply

---

[3] All the earlier publications were recycled, (self?)-censored earlier cookbooks, many of them works by one and the same author: Penka Cholcheva.
[4] There is no information about the printed copies of the first four editions, the last two, in 1971 and 1974 were in a total of 60,000 copies.

with the strong intolerance to the West, typical for the early communist years in Bulgaria.

Contemporary Cookbook, which first appeared in 1964, and *Contemporary Domestic Cooking* from 1969, were both written by (or with the participation of) Cholcheva. *Contemporary Cookbook* was reprinted three times in the sixties, reaching 92,000 copies and was found in three of the households I researched. It shows the first signs of a retreat from the harshest communist years and opens with a short account of the history of cooking, which, indeed, ends with the typical glorification of food under communism. In this context though it sounds more like a compliance with an obligation than a goal wholeheartedly pursued. While it features a greater variety of ingredients, the recipes remain simple and descriptive in the style typical of Cholcheva.

Contemporary Domestic Cooking (Cholcheva and Kalaydzhieva 1969), which came five years later, already manifests a more relaxed air. A new ambition to demonstrate prosperity and worldliness transpires from the pages, instead of the previous 'culture of poverty'. Each chapter is divided into domestic and international recipes, featuring US, British, French, Swiss, Belgian and other, explicitly named, Western cuisines. Also the nutritionist advice is kept short and somewhat subdued, presented more as qualities of the food ingredients. Indeed this book signals the relative 'Thaw', which was short-lived in Bulgaria before the return to the earlier discourses after the Prague revolution in 1968. *Contemporary Domestic Cooking* was also given three print runs, but in a total of 200,000 copies and the book was found in five of the studied households.

Bulgarian National Cuisine (Petrov et al. 1978) was the first compendium, which explicitly focused on national cuisine since 1944. It was released in a total of 245,000 copies, in three print runs[5] and was available in five of the researched households. It was authored by a collective of food professionals in the late 1970s , when political life was dominated by the celebration of the 1,300th anniversary of the first Bulgarian state (681). After having tiptoed carefully around the topic for decades, in the 1970s the Bulgarian communist state became excessively vocal on national identity and turned the celebration into the most ambitious festive project of the century.

Opening with the familiar nutritionist statements that home cooking will 'no doubt gradually retreat, to be replaced by public catering', the authors of *Bulgarian National Cuisine* included an extensive and entirely novel chapter on the history of Bulgarian cuisine. Stating that the healthy diet of the preceding generations was destroyed under foreign influence in the pre-communist years, they praised the communist state for its restoration.

With some minor exceptions, all the five cookbooks offer simple, no-fuss recipes, which do not call for excessive investments of products, equipment, time or skills. The presentation is plain and laconic, consisting of short preparation instructions with very few other attributes: lists of ingredients and illustrations appear inconsistently, and with no information about preparation time, difficulty or other facilitating elements.

The five cookbooks vary somewhat in their attention to detail, and significantly in the type of dishes which they offer. There is also some variation in the intended

---

[5] A tiny (A6, 125 page) book, named Bulgarian National Dishes was published in 40,000 copies prior to that: Shishkov and Vuchkov 1959.

readership: some books focus entirely on home cooking, while others are aiming at combined use also by state restaurants and canteens.

These and other communist cookbooks are discussed in the following chapters from various perspectives. In my analysis I applied Barbara Wheaton's structured approach to studying cookbooks as a historical source (Wheaton 1998). It offers a set of perspectives from which to consider cookbooks in order to extract historical information. These perspectives, which are, really, historical questions specific to cookbooks, focus on what foodstuffs the recipes call for, how the kitchen transpires from the text in terms of space and equipment, what cooking techniques are recommended, what is the concept of a meal, what is the implicit profile of the reader, how the writer comes across, how does he wish to be seen, what ideologies he promotes. Set against the circumstantial framework of the period, the answers to these questions offer numerous insights on private and social economic circumstances, social relations and hierarchies, to name a few. Considered in their context, cookbooks are like flour sacks: they would deliver new insights as long as you 'shake' them. The unassuming tactic of Wheaton is a thorough approach to this 'shaking' and delivers very rich and multifaceted historical information. It also allows freedom as to what techniques to use to read the cookbook. I reached out to different techniques depending on the different questions, stemming from the comparison of the sources: quantitative analysis, microanalysis (as applied by Parys 2013), topical, qualitative and discursive analysis.

My goal in analysing the source material however, went beyond what communist cookbooks meant to say: I needed to know how they were read and interpreted in practice. The cookbooks themselves do not necessarily provide such information, as researchers have explicitly observed (Gronow and Zhuravlev 2011: 25, Albala 2012: 3). To gain access to actual users' practices, I critically compared the triangle of sources: the narratives of the interviewees, their scrapbooks and their cookbooks. In many cases there were gaps, discrepancies, even direct controversies between what the narrators said and what was visible from their written cooking advice. This method proved to be very efficient for evoking memories, completing and clarifying interpretations, outlining inconsistencies and complexities in women's attitudes to cooking and the social context, or sometimes for identifying the influence of post-communist experiences on the recollections.

I also used a broad range of documents to outline the context. Particularly instrumental among them was the archive of **Zhenata dnes,** which was the most important and influential women's magazine, published all through the period. The irregularities of the cookery section in it were researched as part of the context and were used as a supplementary to the commercial cookbooks source.

Diana Velcheva argued that 'from the point of view of the consumer, there is no difference between cookbooks and women's magazines, thus they can be seen as one' (Velcheva 2006: 52). While this point might prove just for the early years of the 20th century, when quite a lot of cookbooks were published as supplements to women's magazines, it becomes more problematic to accept later on, when there was a clearer separation between the two. The commercial cookbooks after 1944, published independently, involved greater editorial efforts and were very often compendiums, meant to cover every need, season, product, or circumstance. Aiming at long-term use, and also, with there being a few on the market, they became normative, generic, household's basic, reference books, connecting the housewives with the fundaments of cooking. Moreover, they were written mostly by professionals in the food sciences and industry.

The magazine recipes, in contrast, became gradually associated with change and novelty. They paid attention to seasonality, fashion, suggested new techniques, introduced new products on the market. Cutouts of such recipes sometimes found a place among handwritten recipes in the scrapbooks. *Zhenata dnes* created – at least in some ways – an alternative to the meta-discourse, walking half the way from the ideology to the actual practices, but also maintaining the ideology of feminism, in a way perhaps slightly more radical compared to the state leadership's policy (as Ghodsee 2014, suggested). The ability of women's magazines to reflect the diversity of ideological interpretations of their historical period has been exploited in the field of cultural food studies (Régnier 2003, Geyzen 2018). I used them as an additional source to draw the context with greater precision. Their main added value was in their higher frequency of publication, which provided a better idea of the dynamics in the ideological discourses through the years, in comparison to the relatively fewer cookbooks. Moreover it presented the interesting variation of the meta-discourse, being both supportive of the ideology and critical of it at times. I followed and analysed the fluctuation of the culinary section in *Zhenata dnes* in size and in character, searching for indications of changes in attitude, of involvement of new products, techniques and equipment, and practices.

For the general context I also used a range of non-fiction books, published between the 1960s and 1989 and discussing the issues of woman's role in the society, the communist lifestyle and the policy and strategy of the state in this field (for example Duhteva and Gerova eds. 1973, Lyutov et al. eds. 1977, Georgieva and Moskova 1981). Another key source of information on state policy and ideology are the extensively published speeches of Todor Zhivkov, and party documents, such as the decisions of the April Plenum and of the 10th congress of the Bulgarian Communist Party, which in 1973 outlined a strategy to elevate women's role in the 'developed socialist society' (BKP 1973). The leader's addresses to party congresses and plenums give insight into the development of the meta-discourse (or of its stagnation). The national archive also preserves a relatively extensive, although patchy, archive of the state administrations, where information can be found on strategies, production, trade and consumption.

The combination of the different sources provided complex and rich insights into the questions I pursued. Still they had their limitations. One of the weaknesses remained the time coverage. A research of the entire four and a half decades of communism in Bulgaria, between 1944 and 1989, would have been a more useful timeline against which to observe the recipe exchange process in evolution, but the lack of access to oral sources from the earlier years impaired this possibility.

Another limitation was the common tendency of the narrators to think of their life as adults under communism as one, and not in evolution – at least regarding their foodways. They were able to distinguish clearly the period between and after marriage, between and after changing their households, or before and after having children. But they were unable to recall any clear division marks, which might have been left by the different political periods – as they stand out from the content of *Zhenata dnes* and the cookbooks, for example. The *perestroika*, which started around 1983–1984 and brought some liberalization and desertion of ideology, was also often mixed up with the post-communist period. Also the narratives suggest that the harsh consumption crisis, which Bulgaria underwent between 1985 and 1989, is sometimes not clearly distinguished from the post-communist crisis of the early 1990s – both related to food shortages and cuts of electricity and heating. This specific of the narratives reduced the opportunity to explore the evolution of their own foodways, instead they are presented as quite static.

One more shortcoming is the absence of men among the narrators. While the national poll found that some 10 per cent of men did use recipes which they wrote down themselves, I was unable to identify such men and include them in my study. The narratives suggested that men who cooked at home and did so regularly, were a marginal part of the male population (only one of the narrators, for example, said that her husband cooked at home). The poll on the other hand did not register the frequency with which men were involved in cooking. As a result I limited my investigation to reflect the perspectives of women, who were the main domestic cooks, the main participants in the process of recipe exchange and also the main intended consumers of the feminist ideology (as it was applied in Eastern European communist countries).

In spite of the conducted national opinion poll, most of this research's findings are not intended to be representative. Founded on constructivist grounds, they reflect multiple perspectives and aim at offering a better understanding of the various ways in which communist reality was conceptualized by and made sense to those who lived it. I very broadly followed Adele Clarke's idea of 'social ecology' (Clarke 2009: 199). My goal through the entire research process has been to investigate how women made sense in their everyday life routine by identifying within it and around it numerous referential points of relevance. Some of them are discourses: of the interviewees, (inevitably) mine, or broadly present in the society in that period through media and other social channels. Some are actants: state institutions, social formations, economic structures and individuals. Some are occurring events: important developments in the context. Some are in essence interactions: practised hierarchies, power relations, emotional attachments. As they are indeed many and diverse, the ambition to make the study non-reductive threatened to produce an incomprehensible result, or at least one impossible to fit to any acceptable format description.

In the process of analysing the interviews, I obtained a detailed map of the importance that the narrators attached to the process of recipe exchange and the resulting scrapbooks. This map revealed a complex geography of meanings, which on the one hand stand out, but on the other refuse to clearly separate from each other and often overlap. Indeed they may be subjected to conditional divisions, but the clusters that they form remain interconnected, somewhat incoherent, and the links between them important and even defining. Trusting that these meanings make an organism, rather than a mechanism, I did not dissect them, but instead applied to them the multi-aspect analysis optics, inspired by Bateson.

PART TWO

HOME COOKING BETWEEN COOKBOOKS AND SCRAPBOOKS

RECIPE COLLECTION AS AN INSTRUMENT

Everyday urban life in communist Bulgaria did not come in a great variety of lifestyles. Women had highly converging patterns for going through their weeks. Eight-hour working days began and ended with some commuting for one to two hours on crowded public transport. Shopping well into the 1980s meant separate visits to the bakery, butcher, fruit-and-vegetable and grocery store, which, queueing included, took over 40 minutes a day. When they arrived at home, the process of cooking and washing of dishes began, taking over 90 minutes a day[1].

Urban homes in the 1970s and the 1980s were typically condominium apartments, where the kitchen, almost always a separate room, varied between 6 and 15 square metres. By 1971 less than 40 per cent of the households used electricity or gas to cook, most continued to do so with stoves burning wood, which also served as house heating. By then 35 per cent had a refrigerator and 23 per cent a vacuum cleaner (Dinkova 1971). In the following two decades electric appliances finally entered most homes and late communism saw its own version of the Frankfurt kitchen with cupboards of plywood, the plastic covers of which easily peeled, and with bad hinges which made the doors hang askew. The porcelain sink and the fridge often leaked, the stove and the electrical plates on top of it were deemed unreliable. Yet, women invested great efforts and time to humanize and beautify their homes. They sewed curtains, tablecloths and covers for the chairs, embroidered tapestries to hang in frames or knitted lace to decorate furniture and tables. Most of all, they cooked day after day: prepared family meals and festive dinners for the very frequent social gatherings at home, baked breads, *banitsas* and cakes, and in late summer organized the family manufacture of preserves, which provided an important part of the winter menu: relishes, compotes, pickles and jams (Shkodrova 2014: 328).

It is in such kitchens that most of the interviewed women had spent many hours cooking. Whatever variety of cookery advice might have been out there in late communist Bulgaria, they were navigating within their own, limited part of it: the told, shown, written, printed or broadcast cooking advice, to which they had had access. Within this pool of possibilities, even more limited were the materials, to which they paid attention and had endorsed as good to use. The principal written sources, which they said they used, coincided with the findings of the national representative poll, made for this research: their ever upgraded recipe collections and a varying number of printed cookbooks.

---

[1] The data is from a 1969 time budget study, quoted by Ghodsee 2014: 551.

All the interviewed women said that the scrapbooks were their main written source. Cathy Ivanova, for instance, pointed out that on 90 per cent of occasions she used her scrapbook and only on 10 per cent one of the three voluminous cookbooks she had. A very similar approach transpired from most of the narratives.

The women differed more in their attitudes to the commercially printed communist cookbooks they owned. Most of them were sceptical as to how trustworthy or valuable the cookbooks' advice was, although in varying degrees, and some did not use or have cookbooks at all. Their opinion of this type of advice was formed by many considerations and one was the insufficient choice of cookbooks on the market. Many of the interviewed women recalled difficulties in obtaining cookbooks in the past. Narrators from the capital and from smaller towns or rural areas equally recalled that cookbooks were purchased mainly with *vruzki* (connections). Elena Salmadzhiyska, who lived in the smaller town of Bansko and then in a village, said that the only option was to be friends with the salesperson in the bookstore – then 'if she gets two copies, she would keep one for herself and give you the other one.'

Pharmacist Sofia Georgieva from Plovdiv recalled a 'marketing' practice, invented as a consequence of this gap: 'In the first place, there weren't enough cookbooks on sale ... But once a cookbook was released, it was problematic to buy it. They would also try to sell it to you in a "package" with other books that were not selling well'.

Lyubka Georgieva for instance explained that she was searching to buy one for a long time to no avail. When she finally purchased one, she decided that it sufficed. Indeed if the three decades between 1950 and 1980 saw a few cookbooks printed, many of them were compendiums and aimed at covering an exhaustive range of dishes. But she said that most of all, she couldn't imagine going through such trouble again to acquire another one.

Many of the women also spoke of being satisfied with the possession of just one or two books, which seemed to be enough for their needs. Commenting on her 'single cookbook', which she in fact bought after 1989 (and ignoring two, which she possessed before 1989 and did not use), Ivanka Atipova, a chemist in Sofia said: 'I had enough recipes'. A few women with a particular passion for good food and cooking had inherited cookbooks from before 1944, which they used with priority. They combined them with cookbooks from the communist period, though, and generally worked with larger quantities of cookbooks at all times.

Speaking of how unavailable cookbooks were, Elisaveta Shkodrova, a chemist in Sofia, pointed out that 'there were just two or three – most of all that one of Cholcheva, and some others, but I probably haven't noticed them and didn't buy them'. Her statement illustrates the already described curious phenomenon of the 'generic cookbook' illusion. An illusion, or perhaps even a delusion, as most of the women proved to know of other books, but were at the same time somehow oblivious of their existence and truly believed that in those years there was only one, single published book out there. Sometimes it happened that days after the interview, while searching in their libraries upon my enquiry, they were surprised to find a few cookbooks from the period, which they owned but said they had completely forgotten about. However many of the omitted books were from the late 1980s, when there was a sudden upsurge in publishing.

This suggests that the national poll, made for this research, might be reflecting the general memories and impressions of the women from the period – and of their use of cookbooks, rather than the actual situation with the distribution of communist cookbooks.

Some of the interviewed women also said that they were never interested in using a cookbook (therefore they never looked for one). Nedyalka Malcheva from the small, nearly rural town of Preslav said that she bought a cookbook once and gave it straight away to her sister, because 'I couldn't care less. Whatever I had learned from grandmothers, from my mother, this is what I cooked'. Her words suggest the possibility that she simply bought that cookbook too late. She possessed a significant collection of handwritten recipes – not only from her family members, but also from neighbours and friends. She also claimed to be a passionate cook, preparing nearly industrial quantities of cookies and other desserts for different occasions, also for people outside the family. Dobrinka Boeva, who lived in Sofia, said that she had inherited a number of cookbooks from her mother-in-law, but never used them, nor did she ever try to buy a cookbook herself. In many cases, it was the scrapbooks that rendered cookbooks superfluous.

Clearly the interviewed women had established perceptions of their cookbooks, and ways to use them, and these were quite diverse. Some said that they learned the basics of cooking from cookbooks and others – that this is precisely what you cannot learn from them. Some stated that they used the recipes as inspiration, others said that cookbook recipes were uninspiring, impersonal and more common, traditional. These perceptions, polyphonic and not always consistent, naturally must have varied due to the use of different cookbooks, combined with different cookery skills and background.

It seems that to the women, cookbooks were at times complementary to, and at other times conflicting with, their scrapbooks source. A finer grained image of their practices and the hierarchies of the written sources came out, when they were asked to compare the two. Their arguments in favour of scrapbooks were aligned along four themes: **adequacy and simplicity, precision, trust, and the level of customization**. Later in this chapter these qualities of the scrapbooks are discussed separately, but with the acknowledgement that they were naturally intertwined.

A MATTER OF ADEQUACY AND SIMPLICITY

The overarching goal of the communist cookbooks to teach Bulgarian housewives how to feed their families sufficiently and efficiently defined their form of compendium, which was supposed to provide a comprehensive idea of correct cooking. In this respect they differed significantly from the scrapbooks, which included only the types of foods in which the particular collector/user had interest (and needed a recipe to cook). The figure shows the difference between the structure of the two sources. The five cookbooks pay more or less equal attention to each segment of the cooking spectrum: from soups and starters, side and main dishes of different types, and desserts. The scrapbooks are dedicated mainly to desserts and dough-based dishes, to recipes for

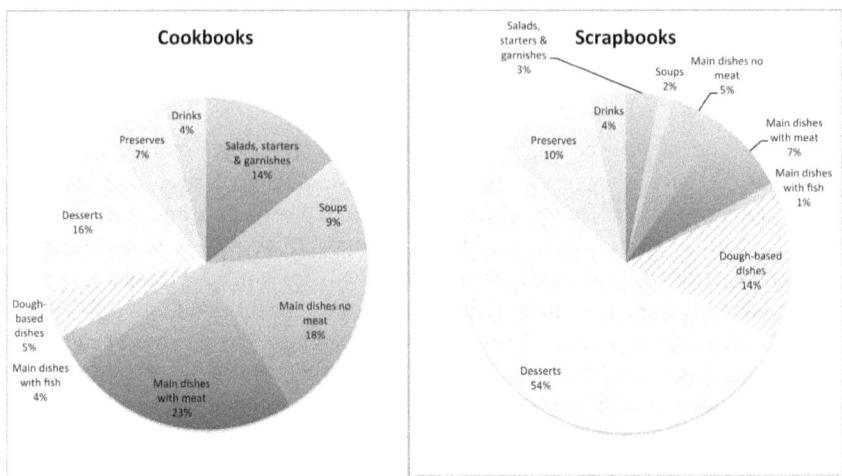

Figure 6 Comparison between recipes, taken from the five cookbooks most available to the households in the study group, and recipes in the scrapbooks (according to the type of dish).[2]

(mostly) fruit and vegetable preservation, and pay in general little attention to any other group of dishes.

The lesser attention paid towards starters, soups and main dishes is probably due to at least two reasons. On the one hand it was rightfully argued (Sharpless 2016: 199) that the exact proportions are more crucial to desserts than to other categories of food. The recipes for preserves were also critical, as the proportions of sugar or salt play a key role in the preservation process. The significant quantities of food which was conserved at once in Bulgarian households, and the extensive period during which the family was dependent on this food, probably raised the value of such recipes even further.

On the other hand one could perhaps argue that the search for variation in the specific cultural framework was expressed more in the field of pastry-making than in the main dishes, which were cooked daily. This might have been the result of the monotonous choice on the market: playing with the same ingredients, changing proportions and methods, may not really create a new main dish, but can produce a different dessert. One proof of this theory is the developments in the early 1990s, when there was an influx of new ingredients on the market, and when the recipes for main dishes in the scrapbooks dramatically increased.

---

[2] The data is based on the quantitative analysis of five cookbooks: *The Housewife's Book* (Cholcheva and Ruseva eds. 1956), *Bulgarian National Cuisine* (Petrov et al. 1978), *Contemporary Domestic Cooking: 2000 Bulgarian and Foreign Recipes* (Cholcheva and Kalaydzhieva 1969), *Our Cuisine* (Naydenov and Chortanova 1955, 1967), *Contemporary Cookbook* (Cholcheva 1964), as well as on 18 scrapbooks. Two of the available scrapbooks were not used in the data set, because they were incomplete and the available parts would have misrepresented the whole. All the sets of cookbooks, which were created by more than one generation, were kept as one, because some of the collections did not allow for clear distinction between the recipes of the different generations.

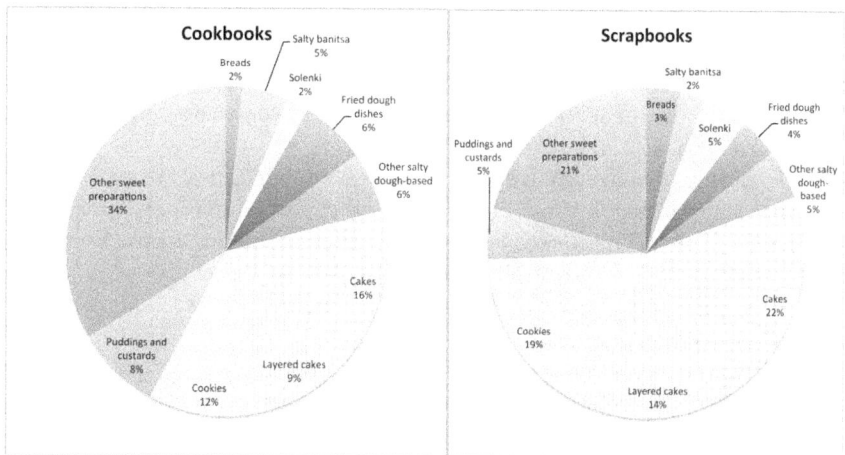

Figure 7 Comparison between the desserts and dough-based dishes taken from the five cookbooks most available to the households in the study group, and those in their scrapbooks.

Another reason might have been that desserts were easier to carry and share. If many of the exchanges were prompted by food shared in small communities, they naturally rotated around the types of food that were easy to take to places and share: baked breads, *banitsas*, dry cakes, cookies.

Therefore, some of the differences between scrapbooks and the cookbooks were the diverging concepts of them as sources and the contrasting ways in which they reflected their users' interests. Comparison between the baking sections offers more insights into the latter (Figure 7). The overall number of recipes for desserts in cookbooks and scrapbooks is different, and a breakdown amplifies the contrasts further and reveals some striking differences. The recipes for cakes, cookies and layered cakes make up 37 per cent of the recipes in the cookbooks' relevant sections, and 55 per cent in the scrapbooks.

Compared to the cookbooks, more than half of the scrapbooks contained the same or (up to three times) larger collections of recipes for cookies, layered cakes, cakes and *solenki*[3]. The comparison shows that the supply of information in the cookbooks was plainly inadequate for the women's interest in these categories: through their networks many of them accumulated more recipes than were available in an entire cooking compendium.

There were also important qualitative differences. For example *Contemporary Domestic Cooking* (Cholcheva and Kalaydzhieva 1972), which featured by far the largest number of 'other sweet preparations', included twenty-four desserts, made with rice or semolina. These two ingredients are more than exceptional in scrapbooks.

---

[3] Varyious salty shortbreads, popular as a snack in Bulgaria.

Equally absent from the recipe exchange were jellied desserts, sweet omelettes, fruit *kisels*[4], which occupied many positions in the dessert sections of the cookbooks. As if to purposefully expand the sections with desserts without offering any useful information, cookbooks included entire lists of 'recipes' consisting of fruits: washed, cleaned, and sprinkled, or not, with sugar.

The women clearly couldn't find in the cookbooks everything they needed, but on the other hand they showed at times a curious blindness towards what the cookbooks offered. For example one of the interviewed women recalled that after the early death of her mother, she was looking for very basic (in her understanding) recipes: how to make *pitka*[5], *banitsa* or *tutmanik*[6], but she couldn't find them in the cookbook. In fact she owned *The Housewife's Book* (Cholcheva and Ruseva eds. 1956), which contained a detailed explanation of how to prepare many sorts of *banitsa*, as well as *tutmanik*. All five cookbooks popular in the examined households boasted extensive instructions on how to make *banitsa*.

Indeed, home-made bread was less present: two of the books, including *The Housewife's Book* (Cholcheva and Ruseva eds. 1962), did not contain any recipes for home-made bread. It is difficult to judge what caused this gap – did it reflect the idea that modern women shouldn't bake bread at home, or some diet-related concerns? The communist industrial production of bread began in Bulgaria in 1952 and after 1973 even the most remote villages were supposed to be supplied with what was called 'factory bread'[7] via the centrally established distribution system (Petrov at al. 1983). On the other hand *Contemporary Cookbook* explicitly stated that 'In the first place the excessive use of bread must be limited' (Cholcheva 1964: 18).

In any case home-made breads, which had a very central role in Bulgarian foodways in the 19th century (Gavrilova 1999: 83), remained very popular among home bakers in the communist period. The scrapbooks provide enough evidence that women searched for more than the cookbooks offered: recipes for home-made bread, *banitsas* and a variety of baked and fried salty dough foods make up one of the biggest sections of the recipes. Endless variations of flour, water, salt and raising agents, combined sometimes with fats, honey, sugar, eggs, milk, yogurt[8], and accompanied by drawings fill up many pages in the cooking manuscripts. Since pulling filo sheets for *banitsa* or preparing 'bathed' or 'beaten' bread required not only mixing ingredients with exact proportions, but the application of very specific techniques and skills, they could be learned more easily through demonstration than through written explanations – especially when the illustrations were scarce and showed mainly the ready-made dish and not the preparation process. It is possible that this was one of the reasons for women to experience this as a gap in their knowledge. Judging by the accounts of the narrators, recipe exchange and scrapbooks were more successful for filling it.

In the narratives the recipes in the cookbooks were repeatedly said to be incomprehensible and inaccessible. Cathy Ivanova for example noted that she turned

---

[4] Fruits in their own juice, thickened with starch – a dish borrowed from the north-east of Europe.
[5] *Pitka* is a round loaf of bread.
[6] A popular soft bread, widely prepared at home with baking soda.
[7] 'Zavodski hlyab' in Bulgarian, i.e. produced in large factories on production lines.
[8] Possibly due to the abundant yogurt production in the country, many cake and bread-based food recipes call not for milk or cream, but for yogurt.

to exchanging recipes because they were more accessible, more 'feasible', with regard to both method and ingredients. To explain, she named as an opposite example Natsko Sotirov's *Contemporary Cuisine* (1959), which she thought contained 'totally unfeasible' recipes, which, seemingly, were meant for professionals (she also possessed *Contemporary Domestic Cooking*, Cholcheva and Kalaydzhieva 1976). Natsko Sotirov, whose book Cathy Ivanova quoted, was a royal chef during the Bulgarian monarchy and was able to publish his book due to his later service as a private cook to the early communist leaders. The book greatly reflected his work in the royal kitchens and until 1989, it remained the most advanced cookbook in terms of level of cuisine, published in Bulgarian. Despite the foreword, which addressed domestic cooks, the book must have been inaccessible in more than one way to Bulgarian housewives. One can only imagine how a recipe for Royal Foie Gras – calling for, besides its central ingredient of fresh cream, Marsala Wine, and truffles – must have sounded to a Bulgarian communist housewife, to whom even the locally grown strawberries were a luxury. But also recipes with more accessible ingredients, which account for approximately half of the content of Sotirov's book, must have been difficult to use. Most of them contain at least one, and often more references to other parts of the book. A typical recipe reads:

Courgettes beignets

Products: 1 kg courgettes, 250 g beer dough
Cut peeled courgettes in slices and add salt to taste. Dip them in beer dough and
   deep-fry in butter. Serve warm as a starter, or as a garnish to meats.

The location of the recipe for beer dough is neither indicated in the recipe, nor in the table of contents of the book. It is also absent from the section 'coating', which explains how pieces of meat (but not vegetables) are prepared for deep-frying. Instructions for deep-frying in butter are given in a separate section for thermal processing of foods.

In comparison with Sotirov's book, the five cookbooks most available in the studied households were far more adequate as to the choice of ingredients, the equipment and the cooking skills and expectations of the average Bulgarian family at the time. They offered recipes, closer to the simple daily foods of the urban and rural cuisines. Most of them were assuming an educative approach to food – one, which would on the one hand result in a more skilful and informed type of cooking. But this was sometimes perceived as making their use more laborious. To prepare a *tikvenik*[9] according to *Our Cuisine,* for example, one needed to read in one place how to make the stretching dough for any kind of *banitsa* (Naydenov and Chortanova 1971: 339) and to find the recipe for the filling elsewhere.

In this regard though Cholcheva's books and *Bulgarian National Cuisine* (Petrov et al. 1978) were simpler and offered more coherent presentations. They featured 100–150-word recipes, which were presented in one place in simple language. Nevertheless many narrators mentioned that they found the use of cookbooks laborious. Mara

---

[9] Filo-pastry pumpkin pie popular in Bulgaria.

Tseneva, who worked as a professional teacher in cooking technology in Shumen, north-east Bulgaria, recalled her impression that people preferred exchanging recipes simply because this was the easier practice. 'It was easier, it was easier,' she reiterated.

But possibly the most significant difference between cookbooks and scrapbooks, when it came to simplicity, was the way they mediated the advice. Recipes in scrapbooks were collected through active listening, tasting and trying out. The exchange of recipes was mostly accompanied by a detailed explanation of the method details and personal recommendations. These verbal instructions were an essential part of the appropriation of a recipe. All the interviewed women with no exception said that when they passed on a recipe, they always told about their own experience with it. Each time they engaged in a transfer not only of recipes, but of know-how, of cooking skills, expertise, experiences, which were not available in written sources, or probably at least not available without expending a more than reasonable amount of effort to search it out and understand it.

In this sense a recipe in the scrapbook was a proxy to already memorized information. They were, as other researchers observed as well, 'designed as a memory keepsake' (Supski 2013: 18), 'memory boxes' (Lakhtikova 2017: 114). Scrapbooks were not entirely a written source, but rather a sequence of memos from a 'multimedia' source of cookery knowledge transmission. Moreover, they were notes from a learning process.

Many women noted that after comparing the knowledge from cookbooks to that from direct sources, they gave up the cookbooks all together. One of them for example said: 'I have been leafing through books, I was interested, I've been searching. But when I saw that . . . there I found the same, but in much less . . . much less well explained than this [pointing at her scrapbook] it is just not worth it.' Another woman, who owned *Contemporary Domestic Cooking* (Cholcheva and Kalaydzhieva 1969), described a similar path of reasoning. She said that after trying for a while to use her cookbook, she developed a strong preference for recipes that are tried. What attracted her was that somebody who had tried the recipe before her, would tell her 'Yes, this is good, this is tasty. Make it, it will be beautiful!' she said.

The scrapbooks offer evidence that dishes requiring more complex preparation were explained in detail and sometimes not only in verbal form: there are multiple examples of written instructions being accompanied or altogether replaced by drawings (Figure 8). This was often the case when more challenging or lengthy technological steps were involved.

Perhaps the popular practices of conveying cookery information in communist Bulgaria can be seen as closer to the archaic ones than to those of modernity – the art of cooking not being subjected to definitions that could be transmitted in writing, but rather comprehended when taught by demonstration. The lack, and the unappealing quality, of the cookbooks (or other sources, based on modern media) in the households contributed to holding back the transition to non-domestic, non-immediate sources.

A MATTER OF PRECISION

Another argument which the interviewed women had against communist cookbooks, was the lack of precision in them. A number of women expressed their mistrust and

 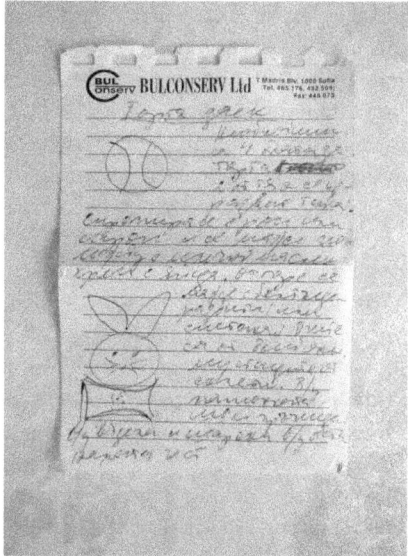

Figure 8 *The diagram on the left (from Zafirka Peneva's scrapbook) shows several designs for cakes. The drawing on the right comes with a recipe for a cake, shaped as a rabbit (from Elisaveta Shkodrova's scrapbook). Drawings were also used to capture the preparation of* pâte feuilleté.

caution when using the cookbooks they owned. Kristin Razsolkova, an art critic in Sofia (who had in her possession *Bulgarian National Cuisine*, Petrov et al. 1978; *The Housewife's Book*, Cholcheva and Ruseva eds. 1956) for example, said that she had encountered many mistakes in her cookbooks and she remained alert when using them. Tamara Ganeva (*Our Cuisine*, Naydenov and Chortanova 1955) shared similar thoughts. Tsveta Tanovska (*Bulgarian National Cuisine*, Petrov et al. 1978; *The Housewife's Book*, Cholcheva and Ruseva eds, 1956) thought that cookbooks were mostly 'didactic, without being particularly precise'.

Indeed, recipes in each of the popular cookbooks offer illustrations of these claims. The instructions on how to make *banitsa* in *Bulgarian National Cuisine* (Petrov et al. 1978: 421), for example, is curious in succeeding to be both confusing to a cook with no experience, and useless to an experienced one. The recipe for the preparation of the filo sheets reads: 'Make dough out of flour [the quantity is specified at the beginning of the recipe], a bit of water [quantity not specified] and salt [specified: to taste] and knead. Roll out filo sheets and bake them.' The recipe does not inform us how thick the dough is supposed to be (and no proportions are given), in what shape or thickness to roll out the sheets, how, or at what temperature and for how long or to what state to bake them.

Our Cuisine (Naydenov and Chortanova 1955), *Contemporary Cookbook* (Cholcheva 1964) and *Contemporary Domestic Cooking* (Cholcheva and Kalaydzhieva 1969) are more precise regarding quantities of ingredients and in their instructions, which are mostly clear and complete. But they also occasionally use vague references and incomprehensible language. *Contemporary cookbook* perplexingly directs the reader to roll out a sheet of dough, 'as thick as a coffee plate', (Cholcheva 1964: 404), or to pour the pudding onto a plate 'shaping it as a pyramid' (Cholcheva 1964: 410). It also follows the unorthodox practice of not giving a list of ingredients, but stating the amount of butter/oil, needed for the preparation – at the very end of the recipe.

Unclear wording, lack of precision or skipped essential information were not unusual for the cookbooks that the women owned. Yet, the scrapbooks were certainly equally, if not more, prone to mistakes. In fact the narrators recalled numerous stories of blunders, which they found (at least retrospectively) entertaining. Maya Mircheva, a linguist in Sofia, recounted an embarrassing situation, in which a young colleague found she had forgotten to write down the raising agent for a cake: 'She was a young bride ... And her parents-in-law were coming for a visit ... Her husband boasted of a cake she was preparing in their honour, and in the end ... It didn't work out.'

Dani Tsacheva, a teacher from the town of Elena in Central Bulgaria, also remembered laughingly an ill-fated recipe exchange between two female colleagues. One of them received a recipe from the other and started preparing it: mixed the dough and put it in the oven to bake. 'Half an hour passed, something was boiling inside, but it definitely wasn't turning into a cake. She called in panic: 'Marietta, (...) it doesn't work!' It turned out she wasn't told to add flour – so she didn't. Why, of course this soup of eggs [that she ended up making] would ... boil ...'

Dani Tsacheva said that in the teachers' room recipes were traded regularly – as were success and failure stories, following their exchange. Once one of the teachers absent-mindedly dictated: 'zest of one lemon and the juice of another'. Her words circulated as a joke around the school for years.

The risk of mistakes in the exchanged recipes was increased by the fact that they were often told by an experienced person to an inexperienced one. They were also often written out hastily or, as the women testified, carried home only memorized. Being exchanged in all kinds of circumstances – on the bench in front of the office, in a bus station, in the bus, on the beach, beside the hospital bed – to name just a few of the situations mentioned in the narratives, there were bound to be mistakes and omissions, unreadable parts. It also happened that recipes were written down on pieces of paper too small to accommodate the complete explanation. There were not many traces of the 'unhurried recipe dictation or copying', of which Lakhtikova (2019: 87) wrote in her reflection on Soviet scrapbooks.

Some of the interesting documents are recipes written on a ticket from the Naval Museum in Varna (Figure 9); on a shred of wallpaper; on a form, titled 'Additional Sheet to the History of the Patient'; on a blood test template (Figure 10); a payment order of the Institute for Invention and Rationalization; a medical prescription; a canteen coupon; an accounting document; a page from the traffic militia's fines record; a library borrowing slip; and a banking slip of the State Saving Bank.

These recipes, scribbled in haste, were sometimes rewritten with greater care in the scrapbooks, with details added from memory, while still fresh. Others were left as they were in a pile – some of the scrapbooks, like for instance the one of Kalina Kechova from Smolyan, consisted entirely of such loose sheets and bits of paper, which were

Recipe Collection as an Instrument 79

Figure 9 *A recipe, written on a ticket from the Naval Museum in Varna, 1976, from the scrapbook of Elisaveta Shkodrova.*

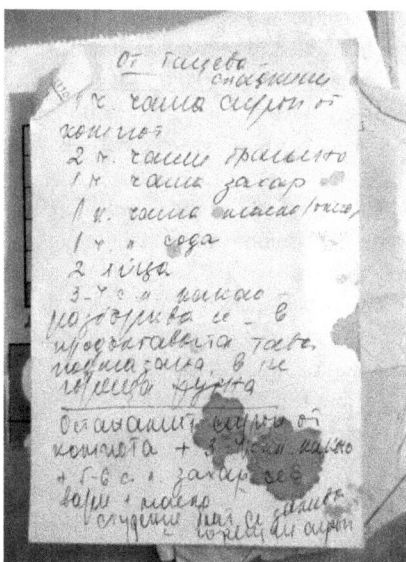
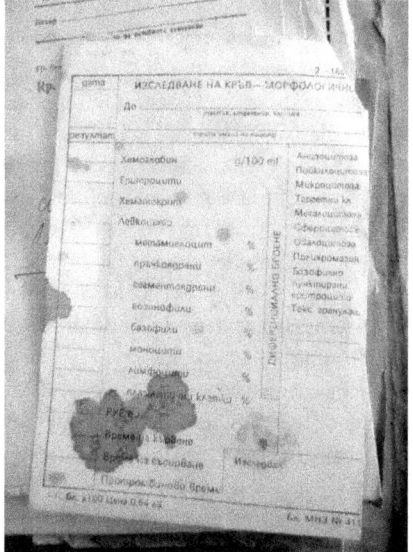

Figure 10 *A recipe, written on the back of a blood test template, from the collection of Lyubka Georgieva.*

never organized, but just kept together in a kitchen drawer. The great advantage of this method of information acquisition was that, if the sketchy notes failed to evoke clear memory of the instructions, their owner could in most cases obtain them again straight from the source.

Mara Tseneva, who had worked as food technologist, said that women found exchanged recipes easier, because they used measures like 'one handful of ...', 'one spoonful of ...', while cookbooks gave quantities in grams. If it was true, it would have been another indication of the communist households' greater proximity to pre-modern times, when traditional cooking did not use exact measurements: cooks had their approximate ways to measure proportions and 'there weren't many delicate dishes, which could be endangered by the miscalculation of a few grams' (Gavrilova 1999: 110).

However the situation was more complex than that. The first edition of *Our Cuisine* (Naydenov and Chortanova 1955), which was aimed at both professional and domestic cooks, consistently used exact weight measures. The quoted quantities were per portion, so that the cook needed to calculate them each time, depending on the number of portions that he/she intended to prepare. The later editions of *Our Cuisine* though were adapted to the domestic cook and all the five books, those most available in the researched households, translated exact measures (kilograms or litres) into the approximate, domestic measures in spoons, cups etc. In recipes they used the two options interchangeably and randomly, even in one and the same recipe. For instance a recipe in *Our Cuisine* for 'chocolate balls' lists the measurements as a mixture of cups (for walnuts, sugar, milk) and grams (for chocolate, cookies).

Indicated in exact measures or not, the proportions of the ingredients may have been the smallest imprecision of all, lurking in a communist cookbook recipe. Very often the method was left unexplained, or was made incomprehensible due to strange wording or unclear references. The cooks were instructed to process the dough 'some more' or 'enough', to spread it in a 'cake form' [of what size or type?] or to shape the dish in squares the size of 'pasti, the sides of which varied from 3 to 12 cm in Bulgarian pastry shops) (Naydenov and Chortanova 1971: 271, 332). The temperatures were indicated only as low, medium and high.

In spite of Mara Tseneva's opinion, scrapbooks suggest that women needed not less, but more precision. The recipes they copied themselves, demonstrated that home cooks were able to handle both. As far as cooking methods are concerned, scrapbooks might come across as utterly inconsistent, with some recipes written out in great detail, complemented with extra annotations and drawings, and others consisting of plain lists of ingredients or barely a couple of lines, capturing the idea of the dish. This seeming inconsistency though reveals one important feature of the scrapbooks: their tendency to be highly customized to the skills and the needs of their owners.

A MATTER OF CUSTOMIZATION

A person who wrote down a recipe, could ask more questions about the preparations, or skip writing the explanations altogether if she knew the method or thought she had memorized it well. This made scrapbooks by far the more economical way of acquiring the needed culinary knowledge: by only asking the specifically necessary questions, and saving time and energy spent reading through pages of superfluous information.

The convenience of the scrapbook-stored knowledge was emphasized in many of the narratives. Kristin Razsolkova, for instance, said that she found the information in the scrapbooks much clearer 'because it was written down by the person himself and he described the method'. Many women spoke of skipping those details which they found obvious. Elisaveta Shkodrova said that she counted on her familiarity with the basic cooking principles and techniques, so she wrote down only proportions or the order of the various operations. 'When there are explanations for beginners, I ignore them ...'. The energy-saving effect of this customization for instance was crucial to Dobrinka Boeva in her decision to completely ignore printed cookbooks – even if she owned a library of culinary advice remarkable for the period. 'Sometimes even if nobody has explained, only looking at a cooked meal, I already know how it is prepared ...'. She said that with such experience, her handwritten recipes are significantly shorter than those in the cookbooks.

Indeed, some of her A4 recipes sheets, typed with a typewriter, contained twelve to thirteen recipes, each of one to three lines. But in her notebook, where she wrote most of her recipes, their length is often the same as in her cookbooks. For instance a recipe for *solenki*, in her scrapbook read:

Solenki

1 cup crumbled cheese[10]
1 cup (or one jar) yogurt[11]
1 tea spoon salt
1 spoon baking soda
flour
Knead into soft dough. Melt a bit of pork fat in the baking dish. Make small balls, put pieces of butter and cheese.
To bake in very hot oven.[12]

A similar simple recipe for salty sticks in *The Housewife's Book* (Cholcheva and Ruseva eds. 1956) reads:

Solenki with Cheese

Products:
1 tea cup milk[13]

---

[10] 'Cheese' was always used for white cheese, similar to feta, the most popular Bulgarian cheese. It was one of two main kinds on sale, the other being *kashkaval* – softer yellow cheese, probably named after the Italian caciocavallo.
[11] There was only one type of yogurt jar on sale, of 500 ml capacity, which makes one cup around half the quantity of one jar.
[12] This line might have been added later.
[13] Could be a mistake, as the raising agent is baking soda and there is no acid ingredient in the recipe.

1 cup pork fat
1 spoon baking soda
¼ kg grated cheese
1 egg
flour as much as it takes
Preparation:
Knead dough from the ingredients and let it rest for 7–8 hours. Shape into sticks, arrange in an oiled baking tin, glaze with beaten egg and bake until golden-red.

The recipe in the printed cookbook does say less in the same number of lines: it does not specify the quantity of the flour, nor does it state what type of dough the cook should aim at, only giving the vague instruction to add 'as much [flour] as it takes'. It also says little about the technology of shaping the sticks or their optimal size and thickness. In her recipe, Dobrinka Boeva also does not specify the size of the 'small balls', or where the cheese and butter should be placed. But she probably knows those things either from experience or because she was told, or, most likely, because she has seen and tasted the *solenki* before baking them herself. In any case she did not miss any essential information for preparing them – which might have been the case with some recipes in cookbooks.

Yet, considering the example above, it is possible that the perception of greater length of cookbook recipes was related not so much to the number of lines to read, but to the whole experience of tracking down the necessary recipe, possibly while reading through a number of others on the way, losing time in hesitation, figuring out the meaning and the method. It is possible that the preference for scrapbooks was not related solely to the actual qualities of the cookbooks. Every practising cook is aware that searching for a new recipe can easily double the time for a dish to materialize, regardless of the quantity and the character of the available sources. The risk for it not working out is also always present regardless of the quality of the instructions, as the cook lacks personal experience with the particular preparation. Feeling forced to process all the ingredients from scratch and to cook daily, mostly after or before work, it is easy to understand that the narrators valued the savings of energy and reduced risk of scrapbook recipes. Any advice, which was already internalized by trying the dish, seeing it, talking about it, and writing down the instructions, required much less effort to recall and apply.

The consequence of this 'economical' approach to recipes, noted for private use, is that they become less comprehensible to the outside reader. Revel (1982) wrote that this makes them removed from the dish itself, divided from it by invisible layers of implicit information and understandings. Moreover, they become coded in a sort of argot, only understandable to practitioners and therefore exclusionary (Revel 1982, as quoted by Pennell 2004: 238). 'The manuscript text is only a fraction and refraction of practice: there are still omissions, elisions and assumptions of intuition,' wrote Pennell (2012: 253).

But indeed the annotations in a scrapbook seem to be only one stage in the metamorphosis, which a recipe undergoes in the cycle of exchanges. Its material form – words and signs, selected to serve as personalized memory triggers – is only a temporary stop. Enriched by the experience of the user, it departs again, now possibly in oral form, adapted to the world 'outside': the giver reformulates it according to his ideas of what the recipient needs to know. Entangled in the everyday communication, what remains is a living construct. Many women spoke of keeping their notes short, but broadening the explanation when passing the recipe over. This meant not only adding the personal experience with the recipe, but also explaining it in a way that is understandable. Of course, also that exchange did not shape the recipe for the use of a broader circle of users, but kept it adapted to the needs of the particular receiver and her/his experience. Precisely this quality – the economy of storage and economy of transfer – must have constituted one of the main advantages of scrapbooks as a source.

Finally, it was not only the level and detail of the cookery advice that was customized. Scrapbooks were also ideologically personalized documents. In an explicit confirmation of the scholarly argument that cookbooks express ideologies (Appadurai 1988, Albala 2012, Shkodrova 2018a), all the five cookbooks, most often found in the researched households, contained sections on the nutrition ideology of the period. Two of those were limited to information and instructions on healthy nutrition, the other three had them integrated in broader, politically charged statements. A few scrapbooks, in contrast, featured such content. Two of them contained explicit political statements and satire, a couple of others included dedications, expressing their creators' philosophy on food and cuisine. But even when individual ideologies transpired on the scrapbook pages, they belonged to the users of the documents, they were not external ideological prescriptions. Moreover, the fact that the political ideas presented went against the grain of the official communist discourses shows that scrapbooks were used as a space for counter-discourses – an argument that is further confirmed by the origin and names of some of the recipes included in them.

A MATTER OF TRUST

There is an emerging tradition in cultural food studies to interpret the exchange of recipes as an expression of trust. The very act of sharing a food recipe is an act of trust, argued Susan Leonardi (1989: 345). Furthermore, using a recipe obtained from an acquaintance, may be seen as a sign of our faith that the person in question would not deliberately let us down (according to the definition by Lagerspetz 1998: 48). Also Pirogovskaya (2017: 337) considered Soviet scrapbooks as embodying 'a specific kind of trust' in community cooking practices and opposed to the 'official' cuisine as a 'system of knowledge' with little credibility.

Indeed in the process of recipe exchange the connection between the giver and the recipient in communist Bulgaria had a very practical value. However, that connection was not necessarily one of faith in the giver's good will or skills. It was a more generic, not necessarily positively charged social relation, in which the recipient in most cases knew well, or at least had some personal impressions of the giver. In this way the collector was able to judge if and how much she could trust her recommendations, or stay alert to their precision, employ her general knowledge on cookery to try to find mistakes or to regulate the taste.

The narratives offered many examples of how recipes were collected within close social networks and from contacts, who were indeed trusted to be knowledgeable cooks. However there were also examples of exchange with strangers, or people who did not belong to the social network of the receiver, or were even at times distrusted. There were also opposite cases when recipes, obtained from trusted sources, failed to pass the approval test of the recipients.

While cases in which the authority of the giver was crucial to seeking an exchange were many, it is difficult to judge how important it was, because in many cases it came together with first-hand experience of the particular dish. As transpired from the narratives, the vast majority of the recipes were written after the dish was tasted: cooked by a friend, who was visited, paid a visit, or brought the food to the common workplace, and similar. The element of knowing the dish had enormous importance in the process and was mentioned by most narrators as crucial.

'Once I have tasted it, and I know who gave me the recipe, I am certain that should I decide to cook it, it will be good', explained one of the interviewed, Atanaska Terzieva, an accountant living in the small town of Radnevo.

When asked to explain their preferences for their scrapbooks, most narrators named in the first place the fact that these were recipes of dishes which they had tasted and liked. Maya Mircheva, Ivanka Atipova, Lyubka Georgieva as well as many other narrators, put it almost in the same words: 'Q: So what was missing in the cookbooks? Ivanka Atipova: Well, there it is written [the recipe], but you haven't tasted it. And in this way [with the exchange of recipes] you get a piece of cake to try and you see that it is tasty, so you tell yourself 'Ooooh, I will make this for the children!'

Also the opportunity to see the dish – its appearance – was an important advantage to the women, who could more easily imagine what they were aiming at – this chance was mostly not provided by the cookbooks, which had very few illustrations, if at all. Explaining the indications of the sources of recipes in her scrapbook – mostly names of women – Lyubka Georgieva said: '[In this manner] I recall what it looked like. I have seen it [the dish], so I can make it in the same way, to look the same as the one that was shown to me'. Many other narratives contained similar statements.

The role of the trust in the giver, of course, should not be underestimated – another excerpt from Atanaska Terzieva's narrative illustrated how it had the power to build bridges between social layers and made women reach beyond the limits of their own social circles. Terzieva's scrapbook contained several loose sheets of beautifully and patiently written recipes. To my enquiry what this was she said that she obtained them from a woman from the ethnic Turkish minority, whom she didn't know herself. She said that the exchange was made via her sister: 'I dare to say I trust my sister on culinary matters'. Her words suggested that the trust in her sister was extended to those whom her sister trusted. Such exchange connected one person to the contacts of another, extending recipes' circulation in broader circles.

The women admitted they had greater interest in trading recipes with peers whom they knew to be good cooks. But tasting the dish was enough to ask for a recipe even from a stranger. Evidence of this was the narrative of Lyubka Georgieva, a syndicate leader in Sofia. As a young woman she worked as a nurse in a hospital, where she took recipes from patients: people whom she barely knew, but whose cakes, cookies or *banitsa* she tried and liked. The leading motivation was not authority, attraction, or any other type of bond with the giver, but the chance of trying – and liking – the taste of a dish prepared by the giver. In such cases the trust, which played a role, was limited strictly to one particular dish and did not necessarily extend to the giver or her social circle. Particular cooking skills, proved in a most direct, fast and convincing way, were exchanged between two individuals as an instance of serendipity.

Investigating scrapbooks in the Soviet Union as expressions of trust, Pirogovskaya (2017: 334) called such exchanges 'short-term solidarities'. While many of them must have been precisely this – acts of benevolence and compassion – they also, in fact, go beyond that. A situation like that narrated by Lyubka Georgieva, when a patient lies in a hospital bed and a nurse passes by and asks for a recipe – especially in the cultural context of the non-monetary communist economies – is essentially an exchange of know-how for the possibility of a better service.

Moreover, the recipe exchange was a normative form of communication between women. This meant that accepting unsolicited cookery advice was seen also as simple politeness. The situation in Bulgaria seems to be very similar to what Pirogovskaya (2017: 352) described about Soviet Russia, where 'Nobody could refuse to share a recipe because it means breaking an unwritten rule of communication and rejecting participation in social bonding.'

Discussing English and American cookbooks from the period between the seventeenth to the mid-20th century, Theophano argued that they 'represented alliances and affinity, and often have been based on shared characteristics of race, class and religion' (Theophano 2002). Indeed, alliances and affinity often played a role in the process. But it seems quite clear that, at least across the communist bloc, women exchanged recipes beyond their networks of affinity. This practice also casts doubts over the argument of Eamon that recipes are 'reliable simply through the fact of being registered: the inscription of the recipe is the 'completion of the trial itself' (Eamon 1994: 7, 131, 360).

On the other hand the low reputation or lack of trust in a person, as a cook or in general, would be transferred onto the recipe itself. For instance Atanaska Terzieva told of a female employee, a subordinate of her husband, who used to regularly send her recipes. She said she hardly knew the woman and tended to interpret the gesture as an act of fawning. Therefore she did not trust her cookery advice. 'He [Terzieva's husband] was in a managing position and the woman, in fact, right, she did her work well ... She was doing, what she was supposed to do ... But it was making me laugh ... he would bring a recipe and would say: 'here is something she sends you' ... I have forgotten already the name of this woman ... So such recipes I didn't trust.'

The recipe exchange was to women the first step in a process of domestication of a recipe. They had possibly tried the dish and knowing the giver in most cases, they had certain expectations from the recipe. But the real assimilation of it took place, as it was tried out, tasted by the family and possibly adapted to the tastes of the household. Not all recipes noted in the scrapbooks made it into the circle of dishes that the cook would consider good and would cook regularly. Sometimes clear indications of failed attempts of preparation, or tastes that did not live up to expectations are visible on the scrapbooks' pages: crossed-out entries, marked with large NOs, or, on the contrary, indicated as excellent with exclamation marks, the annotations of recipes often show the ranking of the particular recipe in the ideas of the housewife.

Thus scrapbooks were documents, in which women stored a synthesis of their cookery interests and experience, of what was already familiar. How well or thoroughly these documents corresponded to the views and practices of their creators depended greatly on how much effort was invested in them. But in all cases the collections were actively pursued rather than simply happening. Even if, as mentioned above, it was a matter of common courtesy to accept a recipe from someone without having asked for it, the main bulk of the instructions related to the details in which the women had an interest. Some of them articulated a specific focus for their recipe search. For example Elisaveta Shkodrova said that since she considered cookbooks outdated, she was looking for, and writing down, recipes which she perceived as new and modern. She explained: 'Everyone wishes to gain new knowledge, to move forward. In this sense we wanted to introduce [in our cooking practice] something better, newer.' Dani Tsacheva also explained that the recipe exchange was indicative of women's wish to strive 'for something new, different'.

A few of the women also spoke of recipes, corresponding to specific dietary adjustments – theirs, or in the family – which were mostly made by modification of existing recipes. Tamara Ganeva spoke of the reduced content of salt, sugars and fats, which her mother found important and which she also followed. Sofia Georgieva recalled not using cookbooks, because their recipes included 'too much frying. I do not fry, because of my husband's health problems'.

Thus the recipes that had passed the test were adapted, became perceived as 'own'. Many women quoted an established practice of divided usage of cookbooks and scrapbooks along the lines 'familiar/unfamiliar'. As an example, Kristin Razsolkova defined her solid collection of recipes, handwritten by three generations, as 'ours, basic, primary', while the cookbooks were to her 'somehow coming from outside'.

Even so, a closer look at women's reasoning over the use of cookbooks shows that their attitude was not necessarily one of mistrust. A number of women mentioned using cookbooks when looking for new recipes and ideas. When directly asked if she found cookbooks unreliable, Tamara Ganeva said 'it was not so much a matter of trust, but of not comprehending well. The way, in which the procedure was described, was not good – the inconsistent way in which the steps were ordered, the skipping of stages ...' She said that when cooking from cookbooks, she always perceived the first time as a trial.

It is not entirely clear if or to what extent recipes from cookbooks circulated in the scrapbooks. I found a clear indication of this only once: in Dobrinka Boeva there were sheets with photocopied recipes from *Bulgarian National Cuisine*, Petrov et al. 1978[14]. The absence of clippings from cookbooks in the scrapbooks could not be interpreted as reluctance to use cookbook recipes, as it was probably due to the common respect

---

[14] The sheets were put together by Boeva's husband and presented 'topical collections', i.e. collections of recipes for a particular foodstuff. For example one of them was for recipes using spinach, collected apparently from different printed sources, and resulted from Boeva's husband's pursuits in ethnography.

for books as material objects. It is quite possible that some of the recipes in the scrapbooks came from cookbooks, as there was a vast body of quite generic cookery advice, variations of which were found in all the types of sources. In any case if recipes were taken from cookbooks and then shared, they must have been amended by each user, and credited to the person who gave them to the collector.

All of this suggests that women thought of scrapbook recipes most of all as reliable. The trust in the giver was only one (and an optional) element that constituted this reliability. Arguably more crucial were the experience of the recipient with the taste of the dish and with the applicability of the recipe.

The great advantage of scrapbooks was that they combined often purposefully sought advice with a record of private cooking experimentation and experience, which delivered a body of familiar, reliable, domesticated cooking advice. Scrapbooks contained trusted recipes and trust, as Fukuyama famously argued, is a mighty saving agent: it allows us to spare effort, time and money (Fukuyama 1997).

In summary, scrapbooks contained customized, processed information, which was easier to use in comparison to the choice of unfamiliar recipes in the encyclopaedic cookbooks. The uncertainties in comprehending written instructions, which women experienced when using cookbooks, were here avoided by first-hand experience, oral additions, the possibility of asking questions, and the visual and taste experience of the particular dish.

The recipe collections, at least to some extent, were instruments for purposefully shaping home cuisine in desired directions. They were by default personalized selections of recipes: a range of cooking instructions and dishes, which had passed through the filter of private taste, adjusted to the individual practice preferences or possible diets. If scrapbooks, just like any cookbook or text ever created, conveyed (at least implicitly) ideologies, these were the private ideologies of their creators: reflecting anything from their love for one or another style of food, to their beliefs in what makes good food.

PART THREE

THE MEANINGS OF SCRAPBOOKS

Analysing the process of recipe collection and the various aspects of its importance offers access to the very core of making sense of everyday life. It allows us to understand the complex ways, in which politics, economics, society and individuals, with their minds and bodies, work together to create meanings and practices. Domestic foodways are outlined here not as standing alone, which they never do, but in their natural, messy and complex context of the texture of everyday life.

Home cooking, and recipe exchange and scrapbooks as its instruments, came out in the narratives loaded with multiple different significances. If the previous chapter discussed the specifics of scrapbooks as a medium for cookery information, this section shows how recipe exchange and scrapbooks facilitated and reflected the various roles/meanings of home cooking. Their instrumentality is examined from four perspectives: how did women construct the meaning of their practices in negotiation with the discursive structure?; what was the economic motivation of their participation in the practice?; in which ways did it relate them to their social group?; and finally, from an affective perspective, what was the emotional value of these activities?

Intertwined on many levels, these aspects are discussed separately with the sole purpose of giving structure and clarity to the data and as a system to nuance their interpretation. But they inevitably are found to merge, overlap and refer to each other.

Such multi-aspect analysis has been advocated by Bateson (1987) to be a necessary analytical approach to social phenomena. I did not have this structure preset during the field study, in fact I stumbled on it accidentally, as this work by Bateson is by now relatively old and not often quoted. But when I read through it, I realized that it wonderfully covers the map of meanings, as I have identified it from the interviews. Its principal advantage is that it validates the complexity of social practices and prevents their simplistic interpretation. It also allows for the construction of a reasonably comprehensive, systematic view of home cooking as practice – and of the more focused discussion of the meanings of recipe exchange and home cooking under communism.

NAVIGATING THE CONTEXT

What distinguished everyday life under 20th century European communism were the high levels of ideological prescriptiveness, which, reinforced by political, social and economic pressures, aimed at changing fundamental social orders and routine practices. The ever-growing inconsistencies, evolution, and polyphony of the ideological discourses notwithstanding, the perception that there was one, solid ideological meta-discourse lived on. Its presentations surrounded individuals in their daily lives, urging them to adapt and amend their behaviour. As the first part of this book showed, despite the gradual validation of consumption and leisure, the social environment in late socialism remained saturated with messages that encouraged modern women to replace home cooking with industrial products and canteen food[1].

The discourses of the official ideology targeted liberating women from household chores. Whatever hidden agendas they might have pursued, there was a positive side to them: they aimed at modernizing everyday life. But how far, and in which way did they find a place in women's actual reasoning? How were they perceived and how did they interfere with the ways in which women saw (and renegotiated daily) their routines in the kitchen?

However fluid ideology might have been in late socialism, and people – accustomed to it to the degree where they did not notice it – most of the interviewed women were well aware of the ideological prescription that home cooking does not become a modern woman. Within a group of twenty women who run households in communist Bulgaria, sixteen confirmed they knew of it. Some stated that it was clearly 'the understanding' back then and that priority was given to public nutrition. Only one said she was never aware of its existence and three showed ambivalence, saying they did not have time to consider 'such things'.

Many answers implied that the women mostly experienced the pressure to reduce home cooking in abstract terms, simply as an awareness that it was out there. Yet a couple of them had personal incidents to tell. Tamara Ganeva recalled how an acquaintance of her father reportedly had said to him: 'My daughter is an intellectual,

---

[1] In this research I use the term 'canteen' for the specific type of restaurants which the communist power created in factories, institutes, administration buildings and educational institutions, and in which employees and students were offered cheap food – subsidized by the state. By 1981 there were 5,690 canteens in Bulgaria, which provided food for 785,000 people, according to the formal statistical data (Hadzhinikolov 1983: 17)

she is not labouring in the kitchen!' Taking this as a personal affront, her father had replied: 'My daughter is also an intellectual, but she spends time in the kitchen to cook excellent meals and her children are healthy!' Both Tamara and her father had clearly found the statement insulting, an indirect criticism of their lifestyle.

Lyubka Georgieva, who was raised in the small town of Dupnitsa in south-west Bulgaria and worked as a nurse in her early professional life in the 1960s–1970s, recalled a face-to-face encounter with social criticism of her strong interest in cooking. She spoke of multiple cases, when her colleagues expressed disapproval of her habit of collecting recipes from patients in the clinic. According to her account it was not a matter of professional code, but more a criticism of her interest in what her colleagues called 'silly things'. 'They thought such things were below their intellectual level', she asserted.

Despite Lyubka Georgieva's recollections, work ethics must have been involved in the discussion – if not in her case, then in many others, as exchanges of prepared food and recipes frequently took place at work. The women's obsession with recipes must have been frowned upon by at least some members of the communist establishment – the management of different institutes and factories. In 1958 even the press criticized the practice. In a publication in 1958 a feature in *Zhenata dnes* described the worries of a certain Darina Georgieva, mildly shaming her for wasting her working hours in this way. The woman was found exemplary in every other way: 'her house is always clean and tidy, her children are neat and at work she is always among the first. But one thing troubled her – cooking'. According to the unsigned article the question worried Georgieva so much that she could not concentrate on her tasks. With her head in her kitchen instead of focused on her work, she was criticized for distracting her colleagues with questions on how to cook this or that (Paneva 1958: 17).

If the idea of women's liberation from the kitchen was formulated in revolutionary terms and disseminated via official propaganda channels in the dawn of the Bulgarian communist era, in the late communist years it seemed to have spread and become accepted by at least some social layers – and not necessarily as related to communism, but to modernity. Some of the interviewed women spoke of this notion as an element of the meta-discourse. Others referred to it as the opinion of 'some', and usually paired it with pretences of intellectuality.

Tsveta Tanovska, today a food and wine aficionado and wine critic, started her household in the 1970s and, building on previous familial archives, developed an exceptionally voluminous, multi-volume collection of recipes. Sitting over a chequered tablecloth in her kitchen, brightly lit by the sun, we patiently went through an entire mountain of familial cooking notes. Her recipe collection included notebooks with recipes, noted by a female relative during a cooking course in the 1930s, and an enormous pile of scrapbooks from three generations, including clippings from before the Second World War, from German magazines, which Tsveta Tanovska had acquired at the price of lengthy queueing in front of the GDR cultural centre in the 1980s, and contemporary additions. Looking at a newspaper clipping from before the late 1930s, on which a Bulgarian actress shared a recipe for French chocolate pudding, Tsveta Tanovska observed: 'For a long time an actress would not do such thing ... Sharing recipes in public? ... Cooking was not among the priorities of the communist housewife.' She said that even if she was never subjected to criticism herself, the 'general attitude' as to her knowledge was critical – to pay much attention to food, to cooking, was regarded as 'philistinism'.

Kristin Razsolkova, a Sofianite whose family had been wealthy before the communist repressions, also recalled that the Bulgarian word for 'housewife' – *domakinya*, had double meaning: it could be used to express appreciation, but also to label someone as a philistine. Elena Salmadzhiyska recalled the derogative use of another word *domosharka*: used to describe women who would rather take care of their homes than submerge themselves in the forms of social life offered by modern society.

Associating 'philistinism' with the old petit-bourgeois lifestyle, ideologists often criticized its manifestations. 'Philistinism was one of the worst enemies of the woman, because it facilitated her enslavement in her household,' warned Rayna Pesheva (1962), a prominent writer on women's issues from the period, from the pages of her book *Bourgeois Remnants in Attitudes Towards Women*. Pointing to the significant improvements in rural housing, she warned that 'the joy from these achievements in some cases evolves into such idolisation of the new home and living conditions, that it replaces all other interests'. This ideological line followed closely the feminist writing in the USSR of radical thinkers from the early 20th century, such as Alexandra Kollontai.

The interviewed women interpreted in different ways the ruling regime's stance on home cooking. Most of them were critical, but some were ambivalent and one was supportive, evaluating it as a progressive measure and an expression of care. All the same, none of the interviewed seemed to have allowed this meta-discourse to affect their own ideas. 'I never wanted to be taken out of the kitchen and I never believed that the modernity of a woman consists of her not cooking,' asserted Cathy Ivanova, who spent the first years of her family life in small-town Bulgaria, before settling with her family in Sofia.

On the contrary, to cook well in the challenging circumstances of communist Bulgaria was endorsed by most as an achievement. They all verbalized differently one and the same thought, which engineer Lilia Dencheva from Sofia summarized as: 'Every woman wanted to be a good housewife'. To cook a meal, a dessert, to create a good atmosphere at home, was seen as a natural thing for a woman to do, believed Dani Tsacheva, who was born in the wealthy town of Elena in Central Bulgaria and later in her life moved to work as a teacher in Sofia. Bozhurka Velkova, who grew up in a working-class family in the capital and took jobs in cafés and in shops, recalled that good housewives were greatly appreciated and their well cooked dishes frequently provoked explicit approval: 'Look at her! An awesome housewife!'

All the interviewed women kept finding home cooking essential, desirable and deserving of admiration. Their narratives spoke of how intrinsic it had remained to their social roles, as they saw them – confirming what has become already a trivialism: that despite their ambition to revolutionize genders, communist societies preserved much of the patriarchal order of the past. However this ideal, incongruent with the tenets of proletarianism and essentially bourgeois, was pursued within the specific communist and ideological framework and possibly had absorbed elements from it. One of them could have been the women's tendency to achieve it at any personal cost. To smoothly incorporate home chores into the routine of working women was one of the most obvious standards of individual success. Many of the women spoke that they were proud to find time for everything. Dobrinka Boeva, who started her household in Sofia in the 1970s and 1980s, was one of the women who spoke with pride of their ability to combine the many obligations efficiently. She said she saw home cooking as a duty, for which she always found time.

But the women also offered a peek at how draining the efforts were that they invested in order to succeed, just like the unmerciful 'people's teacher' Puhovska instructed them from the pages of *The Housewife's Book* in 1956: 'with all their heart and abilities', 'daily and with no interruption', 'fighting fervently' and as a 'wild current' (Cholcheva and Ruseva eds. 1956: 10–17). One of the revealing statements in this regard was made by Elena Salmadzhiyska, who was born in the isolated mountain village of Osikovo, then moved to the town of Bansko and later to the village of Mikrevo: 'Everything that I did, I did it for my own satisfaction, to make my family feel happy, to give ourselves a good life. At times I was falling asleep [from exhaustion] on the tiny sofa, but I didn't complain. I liked it.'

IT IS ALWAYS 'THE OTHERS' WHO DO NOT SHARE ENTHUSIASM FOR HOME COOKING

On the surface of it, most of the interviewed women did not seem to find tensions between their cooking-related practices and the ideological urges to modernize by spending less time in the kitchen. They always assigned these perspectives, unappreciative of home cooking, to the 'others', even if they defined these 'others' in different ways.

To some the division ran between small and big towns, or rural and urban areas. Several of them insisted that the irrelevance of the meta-discourse prevailed in the villages. 'Here, in the countryside they couldn't break the connection of women with their families,' contemplated Dani Tsacheva on the situation in the town of Elena. Nedyalka Malcheva lived most of her life in the small town of Preslav, north-east Bulgaria, combining her domestic duties with a job as a telephone operator and with farming a patch of land behind her condominium, from where a significant part of her family's food came. She claimed that she was never aware of any efforts to discourage women from cooking. 'No, dear, no, no, no. I have lived in an environment, in which we had no free time to think of such things. (...) we were raising cattle, we had crops, strawberries, raspberries, potatoes to take care of. We didn't have time to think that we shouldn't cook.'

Lyubka Georgieva, who was born in the village of Samoranovo, south-west Bulgaria, before moving to the nearby town of Dupnitsa, also thought that such ideas had no power over rural life: 'I know that such ideas existed. But being born and raised in a small village ...' she said that these notions had bypassed her parents and they did not plant them in her.

Also class divides were seen by some as a border line, rendering non-cooking ideology as alien. Perhaps the most widely spread was the perceived opposition between those defined as common people and those who showed pretence of being intellectuals. Such an explanation was offered by Vanya Pinteva, who used to work as a prosecutor, and Maya Mircheva, who lived in Sofia. They both disassociated the discourse from the official communist ideology, of which they were supporters (this was still the case in the period of the interviews). 'Of course, there are always people who consider cooking to be beneath them. I think this is simply because they cannot cook and do not dare to admit it,' said Maya Mircheva. She referred to a friend of her mother, who always ordered her food from a restaurant. '[She would say]: 'I can't be busy with such things!', although what kept her busy if she didn't work …? She was presenting it as if it was beneath her to spend hours in the kitchen for something which would be gulped down in half an hour …'

Vanya Pinteva generalized more than Maya Mircheva, defining this discourse as a 'mania of a certain social layer of people, who consider themselves superior'. Similar was the interpretation of Kalina Kechova, who was born in a small mountain village in the Rodopi and moved to Smolyan, where she took a sequence of menial jobs. She said she didn't see this attitude as grounded in the ideology, it was more a social pose of those women who tended to looked down at other people.

However some of the narrators clearly related these discourses not only to the official ideology, but to the political establishment. Elena Salmadzhiyska thought that this was a policy concerning the 'upper classes', while 'nobody has ever thought of 'liberating' the women in the villages'. The 'red bourgeois', as they were popularly known, were constituted as a class under the totalitarian rule of Todor Zhivkov, whose entourage used to ensure the loyalty of a growing circle of people by giving them a wide range of privileges. Among them were monthly financial support, and priority in anything from study or job opportunities to purchasing an apartment, a villa or a car (Kovachev 2013). The existence of this class and its social advantages was a strong demotivating factor to many, who stayed out of it because it conveyed the notion that communism was more communism to some than to others. Its members were disliked and it was precisely to this class, that Elena Salmadzhiyska assigned the idea of cooking as non-modern. She identified them as people, 'who were higher in the hierarchy' of the regime. Sofia Georgieva made an unprovoked association between the idea to reduce home cooking and the new upper class.

To Dani Tsacheva similarly, the disseminators of such attitudes were 'orthodox female communists … whose life was spent on political gatherings … Those were running around. They didn't have time. They believed that this was the new life'.

This perspective over the association of orthodox communists with the non-cooking doctrine was grounded in various circumstances. One was obviously the involvement of this layer of the society in propagating such discourses during various grass-roots activities (for example party meetings at the workplace). But there was a side to it that has been little researched and which related to the privileges of the political establishment, to which many lower standing communists aspired or partially participated in.

Some autobiographical writing of people, who belonged to this establishment, do indeed expose a lifestyle in which cooking was marginalized. Two interviews from the already mentioned People's Memory Archive[2] suggest many meals were taken in restaurants and servants were employed). One of the women recalled that her husband did not think highly of housewives who did a lot of cooking.[3] Another striking example of how the life of the upper classes was arranged in regard to food gives a short autobiographical story in *I Lived Socialism*. The author, who was a child in a family from the establishment, recalled his astonishment when discovering that not every Bulgarian family had its food delivered daily by car from the restaurant of hotel *Rila* in Sofia (Ivanov 2006: 325–326). His encounter with reality occurred when he decided to ask his friend if in their house too food sometimes arrived late. When he finally grasped that most people have to actually buy and cook their meals, he thought it was 'impractical, to say the least'.

This evidence suggests that the non-cooking doctrine, while propagated under communism, was mostly accessible to the upper classes. From the point of view of the average Bulgarian, it did not look exactly affordable. Ivanka Atipova, who followed her husband to live in a small mining town next to Yambol before she moved to Sofia in 1982, curtly commented: 'I don't know if they tried [to liberate the women from their kitchens], but they failed.'

Thus it was 'them', an ever-changing, but always dismissible category of people, who might have had other ideas about home cooking. The interviewed women found it less easy to dismiss their own social circles: family and peers, who all seemed to validate and reinforce women's connection to cooking. Many narrators sought legitimacy of their lifestyle in the discourses that were dominant in their immediate environment – to which the 'non-cooking' perspective was in all cases foreign. Sofia Georgieva referred to her upbringing just as Lyubka Georgieva did. Tamara Ganeva, who spent her youth in Karnobat and Sliven in East-South Bulgaria and was born in the family of a school director and a prosecutor said: 'I have been raised with the idea that one eats only at home.'

She and Kristin Razsolkova both referred to their parents and grandparents, who were dedicated to the culinary art. Many others spoke of the preferences and routines of their husbands. Searching for explanation of her intensive home cooking, Dobrinka Boeva for instance remarked: '... such were the expectations of my husband. And so I raised my sons.' Dani Tsacheva also quoted as important the habits and expectations of her husband, who according to her was raised in a family where food 'traditions were laws'. She, like many others, revoked also the dominant authority of the mother-in-law: '... His mother was a very good cook, an excellent cook. She was very good at desserts and he was used to eating really good stuff.'

But even more importantly, most women differentiated the discourses in official platforms from those circulating in society. They gave priority to the social ones. The

---

[2] People's Memory Archive contains 90 biographic interviews or autobiographic writings, collected by sociologist Galya Misheva at the Critical Social Studies Institute at the Paisiy Hilyandarsky University in Plovdiv, Bulgaria.
[3] The two interviews of the archive, which is only accessible to researchers, are with reg. n. 2032-II and 3003-II.

passion for recognition, which some of them demonstrated that they had pursued by developing their cooking skills, can only be explained against a social environment in which significant value was attached to home cooking. While offering details on the mechanisms of recipe exchange, Lyubka Georgieva used emotionally charged language: 'Oh, I was so ambitious! ... at the beginning I was very careful to do it in beautiful handwriting. But I wrote, and wrote, and wrote ...'. Not letting the negative attitude of some colleagues stand in the way of her enthusiasm, she said she cooked and experimented in the kitchen 'day and night'.

Contemplating the cooking passion she developed in her youth, she commented on her upbringing: 'Mind that I was raised this way, I was taught that it is not right for a woman not to be able to cook, that a woman must be able to do anything ... I have accepted this, that it must be so. And for this reason, trying to understand myself and this insane drive back then to cook, cook, to try everything ... – it was out of desire to prove myself, to prove that I was a mature woman at the age of twenty. Funny, but such were the times ...'.

A similar striving for recognition, which is expressed in frantic efforts to master the culinary art, was also formulated by Bozhurka Velkova. Speaking with awe of her mother-in-law, whom she defined as a uniquely good housewife, she exclaimed: 'I started learning with great enthusiasm, wanted to become a tiny bit like what she, with all her skills was ... To me everything was new. I wanted so badly to soak everything up and I wrote down every single detail, everything!'

Clearly behind the shared association of the non-cooking ideologies with 'the other' stood various explanations. Considering that both supporters and critics of the communist state were able to accommodate home cooking as part of their self-identification suggests that the processes were more complex than simply aligning yourself with the communist ideas or not. In them sources of the discourse were relocated to accommodate personal political views and the definition of modernity was renegotiated to include the 'old' practice of cooking.

Three aspects of the routine food practices are examined further on in this chapter, to allow for a closer look at how state economy and modernization, gender, social and political divisions, matters of authority and trust, habit and taste shaped the women's individual ideas of home cooking. The first part examines men's role in domestic cooking; the second is an enquiry into how the most available form of ready-made food – meals cooked in state canteens – affected domestic food practices; the third one looks at how communist modernization ideologies influenced the ways in which the interviewed women made sense of home cooking. The popular social understanding of the role of the woman in the family clearly played a role. But did the pressure of the ideology have an impact too?

SHARING THE KITCHEN WITH MEN

The idea of men helping in the kitchen only really appeared in the increasingly polyphonic public discourses in Bulgaria in the 1980s. Moreover, it seems that it stayed there: on the pages of the women's magazines that promoted it.

A survey in *Zhenata dnes* (Spasovska 1974), claiming that on average men spent 8 minutes a day working in the kitchen, while women spent 88, stated that men from the cities and with higher education tended to devote more time to cooking/cleaning the kitchen. However the personal perceptions and memories of the interviewed women did not offer any indication to confirm such a statement. They were equally consistent across the urban–rural, class or generation divisions: kitchens were 'definitely female territory', as Maya Mircheva put it.

The narrators' reminiscences of the participation of men in home cooking were quite uniform. Dani Tsacheva spoke of a very clear distinction between male and female work in her generation. To explain how strange cooking was to their partners, two of the women reacted with the same exclamation: 'they couldn't even fry an egg!'

Mara Tseneva's husband, who was present at the interview, nodded at this statement. He added that he knows how to prepare coffee and tea and he can actually boil eggs. But not fry them. 'I am not interested, nor do I feel any desire [to cook],' he explained. Violeta Kaloferova, an engineer from Sofia, reacted to the question if men ever cooked at home with laughter. Dani Tsacheva suggested that it was a very exceptional role for a man and said that it was perceived as humiliating. According to her those men who did that risked being laughed at and called 'effeminate'.

In fact men had their roles in the kitchen, but these were hardly related to everyday cooking. Particular types of operations or certain types of food were considered their prerogative and were far from shameful – they were even a source of pride taken in trading with advice between men. Men's involvement was often related to seasonal cooking and/ or meat. For instance cutting or curing meat was considered acceptable and even sometimes typically men's work. I encountered a curious illustration of this fact, when in the flea market of Sofia I purchased a copy of *Home Preservation of Meat and Fish* (1959) by Marin Marinov. The title page was signed off by the author to another man (Figure 11).

The reminiscences of the narrators confirmed the legitimacy of men's involvement in activities related to meat and fish. Bozhurka Velkova recalled her husband always cleaning the fish which she was to cook, and said that only men prepared home-made charcuterie: *lukanka*, *sudzhuk* or similar.[4] Ivanka Atipova also remembered men trading recipes for how to prepare various parts of a slaughtered pig. Recalling her years in a miners' town near the Turkish border in south east Bulgaria she said that they often gathered in these periods to process the meat together. Lyubka Georgieva remembered her father preparing lard with herbs, and Vanya Pinteva recalled a relative making *lukanki* and *pusturma*[5].

Their accounts were consistent also with some male perspectives, which I was able to record in 2016 for another research project. One of the prominent chefs of sushi in Sofia, Petur Mihalchev, recalled the fascinating urban hunting practices of his father, who trapped pigeons in sacks in the attics of Sofia buildings and dried fish on their city apartment balcony, leaving the next-door cat staring at them hypnotized for days.

---

[4] *Lukanka* and *sudzhuk* were the two types of dried sausages most popular under communism in Bulgaria. *Lukanka* is usually long, flat and less dry. *Sudzhuk* is shaped as a horseshoe and dried longer. Both were eaten mostly without further preparation.

[5] A type of high quality dry meat.

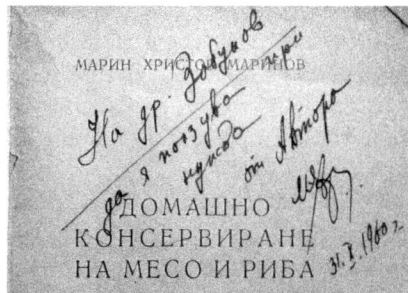

Figure 11 *The cover of* Home Preservation of Meat and Fish *(1959) by Marin Marinov and a dedication, penned by the author to another man, a Dr Zabunov, which reads: 'To use in case of need'.*

Another territory, which was accessible to men, was the preparation of alcoholic drinks. Kristin Razsolkova gave as an example her father's hobby of making egg cognac and *mastika*[6].

This separation of roles in cooking was in fact inherited from pre-modern Bulgarian society. In the 18th and 19th centuries 'the specialists in roasting, preparing *pusturma* and *sudzhuk* were usually men' (Gavrilova 1999: 108). Similar arrangements were observed in many parts of Europe – in Hungary men cooked when out hunting, fishing, or working in the vineyard. They learned from each other and cooked dishes different from those their wives would. They prepared fish on the grill, or baked in clay, or made fish soup boiled in a kettle, while women put fish in soup thickened with cream, stuffed it, or made it into a fish loaf with cabbage (Szilagyi 1997 as quoted by Knezy 2003: 140).

In communist Bulgaria, where in the 20th century many rural and pre-modern practices were transferred from villages to towns and cities, it was quite usual for city dwellers to prepare cured meat: mainly sausages, which they hung to dry on the terraces of the apartment blocks. But it was not a practice in every family like canning vegetables and fruits was. In any case if a man cooked, it was exceptional, usually unrelated to everyday routines or was paired with the absence of a woman in the household: temporary or at all.

---

[6] *Mastika* is a drink with an anise flavour, similar to the French *pastis*, the Turkish *yeni raki* and the Greek *ouzo*.

Among the core group of twenty interviewed women only one said that her partner cooked with a certain regularity. The husband of Dobrinka Boeva, who was a professor in Turkic languages with an interest in ethnography, was described by her as an enthusiastic and daring, experimental cook, who collected recipes during his travels and then tried them out at home. Boeva though also emphasized that it was only her husband among the men she knew who would cook. In contrast, Sofia Georgieva's husband was a professional cook. But both she and her daughter Veselina, who was present at the interview said that he never took part in home cooking.

The marginal role of men in domestic kitchens was reconfirmed by the description which the narrators gave of men's involvement in recipe exchange. Some of them did not remember any male participation. Others recalled single cases, which they had memorized as curiosities. Tamara Ganeva, for instance, told a story of a neighbour who held her mother in high esteem, and once came to their house to give her an inherited recipe for a rare dessert. He expressed trust that he was leaving the recipe in good hands.

Maya Mircheva recalled a letter, which she had received from a dear male friend, living abroad, and which consisted of a recipe. In her scrapbooks Tsveta Tanovska had an entry, indicated as given by someone called Nikolov. She was unable to evoke the identity of that person, but she said she remembered the page well because it was so strange – the only one with a male name as a credit. Elisaveta Shkodrova said she had two male colleagues who cooked, from one of whom she had taken a recipe for meatballs.

Apart from these rare cases, men were involved sometimes in the exchange of recipes as mediators. Many of the narrators remembered situations when they brought food, which they had prepared at home, to their workplaces and when men, after trying it, asked to take the recipe to their wives.

Tamara Ganeva added a unique detail. When someone was about to give a recipe to her mother, it was often her father who wrote it down: he was accustomed to assume the role of technical facilitator in the culinary exchange. 'I have no idea why, perhaps because, when we were visiting someone, the hostess would give the explanation, my mother would enquire about details, and my father would write it down,' said Tamara. He was also known for – and possibly proud of – his beautiful handwriting.

The interviewed women rarely spoke of men's marginal role in the kitchen with irritation. Possibly because of the time distance and the changed circumstances in some cases, a few of them expressed some emotion about having to do the work on their own. In one of the few such cases, after briefly describing her husband's help, one of them exclaimed: 'You know which is the most resilient pack animal, right? The Bulgarian woman! That's it!'

But rather than with frustration, some women spoke of men's participation with a slight disregard. If irritation was expressed, it was rather with the men's involvement than with their absence. One of the women described her father as always present in the kitchen, but not as a doer or a helper, but as a consumer and a critic. 'He was an active participant. I mean – he always had an opinion. And when my mum died, so I had to cook, he was like . . . "Your mother made it differently!" However, she also recalled some attempts on the side of her mother, when still alive, to claim at least some help: every Sunday she woke her father up and handed him a primitive plastic device to beat egg whites stiff. What justified her demands was that the egg whites were needed for his favourite pudding.

The role of men as critics and consumers in the home kitchens came up also in other interviews. What remained doubtful though, was how the women would have looked upon men's potential increased involvement. The language, used by one of them to describe such cases, showed sarcastic distrust: 'I've heard of men, who cooked at home – i.e. most of all liked to stand in the way of their wives in the kitchen [laughter], to offer advice and to criticize'. Her words suggest that, having assumed the role of the cook at home, she did not trust men's skills or sense as cooks. Also other recollections implied that men's activities in the kitchen would have been taken as a nuisance, rather than help.

Was it communism, Balkan customs or the 1970s, but men seem not to have been that welcome in the kitchens: in Bulgaria, and across the region. 'If your husband finds happiness in cooking, do not take this happiness away from him', somewhat desperately pleaded a popular male chef from the Slovenian television screen in 1968 (Tominc 2015: 32) – 'Let him help you, right? When he gets used to it, he might start doing it himself.'

Some recent studies suggest that women's hostility towards men's participation in cooking might be more omnipresent than one might intuitively think. Recent research in Belgium highlighted that this is a general phenomenon, spread at least across Europe, but very likely beyond it as well. Examining the situation in families with different ethnic and social backgrounds, Sinem Yilmaz found that even women, who did not experience pressure to perform alone in the household, and who are in a position to assign various tasks to their partners, take over the cooking. One of the women, interviewed for the research, was quoted as saying: 'I do not want my partner to come to the kitchen to do something. There are things that I just want to do myself. On the one hand, I think that if I take care of it, it will be done properly – I am a better cook (laughing). And I want to make sure my children eat certain kinds of vegetables or whatever. On the other hand, taking it all on myself is very tiring. You need to search for a balance.' (Yilmaz, Putte and Stevens 2017: 10–12). A newspaper article which presented this research also quoted a survey of the European Commission, according to which more than 30 per cent of Belgians consider men less competent in household matters (Vanhecke and Eckert 2016).

In any case it seems that there were few occasions when the interviewed Bulgarian women were irritated by the incompetence of their men. Their husbands mostly kept themselves out of the kitchen. Bulgarian philosopher Raycho Pozharliev argued that in the communist era the lack of interest in food preparation among men was predetermined by the non-individualistic and non-prestigious character of cooking, the lack of ingredients and culinary traditions, which made it more difficult to see home cooking as entertainment and hence it held no attraction for men (Shkodrova 2014: 291). In fact the single case in the collected private stories endorses such an interpretation of the men's behaviour. Dobrinka Boeva's husband did not simply cook at home, he was actively seeking and adding intellectual value to it in line with his ethnographic interests.

In any case the narratives demonstrate that if the communist modernization saw any changes in the ways women defined their gender roles in the kitchen, they did not involve shifts in men's gender roles in the same area. The division of territory remained at the pre-communist borders. Family and broader social circles played an important role in the preservation of the traditional model, in which women have internalized home cooking as a crucial element of their gender roles and have given it a central place in their lives. Parental, familial and social expectations and values had shaped women's own views, turning them into both object and subject of the discourse. They were as much complying with it as they were reproducing it, reinforcing it, legitimizing it from one generation to another.

Clearly, if women were able to appropriate certain freedoms, these were not achieved via equality in the household. But if pushing men to share the burden of household chores was not part of the early communist plans, what was the impact of the alternatives to home cooking – those measures, which the communist state actually had in mind, when speaking of the women's liberation from their work in the kitchen?

STATE CANTEENS: TO USE OR NOT TO USE

As previously discussed, the state planned to take the production of food out of the household, and its strategy included various elements. But only one of them was in place early on and accessible to many: the canteens.

Indeed, all the interviewed women said that they had access to canteens and canteen food under communism. At the same time only one of them confirmed that she had used such food at home regularly. Three others described difficult periods of their lives, mostly when establishing their own households, when they found themselves forced to use it. Their view was that this was a last resort solution: one of them said that she fell back on it, when she had no kitchen and had to use her stove to keep her books in.

Many reasons why women avoided using canteen food came up in the narratives and very few of them were related to practical difficulties. What turned out to be the principal objection concerned the taste of the canteen food, which many narratives related to the preparation practices, to the methods involved in cooking for many people at the same time. One of the women said that in such circumstances it just 'couldn't be as tasty as at home', another observed that the food was reheated and hence not tasty and many others made similar remarks. In all the narratives canteen food was deemed inferior to domestically prepared meals. But there were also cases when it was defined as plainly inedible.

Violeta Kaloferova, who worked in the state administration and had access to a ministry canteen, said that she preferred the simplest sandwich to what was served there. She criticized the menu and the cooking skills of the personnel: 'They were preparing some puddings, which I generally dislike. But I do like rice in milk – I cook it myself. I tried to eat it there ... why, it was inedible!' Between all the narrators only three recalled experiences in canteens in positive terms, but even they did not make use of canteen food to feed their families.

The partially physical reaction to the canteen food, the dislike of its taste, was in almost all cases paired with lack of trust in the canteens' cooking practices. These doubts seemed to be cast over the entire public nutrition system, but were particularly pronounced about canteen food. The women though it was meant to be cheap and nutritious. If it happened to be bad, it would be difficult to object, like one would do in a restaurant: the work environment obliged them to keep their discontent to themselves.

The women's mistrust was based as much on publicly and socially disseminated discourses as on personal experience. Some made observations about the hygiene in the kitchens, others spoke of dubious ingredients. Lilia Dencheva recalled reading a story in the press about an incident with bad canned food, used in the preparation of a canteen meal. She remembered how striking she found the arguments put forward in favour of canteen food. 'The reasoning was that if you use a can accidentally containing a poisonous mushroom at home, you could die. But if the mushroom's poison is spread between so many meals, the worst that could happen is that you feel a bit bad', she recalled.

The mistrust, with which ready-made food was widely eyed, was often reconfirmed by private experiences. When Tamara Ganeva's mother heard of the opening of a new shop in their home town with prepared food under the slogan 'To liberate women', she exclaimed sarcastically: 'Right, I will surely feed my children with potato patties, fried in burned oil!' Tamara Ganeva remembers the scene, because afterwards she, a youngster at the time, nevertheless decided to buy a potato patty. She did so once, only to discover that her mother was right: 'It was indeed fried in burned oil and stank'.

Historian Nenov (2006) argued that 'the artificiality of the city in the modern era, which has penetrated even physiology' was putting off those who were unused to urban life, and was encouraging them to keep the village as a source of their food supplies. The narratives, though, revealed that however abstract fears might have interfered in the narrators' reasoning, they mingled with first-hand experiences, which quite consistently led women away from what the state offered them to ease their lives in the kitchen. Sometimes such experiences were personal, at other times they were shared within their social circles. Dani Tsacheva remembered how a relative of hers was working in the kitchen of an orphanage. 'She so often felt like crying because they [her family] were honest people, they couldn't accept such a thing ... The chef ... was stealing from the children! He pocketed butter, cuts of meat ...!'

Information about poor practices in the food industry spread also due to the mass participation of the population in brigades. In the autumn students of universities, higher grades of school and various groups of professionals were obliged to help with harvesting and processing the yearly yield of fruit and vegetables, and many of them took shifts in food processing factories (Shkodrova 2014: 67–90). Dani Tsacheva recalled how her brother came back from a student brigade, saying: 'Never again will I eat from an industrial can, never again!'

Stories of canning unwashed, spoiled fruits, cockroaches, cigarette butts, of reckless students putting their muddy boots on the belt with fruits just before they were canned, flooded communist folklore. Studying the mistrust in industrial food from a post-communist perspective, anthropologist Jung observed that despite the affordability and the declared 'standards and control', Bulgarians found the prospect of purchasing jars that had been factory-produced under communism unimaginable – not only out of safety concerns, but because of the suspected poor quality (Jung 2009: 32).

The idea that most of the available food prepared outside the house was 'rubbish', transpired in many of the interviews. In this spirit was the reaction of Elisaveta Shkodrova: 'Why would I take food from there [from a canteen], how do I know how it was prepared and with what – if they didn't use some leftovers from the day before ...?'

The ideology on which canteens were based was part of the trust problem to some of the interviewed women. Lilia Dencheva, for instance, was critical of the communist canteen policy, describing it as a petty economic guile. She thought that 'the goal was simply to use all the products – all of them', to avoid waste, rather than 'them [i.e. the state] being concerned with what keeps you busy at home'. Dani Tsacheva, who voiced in her narrative an open disapproval of the former regime, formulated her criticism in political terms: 'They have established these canteens to help women, right ... The message was: a woman doesn't need to cook. She needs to reach her production targets, she must ... be *udarnik*[7]. ... (...) But they were feeding people with junk!'

On the other side of the spectrum of political attitudes to the communist state, Vanya Pinteva interpreted positively the ideological background of the canteen meal: she pointed to the system's efforts to create comfort and convenience for women. But when it came to her use of canteen food, these reminiscences became somewhat contradictory. She said that there were very good quality canteens, 'just like restaurants', with 'excellent quality control'. But elsewhere in the conversation, among the reasons not to use food from canteens as takeaway she stated that home-made food is 'tastier and cleaner' (together with the fact that she liked cooking, and 'because I have a family too, and they also need to eat'). Once more the idea of feeding your own family with canteen food seemed not just dismissed, but inconceivable. Families were a principal reason for the women's dismissive attitudes towards canteen food. In their narratives though it was not simply an alignment to a patriarchal order.

Some for example said that bringing home canteen food would be shameful. One of them was Mara Tseneva, whose work was related to the public nutrition system. She explained that on the one hand she felt embarrassed to tell the cooks to pack food 'in a jar' for her. On the other hand she also found it embarrassing to feed her extended family with such food. 'I lived with a father-in-law, a mother-in-law, I had two children. To bring a jar for them to eat? I was cooking, I was cooking'.

Her reflections speak of feelings, stemming from a very traditional family set-up and are radically different from the mode of thinking, advertised by *Zhenata dnes* – one of the changes promoted by the quoted article on canteens was precisely to shift the meals of elderly members of the family to canteens to lessen the burden on their daughters (-in-law) (Koleva 1958). But in reality starting a family in all cases reduced or ended women's use of canteen (or other ready-made) food. Elena Salmadzhiyska recalled having bought prepared food as a student in the town of Bansko and to have ceased the practice when she married – for financial reasons. Vanya Pinteva also said

---

[7] *Udarnik* was the regime's way to label super-performers in production, the movement was known as Stakhanovite in the USSR.

she lived through her student years 'on Russian salad and meatballs' from the culinary shop. Later on, as a prosecutor in Sofia, she enjoyed her social life and gladly visited restaurants and superior canteens, but prepared food for her family at home. She said that she lived next to one of the few culinary shops in Sofia, but hardly used it.

This change can be associated with expectations about the women's role in the household in Bulgarian society, which remained patriarchal. It could be asserted to some extent, that the patriarchal set-up not only prevented the rearrangement of gender roles in the kitchen, but blocked women's options for easing their tasks by making use of the little help that the communist state was able to provide.

However there is more to that than just the understanding of authority or the weight of older generations' or men's opinions. Giving up the easy pre-cooked or ready-made formulas had also to do with the transformations of the economy and the social importance of the meal, which a marriage and, especially, the birth of a child in the family cause. The required volume grows, specific diets and tastes of children add to those of adults, the dinner as a social event gains complexity, where different horizontal and vertical relations are practised. As many anthropologists have argued, consumption rituals express social relationships of inclusion and exclusion (Douglas and Isherwood 1979, Miller 1987, Tomlinson 1990, Valentine 1999). The family meals, in other words, turn into times for practising family life. In their early exploration of the links between women, food and families, Charles and Kerr (1988: 17) established that the understanding of a 'proper meal', apart from being related to the idea of healthy food, is of 'a meal eaten together as a family'. It is on these grounds that they were seen as constitutive to women's identity. The social importance of the familial meal was that it created an arena, in which women were able to assert their personality and authority, their position in the family and in the society, and their emotional rights with regard to their relatives, in particular their children. It was clearly used as an instrument of self-identification. One illustration was the statement of Lyubka Georgieva that she liked canteen food but never used it at home, because 'I wanted to prove myself so badly! And I was taught that a married woman should cook'.

An interesting example, contradicting the simplistic interpretation of women's ideas as imposed by the authority of other members of their family, was given by Tamara Ganeva. She recalled how her father, wishing to relieve his wife of some household work, suggested using canteen food at home. Her mother refused, and her arguments, as accounted for by Tamara Ganeva, had to do not so much with her love of cooking, but with the importance she found in the entire procedure of eating. 'She was saying that food is more than what we see in our plates (...) She taught us a whole philosophy, culture of eating', emphasizing the social and aesthetic importance of the familial meals.

Another trace of how home-made food was used to build and sustain identities is contained in the complaints about the 'anonymity' of the canteen food. In this sense it was seen as an opposite of home food – a binary opposition, which resurfaced often as a motivation to collect recipes and not to use the officially printed cookbooks, which were claimed to be too 'restaurant-like', too 'official', 'functional' (i.e. aiming to only satisfy hunger), and 'lacking character'. Home cooking, in contrast, was defined by many narrators as the standard of the times, the targeted level, the epitome of the very understanding of good food. This idea has been reinforced by the interaction between generations in the family. Admitting that sometimes her children liked ready-made food, Lyubka Georgieva said: 'But I always tell them that it is not cooked as you would cook it at home.'

As Tsveta Tanovska pointed out, 'the very understanding of cuisine, of cooking' was not restaurant-made, but home-prepared food. To many of the narrators home cooking was self-evident. There was no articulated idea of an alternative, even if they had the canteens at their disposal. The ideas of many of them demonstrated how ingrained was the discourse that family food is cooked at home, how unwavering it remained, and how decisive was its structural influence in the sense which Bateson attributes to it: a behaviour so standardized, that it seems to be the only logical one.

Considering the impact of shortages on the traditional model, one could reasonably argue that deficits – which in practice resulted in daily waiting in long queues, not finding necessary products, not having significant access to partially processed food – would push families away from home cooking. If it is too difficult to find the ingredients for your meal, if you need to do gardening yourself to obtain supplies, if you need to cook everything from scratch, if you do not have access to modern appliances and need to perform all the cooking processes in a traditional, labour-consuming way, one would expect that it would be easier to give in to the ideological appeals and make use of the food available at low prices in the canteens.

Ready-made food, when available, was an opportunity to save time and effort. But a complex set of considerations acted against its use, for only part of which the patriarchal thinking was responsible.

The narratives certainly illustrate that home cooking, just as every other sphere of private life, was a subject of contests between the polyphonic meta-discourse, based on communist ideology, and 'grass-roots' views. These competing, contradictory ideas coexisted, while to a great extent ignoring each other: neither did the meta-discourse that implied the existence of 'subjects' and the need to control them, much affect the views of these same 'subjects', nor was it significantly affected by them. Mostly, the existing conflict was hardly recognized. It was not perceived as part of daily life reasoning. Yet there were areas, where it was more visible and conceptualized: the zones, which some 'subjects' deemed forbidden or inaccessible.

SPACES OF TENSION, SPACES OF FREEDOM: THE WESTERN, THE BOURGEOIS AND THE INDIVIDUALISTIC

Concealed by the Iron Curtain, the 'West' held a special attraction for peoples under communism. The little that penetrated through the cracks in the fence mesmerized the imagination of many and was further imagined into a phantasmal world of plenty, luxury, of mind-boggling colours and smells, of a lifestyle as unachievable as heaven. The anti-Western propaganda significantly contributed to the idealization of the image and to the intensity of the desire for it.

Yurchak spoke of the 'West' as an 'archetypal manifestation' of an imaginary 'elsewhere', that is not necessarily about any real place' (Yurchak 2006: 159). However, there is enough historical material to suggest that the abstraction of the idea of the West might have been variable in time and between the different communist peoples, some of whom lived in greater physical proximity to the West. The immediate, non-abstract experience of many Eastern Europeans with the Western world or its material manifestations clearly stands out from some recent historical research (Grigorova 2013, Bren and Neuburger 2012, Reid and Crowley 2010, Guentcheva 2009 among others). Especially under late communism, the Bulgarian seaside resorts attracted significant numbers of Western tourists, whom the state deemed useful to cover convertible currency gaps in the budget. Even if different measures were undertaken to reduce Westerners' contacts with locals, their presence left traces. Also more Bulgarians travelled abroad, in particular from the 1960s on, when the state tried to intensify its commercial contacts with the West. The higher party echelons established nearly 400 state companies abroad (Hristov H. 2015) and employed people to work in international transport, construction projects, in healthcare and others areas.

These processes somewhat opened the door for Western material culture. While it remained accessible only to a few, it gained visibility and emphasized stark differences between the two worlds. These contrasts were often embodied in novel, or insufficient food products. 'Even small commodities from the West are believed to have almost magical significance: bubbles of chewing gum and instant soup cause excitement and euphoria. They represent' something incredible and unbelievable . . .', wrote Baločkaite (2011: 420) about Lithuania. Similar perceptions were observed in Bulgaria, as multiple reminiscences from the communist era suggest (one example being the biographical stories, collected by Gospodinov (2006). The private narratives, and to some extent the scrapbooks, gave interesting insights into how the general idealization of the West affected the field of gastronomy in communist Bulgaria and how, in a way, food proved to be a conservative field in this respect.

One of the peeks into the other world which the peoples across the Eastern European communist states were granted, were the restrictive hard-currency shops, which were opened in the big cities of the Communist bloc in the 1960s. If until then the Western world might have been not 'any real place in particular', these shops translated the abstract ideas into smells, looks and tastes, into concrete objects of desire. In the midst of persistent deficits, the newly established shops were selling Western goods, otherwise unavailable on the local markets. The mode of sales, though, was forbidding to the general population: the goods were to be purchased with dollars or other kinds of convertible currency (which Eastern European money was not) and thus were only available to foreigners, members of the political establishment, a few privileged in their professional groups that enjoyed freedom of movement, such as workers in international transport and construction companies (Shkodrova 2014: 130). The aim of these shops was to help the governments with covering their constant deficits of hard currency. But the result was that they became both a blatant crack in the propagated image of the communist bounty, and a blow to the claims for egalitarian society.

The Bulgarian shops of this kind, the CORECOMs (an abbreviation of Comptoir de représentation et de commerce) offered a range of deficit goods, such as coffee, cocoa, chocolates, chewing gum, blue jeans and electronics. Sources suggest that the food products from these shops were an object of desire and a symbol of the inaccessible Western lifestyle (as illustrated by many of the private stories, written in 'I Lived Socialism', Gospodinov 2006). One of the narrators recalled her distress when her very young daughter fell for a pair of brightly coloured flip-flops in one of these shops and she had to put up a fight with her partner and with the saleswoman to obtain them. 'CORECOMs drove me crazy! They just pushed my buttons so well!' she exclaimed.

The communist state boosted the imagined value of the Western goods with many of its practices, and CORECOM was only one of them. The policy to release rare imported goods around celebrations had a similar effect (Guentcheva 2009: 9) – the logic behind this was to boost the holidays, but it also boosted the perception of rare Western goods as festive and precious.

Along with food products, recipes too, coming from the other side of the Iron Curtain, held a strong attraction for some, of the 'mundane, yet exotic', in the words of Yurchak (2006: 159). Their affiliation to the other world, the world of dreams and possibilities in many Bulgarians' imagination, made their appeal extraordinary. Several of the women recalled their thrill at their encounter with 'true' Western recipes, since those in the communist cookbooks, purged in the 1950s but returning in the 1960s, did not seem to count. Tamara Ganeva for instance recalled her excitement when in 1972 she held in her hands for the first time a French magazine. 'It was a great event!', she exclaimed.

In similar terms Tsveta Tanovska spoke of her travels to the German cultural centre in Sofia, where she was looking for German culinary magazines, her 'small door', as she called them, to the tempting world beyond the Iron Curtain. She either copied recipes, or sometimes was able to acquire the magazines themselves, which she saw as a significant personal achievement. The access to the several similar foreign cultural centres was difficult and very contested. Another narrator, Sofia Georgieva commented bitterly how in a struggle to access the Czech centre she lost a jewel dear to her, that she had bought in the German centre.

A frequent source for foreign recipes were magazines, brought by people who travelled abroad or incoming tourists. The interviewed women, who collected such recipes, were not particularly picky. They said they took any recipe that came their way, from any source, sometimes making efforts to put their hands on a piece of information, of the content of which they had no idea. 'We tried to learn recipes from whoever would come from abroad', explained Dani Tsacheva, asserting that her interest was widely shared among her social circles. She obtained some cookery advice from people working in international shipping, and generally used all possible channels for such acquisitions.

Sofia Georgieva also mentioned her interest in foreign, privately imported recipes. She gave an example with a pizza recipe, which her professional musician friends brought back from Italy and which immediately became a success in her household – long before the communist version of pizza appeared in the capital in the 1980s.

But if Sofia Georgieva made use of that pizza recipe, it was not always the case with foreign recipes that the interviewed women had collected. Sometimes the advice came in unfamiliar languages and translation had to be arranged. It transpires from the narratives that other obstacles also counterbalanced the personal enthusiasm of the cultural encounter: lack of knowledge of the ingredients or cooking techniques employed, and absence of products and equipment.

Due to their general inaccessibility, many of these recipes could not gain much importance to the communist households, as Dani Tsacheva, Tamara Ganeva or Tsveta Tanovska acknowledged. Despite the significant efforts to obtain such recipes, visible on the pages of her cookbooks, Tanovska said that they were practically 'completely alien objects'.

Discussing the attitudes of Lithuanians to the material wonders of the Western world, Baločkaite argued that they had a magical aura, but were considered in general unnecessary. 'The West is perceived as a fantasyland, but not as a serious alternative to daily existence. The magic of chewing gum is hard to resist, but the political message is not treated seriously'. It is difficult to draw identical conclusions about Bulgaria on the basis of this research. People did collect and use at least some of the Western recipes, as the narrators' accounts suggested. But more importantly, whenever they did not, precisely the uselessness of such recipes, their complete practical superfluousness, made their collection a political, rather than a pragmatic gesture, an act of deliberate and enthusiastic cultural transgression.

On the other hand not all the interviewed women showed themselves sensitive to the appeal of the Western recipes in the past. Some of them would refer to their settled, locally-grounded tastes in food to explain their lack of interest. Lyubka Georgieva for example identified herself as a traditionalist and stated that she never had an interest in any foreign cuisine, even today and contrary to the daring food choices of her children. Two other women expressed similar thoughts. One stated that she has always stayed within the range of dishes cooked traditionally in her family, and in general had never considered recipes in terms of national origin. In another moment of the conversation she mentioned that she never paid attention to foreign recipes in the past. Even her scrapbook though contains multiple recipes, crediting the German magazine *Burda*, and the recipes in her collection include a broad range of recipes, coming with their French or central-European (Austrian, German) names – probably coming from the cosmopolitan Bulgarian cookbooks from before the Second World War.

BOURGEOIS ANACHRONISMS

The pre-war culinary literature was another object of the communist stigma. It was anathematized by the early ideology as decadent throughout the entire urban culture of the pre-war period. While here the ideological wall seemed to be more fluid and porous, the wealthier lifestyle, reflected and perpetuated by some cookbooks, was clearly disapproved of by the new meta-discourse. Names were purged, references to cuisines were reduced, the variation of products was changed and adapted to a poorer and less joyful market. Most of all, cooking and eating were no longer legitimate sources of entertainment: they were seen as instruments in the mission of feeding a hard-working nation and were a responsibility, a duty, which should not be taken lightly (Shkodrova 2019).

Many of the interviewed women explicitly expressed preference for cookbooks from the period before 1944 to the publications from the communist years. Such sentiments were not exceptional in communist Eastern Europe. In Czechoslovakia, for example, 'well-thumbed and torn copies' of pre-war cookbooks were 'handed down from mother to daughter as precious gifts during the period of communist totalitarianism, when it was difficult to get hold of culinary literature of any quality' (Petranova 2003: 176).

The interviewed women, who said they had preferred pre-communist cookery literature, gave a variety of arguments. Some of them concerned the quality of the instructions in the later cookbooks. Others stemmed from what the women saw as a different meta-discourse, clearly indicating the ideological, political connotations of their attitudes. The latter were not related to the practice of cooking, but to the way in which it was conceptualized.

The practical advantage which the older cookbooks held for some of the narrators, stemmed from their greater trust in the authors and the publishing system. Dani Tsacheva for example thought that the older books possessed more precision and that those who wrote them had indeed tried the recipes – something, which she apparently did not believe was the case with the books published in the communist years. Similar to the attitudes to foreign recipes, there were narrators who found the older recipes unusable, but at the same time valuable. Speaking of a Bulgarian cookbook from 1895, Kristin Razsolkova stated that not all the recipes were understandable, as they contained words she did not know or could not translate. But she nevertheless valued the book, because 'the attitude is interesting. From the pages just radiates the European cookery (...) many things, which somehow are not in our foodways, in our everyday life.' She thought the spirit of the pre-war books 'held more charm, greater value' to her family. Having experienced only the ruins of the aristocratic life which her family had had before 1944, Razsolkova nostalgically saw in the old cookbooks a different, more cosmopolitan and elegant Bulgaria than the one she was forced to live in.

Others among the interviewed women had a different way of framing the same contrasts: Cathy Ivanova distinguished between the 'professional cooking' character of the communist books and the 'homely' spirit of the pre-communist culinary literature. Tsveta Tanovska said that what mattered to her was that the pre-war books discussed food not only as nutrition, but also acknowledged the beauty and pleasure of it. The ideological grounds of these preferences transpired also from the words of Dani Tsacheva, who curtly commented: 'As a local wise-cracker once said: back then [in pre-communist times] even the mud was better'.

Yet there were also women, who dismissed the pre-war cookbooks even if in theory they were curious about them. Elisaveta Shkodrova said that whenever she encountered old recipes, she found them rather odd. She referred to some ingredients that were mysterious to her. 'It took me a while to find out what *sharlan* was...' *Sharlan*, a word for cold-pressed, unrefined sunflower oil – the sunflower version of cold pressed extra-virgin olive oil, was absent from the language of communist Bulgaria, as was the product itself. This made Elisaveta Shkodrova think of the recipe as old-fashioned. 'They were advising how to reduce the smell of it ... Why, I wouldn't even use it, since we have double refined oil ...'

In fact the inaccessibility of cooking literature in general – pre-communist or communist – was predefining the ideological quality of the most comparative judgements. With most women having one or two communist cookbooks at hand and very few of them having any access to older ones, variations, contrasts and changes were not necessarily evident to the generations of late communism. Still the special interest which some of the women expressed towards these pre-communist books shows that at least some circles were able to identify the spirit of the ideology in the communist literature and valued the opportunities to avoid it.

When it comes to political aspects of everyday food practices, communist societies were able to invest subversive meanings in most unexpected ways. One of them was by building hierarchies, only understandable within the local cultural frameworks. Anya von Bremzen spoke of people in the Soviet Union expressing their 'culinary nihilism and their disdain for Brezhnev-era corruption and consumer goods worship by eschewing meat, fish, or fowl together in their Olivier [salad]. At the other end of the spectrum, fancy boiled tongue signified access to Party shops; while Doctor's *Kolbassa*,[8] so idolised during the seventies, denoted a solidly blue-collar worldview.' (Von Bremzen 2013: 242).

Such stratification and attaching of political meanings to food products was also observed in Bulgaria. People were divided between those who drank rakia (low working class) and vodka and cognac (middle, upper-middle). Certain jams – of green figs, green walnuts, white cherries – were considered more decadent and somehow non-compliant with the 'culture of poverty', than others. It is difficult to judge to what extent these symbolic hierarchies were generally accepted.

Tamara Ganeva gave voice to some popular ideas of foods with certain political connotations: 'There was something terribly wrong with the mentality of this political establishment! Non-refined oil, confectionery chocolate, cream of tartar, carob – piles of things, which were widely used [before the Second World War]– disappeared. One was supposed to preserve what they knew from their villages – because this is where they all came from! All the rest was [pronounced to be] old-fashioned and bourgeois...'

Many products indeed vanished from the market as a result of state decisions – into this group fall Brussels sprouts, artichokes, endives, and asparagus, which were known and used in Bulgaria in the 19th century (Gavrilova 1999: 94, 180). But it was also possible that dismissing these vegetables as unnecessary luxury, as one of the follies of the former aristocracy, was just an excuse and that there were practical reasons behind this act. In any case once again, it seems, that the communist establishment was falling into its own trap, as what was labelled as unorthodox became only more desired, or associated with old-style wellbeing, ultimately of better quality.

Much of this underlying politics of food remained ambiguous. Ideology in the realm of everyday life often went only half articulated and mostly inconsistent. It easily allowed for contradictory interpretations. The interviewed women testified that they both saw and did not see the ideology, encoded in cookbooks. While speaking of the pre-war cookbooks as embodying a more refined food culture, they seemed to be mostly nonperceptive to the ideology in the new ones. Tsveta Tanovska thought that this sort of blindness could be explained with a joke: 'Why, your husband has such bad

---

[8] A popular type of sausage.

breath! How can you bear this!?'–'I have never known a man with better breath, so I didn't know it was unbearable.'

This is a situation of the sort that British sociologist Anthony Giddens must have had in mind when arguing that while actors' interpretations of their own lives should always be taken into account, meanings should be sought beyond these interpretations. As a significant part of social life is so routine, it is taken for granted, the actors sometimes being unable to even acknowledge it (Giddens 1984: XXX–XXXI).

A very similar idea stood behind American anthropologist Bateson's suggestion that 'a structural aspect of unity' should be one of the key perspectives, from which each social phenomenon should be considered (Bateson 1987: 75). He defined this structural aspect as 'cognitively consistent' behaviours between individuals of a certain social group in a specific context. He spoke of patterns of thought so standardized among individuals, 'that their behaviour appears to them logical'. Such structural patterns of thinking form an important part of the context (Smith and Watson 2010) and are involved in the sense-making process (Charmaz 2009; De Jaegher 2016): even without being identified, recognized, articulated, they co-produce the meanings, which people find in their everyday life.

A SEA OF PRIVACY IN THE DESERT OF THE COLLECTIVE

At the source of the Bulgarian communist practices, the Soviet Union, kitchens were eyed with suspicion as dangerous places. They allowed for privacy and individuality which were concepts disliked by the regime because they contradicted the idea of collective life and diminished the regime's ability to rely on mutual surveillance, allowing the opposition to flourish. 'The most important part of kitchen politics in early Soviet time was that they would like to have houses without kitchens,' remarked Russian journalist Alexander Genis, 'Because the kitchen is something bourgeois. Every family, as long as they have a kitchen, they have some part of their private life and private property," (The Kitchen Sisters 2014). The possible desire to have a separate home was denounced as individualistic and bourgeois, private kitchens were seen as misleading women into cooking at home (Reid 2002: 244).

The Soviet communists' response to the threat of the private kitchens were *communalki* – the shared apartments, where many families lived each in a room and shared the kitchen of the once spacious apartments of the former aristocracy. The Bulgarian communist regime was prone to similar solutions in its harshest 'Stalinist' period until 1956. The urban properties of the wealthier class were expropriated to accommodate people who were loyal to the party: whether urban, or coming from the rural areas. This practice died out at a later stage, when the construction of new neighbourhoods with concrete condominiums provided many city dwellers with mostly small, but all in all functional flats (Kiradzhiev 2010: 130).

In the newly acquired or regained private kitchens many found the freedom to manifest their individuality, be themselves – in their cooking or in their political views.

People gained or regained the kitchen as a space in the modest average communist homes of the 1960s, and at the same time, in a sense, home cooking was reclaimed from the austerities of the war and post-war periods. The kitchen spaces, humble as they were in concept and in execution, became the centre of the late socialism's mini-renaissance of individualism. As Oldenziel and Zachmann (2009: 8) noted, 'in the earlier century, the parlour had been domestic reformers' iconographic centre, but in the twentieth century, the kitchen became the stage where social actors performed a domesticity (...)'.

One of the reasons for the kitchen keeping such a prominent place in the people's lives was its multi-functionality: in the Soviet society, argued one of the most prominent Russian researchers of Soviet *communalki*, Ilia Utehin, it was a unique space, where you could smoke or read a newspaper, something that it is completely unacceptable to do in the toilet or in the bathroom (Utehin 2001, as quoted by Nikolova 2015: 194). The interpretation of kitchens' multi-functionality as a result of the Soviet urban practice to settle several families in one flat seems dominant in the Soviet cultural studies. A closer look at the history of everyday life in Bulgaria though raises questions as to whether the same reasoning applies: did the same status of the kitchen in Bulgaria reflect the period of communal living in the 1940s and 1950s, or was it rather a reflection of the usage of living space in the Bulgarian pre-modern society? Until well into the 19th century families resided mostly in one single space, where they worked, cooked, ate, met guests, and in many cases also slept. Even when the urban housing developed in the second half of the 19th century and the rooms in the houses of the well-off families multiplied, everyday life remained concentrated in two rooms: one to sleep in and one for all the other activities of the day (Gavrilova 1999: 63–67). Only since the last decade of the 19th century did the kitchen slowly settle in the landscape of everyday life (Gavrilova 2016: 143–146). This data suggests that to most of the hundreds of thousands of people who migrated to the cities in the late 1940s and in the 1950s, a separate kitchen must have been a novelty. The modesty of many of the newly built flats could have encouraged them further in preserving the multi-functionality of the space.

The kitchen as a special nexus between the liberties of private everyday life and political freedom did exist to some extent in Bulgaria, as the story of Tamara Ganeva, quoted in the introduction, suggests. Hiding the evidence of her interest in the dissident movement among her cookbooks is one of the ways, in which her association of the kitchen and cooking with freedom found expression. Certainly, not every woman in Bulgaria in those times had a similar story to tell – the attitude of people to the communist state greatly varied and the numbers of those who chose forms of escapism, was significant. But among the interviewed women several more spoke of home cooking or/and of the kitchen as a political resort.

'There were many constraints. You can't say this, you can't say that – or someone will think you are opposing the power...', reflected Dani Tsacheva. While clothing or haircuts were controlled and censored, cooking allowed for 'the beautiful, the different, the new, for free choice ...' In it 'nothing was forbidden' and it was safe, said Dani Tsacheva. She recalled that even her father, a committed communist with idealist ideas, engaged in political humour in the kitchen. '*Drob-surma*[9] with chicken?!? And why not

---

[9] A dish, made of lamb meat and liver, and rice.

with lamb? Because all the lambs departed on a transcontinental journey!', she recalled her father joking over the communist export of food, which left empty the shelves on the domestic market, and made one of the most treasured kinds of meat, lamb, a rare luxury.

Political views, which were normally considered unsafe, often found their way out around food. The criticism of the communist power during the later decades of the regime coming from the restaurant tables of intellectuals' favourite hangouts has been a recurring memory (Shkodrova 2014: 197–227). Private dinners provided even better terrain. Elisaveta Shkodrova reminisced that her circle of friends found private gatherings much more liberating than dinners in restaurants. 'In a public place – outside, or at work, things were told less explicitly. At home everyone was open about their opinions of other people, superiors, government, of international politics if you wish ... We criticised everything, of course, back then this is what everyone did: everything was criticised, but covertly. Otherwise [in public] we were all supportive.' Shkodrova's circle of friends traded political jokes and had their witticisms, like for example calling the Russian salad Soviet and scooping some from it onto someone's plate as a reward for his alleged loyalty to the USSR.

Apart from some lurking political discourses, the privacy of the kitchens was most of all experienced as an opportunity for expressing individuality, free from ideological restrains. 'There was freedom in cooking. When you close your kitchen door, nobody will come and tell you what to do and how to do it', reflected Dani Tsacheva. She and many others spoke of their kitchens in a binomial opposition with the outside world, which was one of a formalized collective order. In this collective order individual achievements were mostly neither stimulated, nor recognized. As Tamara Ganeva observed, '[i]n all other occasions [but cooking] success was always a collective matter. For instance if I am a good teacher, that is because I am part of that particular collective. Individuality was not allowed to be manifested. Everything was collective.' Cooking, in contrast, was the one popular individual achievement.

PRESSURES REVERSE THE PERSPECTIVE

The perception of ideological coercion – in general or in home cooking, – was clearly a variable among the interviewed women. But if regardless of it all women deemed cooking indispensable and desirable, did it mean that the ideological pressures didn't play a role? Why was the renouncement of cooking always perceived as so alien? Not only impossible, but unwanted?

The narratives offered one answer to this question by bringing up a somewhat unexpected perspective. They revealed a tension, formed not in reaction to the political ideology, but to the reality which it had produced. Those, who did not feel pressurized by the communist ideas of modernity, did feel under the pressure of the actual communist-style modernization. In other words those women, who did not experience their everyday life being manipulated with political purposes, experienced as a pressure the consequences of their compulsory employment and the many other obligations, which the reality of communist everyday life made them face.

Under communism the state economy employed the entire female population of active age. It was not a matter of free choice, in the sense that no deviation from this path went unnoticed and the social and peer pressure was relentless. In fact it was difficult to draw a line between state and social pressure, as the politics of the communist leadership were supported by Communist Party members, who were present across all social layers and economic fields, and were supported by the activity of party-controlled organizations like the Fatherland Front and the syndicates. The archive of FF shows that all its network was cooperating with the militia in launching administrative punishment against 'incorrigible idlers and morally rotten elements' (CSA 417-4-42 1968: 50), a category in which one would end up, if one refused to be employed.

The new urban life, involving commuting and full-time, with often long hours at their employment left little room for housekeeping and cooking and put pressure on women to reform their ideal of their domestic role into a more time-sparing one. The practice of home cooking became one of the most contested points. If ideology could be ignored, the employment, occupying around sixty hours a week of Bulgarian women's time, could not.

While recalling her years as a young bride, Bozhurka Velkova offered an insight into how the shift to a modern lifestyle has affected women's idea of home cooking. Her mother-in-law, who was of age and with many children when the communist state was formed, remained unemployed. Having invested all her life in maintaining her household, she had developed excellence in domestic matters. Coming from a working-class family, Bozhurka Velkova saw her skills as outstanding. She found her mother-in-law 'very respectable', a role model. From the perspective of a worker with 'no time and no possibilities', she said she saw the life and the status of her mother-in-law as highly desirable, a sort of luxury.

Kristin Razsolkova made a similar point, reflecting upon the household practices of the pre-communist past in her family. She saw them as exceeding by far in sophistication the realities of a woman under communism. She said once households were maintained in a manner unimaginable and unfeasible under communism, or nowadays. She spoke of the different pace of time, the changed rhythm of life, with nostalgia.

The realization that the working woman could only dream of becoming as good a housewife as those from the previous generation, seems to have played a role in flipping some women's ideas of the importance and the status of home cooking regardless of their political beliefs. Tamara Ganeva, who perceived the members of her family as people with interest and respect towards food, made an important observation, which shed light in the same direction: 'Women complained not so much about being obliged to cook, as about not having time to cook. And these are two different things.'

Her words must have been indeed echoed by many, as statistical surveys from the late communist period suggest. As Ghodsee noted, 'women wanted to be both mothers and workers. They merely desired help in balancing these two responsibilities' (Ghodsee 2014: 552). The consequences of the pressure, which communism built on home-cooking practices both with its reality and its ideology, paradoxically resembled the one felt by working-class women in the United States. Not having access to the domesticity enjoyed by the upper-middle classes, they developed a cult towards it (Dantec-Lowry 2008: 110). It seems as if the social system in Bulgaria, which was supposed to remove class divisions, was just as susceptible to them as the American one. Still, in communist Bulgaria this dream was more discussed than actually pursued, according to polls from the end of the 1960s – possibly for the lack of feasible paths to do so.

The pressure building up against home cooking in this context seems to have produced an unexpected side effect. It had reversed the perspective, and if any part of the female population entered communism by seeing their home cooking as slavery, by 1970s some thought of it more as a privilege, even a right, conceptualizing it as such namely because they thought it was partially lost (Shkodrova 2019).

This process resembles in a way the reactions toward the Soviet campaign against clutter and over-decoration at home: instead of diminishing people's tendency to practise it, 'the so-called domestic trash rebelled against the ideological purges and remained as the secret residue of privacy that shielded people from imposed and internalised communality' (Boym 1994: 150; Reid 2002: 250).

Similar 'flipping' of the perception of household chores was observed by Liora Gvion in her research of the Israeli kibbutz. A first generation of women, who were among the founders of this form of communal life, had reformatted private cooking and childcare into communal work: their children grew up without an individual mother, raised in a communal kindergarten, and they ate in a dining hall food, prepared for their community by paid workers.

The second generation of women: those, who had been raised in the kibbutz circumstances, decided to scrap the forms of extreme collectivism, which their mothers continued to defend. Owing to the circumstances under which they were raised, they came to see home cooking and childcare as privileges (Gvion 2015: 170).

Quite ironically, in both communist Bulgaria and kibbutz Israel the elimination of home cooking was at first seen as a revolutionary act of liberation. But in both cases the pressure of this 'liberation' (or in the case of Bulgaria the coercion to it) reversed the perspective and made individuals perceive household chores as desirable, even as a sort of a right. The longing for more time spent in the household, and the enthusiasm for perfecting householder's skills in Bulgaria matches the willingness with which Gvion describes the second-generation kibbutz women applying themselves to work in their reclaimed homes (Gvion 2015: 166). In Bulgaria the peer pressure between women made a great contribution towards this flipping. It is not necessarily the case though in the kibbutz, where the first generation of women were discouraging of their daughters taking back their household work. The data, presented by Gvion, sheds no light over other possible causes of the flip, preventing me from taking this comparison further.

DOMOSHARKI WITH FEMINIST TENDENCIES?

Considering the differences in the interviewed women's discourses, it is clear that generalizing would mean compromising. However, there are some points of intersection between their opinions and experiences. To summarize, home cooking remained an unwavering element of the ideal woman's profile in spite of the unfavourable ideological context. Patriarchal values played a role in the process, but they were not the only factor. The assertion that 'women became as free as men to work outside the home while men remain free from work within it' (Massey and Kahn 1995: 360) describes the situation only partially. In cases where women felt that they were being reprimanded or deprived of the possibility to cook as part of maintaining their family and household, they started seeing home cooking not only as their duty, but as their right. They did perceive the discourse that home cooking is old-fashioned as a contestation of power. It was always attributed to the 'others', whatever the definition and content of this category was in each particular case.

If only a few of the women had sensitivity towards the ideological pressure of the system and conceptualized it as such, those who did reacted against it. On another level, many women who did not feel pressurized by the ideology, did feel pressed by the modernization which was grounded on it. They rebelled against it too, without formulating the tension in political terms. In both cases the pressure acted as a reverse motivator (to its intentional effect) and boosted women's interest in home cooking.

How far such conceptualizations of everyday acts can be interpreted as resistance is a question which historians and sociologist debate. One of the discussions takes place within the historical and cultural studies of communism, where lately there is an increasing appeal to abandon binomial thinking as simplifying and ignoring the fluid quality of the social convention, where values were constantly renegotiated. A growing number of writers concentrate instead on the ways in which the worlds, created by the ideology, were lived in – in this spirit are the writings of Svetlana Boym (2001), Rasa Baločkaite (2011), Svetlana Alexievich (2013), and especially of Alexei Yurchak (2006). Pointing out that to many, living state socialism 'meant something quite different from the official interpretation, provided by state rhetoric', Yurchak argued that new language is needed, which would allow space for the 'seemingly paradoxical mix of the negative and positive values, of alienations and attachments', a language 'that does not reduce the description of socialist realities to dichotomies', but offers an explanatory framework as well for the 'creative, imaginative and often paradoxical cultural forms' of social life (Yurchak 2005: 8–9).

These views seek ground in the postcolonial theorists' thought and mean to stay clear of exaggerations in the discursive interpretation of behaviours. As Ashcroft (2001: 44) stated, 'The subject [in an oppressive regime] does not resist and does not criticize. He consumes the dominant discourse for purposes far different than those foreseen by its disseminators'. Also outside historical studies the notion of resistance has been recently subjected to a discussion, as the term is used in contrasting ways throughout the existing literature. Ore (2011: 691), for example, asserted that resistance lies more in the results than in the intentions of an action, while Rubin (2014: 2) maintained that the term 'implies consciously disruptive, intentionally political actions'. He argued that it is more fruitful to distinguish 'resistance' from 'friction' – the term, which according to Rubin should signify the instinctive resistance that humans necessarily or naturally enact in extremely controlled environments.

Some researchers speak alternatively of 'macro-resistance' and 'micro-resistance', the second describing 'the daily practices of individuals as they continue to live their day-to-day lives' (Haynes and Prakash 1992, Dutta-Bergman 2004, Dutta 2008). Others, such as Crewe (2007) or McEvoy (2000), make distinction between 'coping' and 'resistance'. Crewe accepts Buntman's (2003: 237) definition that resistance consists of 'actions and practices designed to dilute, circumvent, or eliminate the imposition of unwelcome power'.

Indeed applying more nuanced terminology is beneficial to the understanding of human behaviour, which certainly is far more complex than social sciences, and in particular history, tend to acknowledge. If applying the finer 'scaling' of the resistance phenomenon, suggested by Rubin (2014), Haynes and Prakash (1992) and Dutta (2008), routine actions, which presented circumvention, dilution or elimination of the ideology without the acts being conceptualized as such, can be defined as 'friction'. Micro-resistance could be seen in those everyday-life actions, which presented incompliance with the ideology and were conceptualized as such. Finally actions, which did not remain within the routine daily life practices and intended political disruption, can be termed 'resistance'.

The collected narratives suggest that the alternative consumption of the dominant discourse was only part of people's everyday life and to many it coexisted with criticism, friction and micro-resistance. The dominant discourse may not have been antagonizing the citizens on a daily basis and may not have clearly defined their morals, but it did define at all times layers of meanings, motivating actions of everyday life. In this particular case it added value to obtaining a foreign recipe, which was seen as pragmatically useless but symbolically important, or escaping the spirit of the communist cookbooks and reaching for the denied luxury of the past, looking for an unproblematic corner of freedom of choice, expression and criticism.

While binary reasoning without sensitivity to details and exemptions can indeed produce blind spots in any attempt at interpreting communist societies, the binary framework is at the same time essential to any attempt to conceptualize the period. I hold that its dominance in political and social analyses in the early post-socialist years is due precisely to its persistence if not in living daily life as such, then in its conceptualization by the very people who lived it. Consciously or not, it did affect the meanings of many daily actions.

In summary, as the narratives suggest, to many if not most people daily life did have a binary texture, with omnipresent elements of perceived obstruction, with a lasting, even if fluid division between 'them' (i.e. those at power) and 'us'. The suppositions were ingrained in daily actions, and perhaps more often defined the meanings than was actually articulated. The restrictions, the ideological prescriptions, the existent borders of forbidden and permitted, of regulated in general, affected the meaning of many daily actions of life, which Baločkaite (2011: 421) analysed as just being lived[10]. Some narratives demonstrated that the opposite was also in place in communist societies – even when performing activities on the margins of what was regulated by the dominant discourse, individuals still happened to conceptualize it as (micro-) resistance.

---

[10] While building her argument against 'binarity' of socialism, Baločkaite quotes an interviewee saying 'I don't know how to explain whether we believed (in the Soviet regime) or not. We lived, and that's all'.

If people did not feel that they were able to break the system, they certainly experienced their small acts of trespassing against the Iron Curtain as an opportunity to break free from the system. They arranged pockets of freedom for themselves.

The arguments, drawn on the postcolonial theory of Ashcroft, state that under communism people practised 'withdrawal from politics, the excision of the political from daily life and the cultivation of a space of one's own, uncontaminated by politics.' And while the object of this observation can be interpreted as the existence of a zone free from the binary model, it can also be seen as an attempt to escape oppressive dominances, the very act of which escape is one of acknowledging them as perceived. Individual 'spaces of their own' were certainly not uncontaminated by politics, on the contrary, they made sense as political statements. In each case the meanings were negotiated with this dominant framework. If people persisted in practising escapism, it was because they felt pressure in the private zones, far beyond what they thought should be the limits of the public.

Observing evolutions in the meta-discourse, researchers of communism have also argued that it is being 'renegotiated'. The term, used by Yurchak, Baločkaite, and Bren, among many, signifies interaction between the different social levels, as a result of which the discourse has gradually evolved. However in many cases there was an intermediate level – in the case of the researched field that would be the authors of the cookbooks, which perpetuated the discourse: producing cookbooks in the intersection of what they thought desirable and acceptable. It would be interesting and important to study further how far the resulting discourse, found in these books, was indeed 'negotiated' in the sense of being shaped by interaction between the levels, or was it instead spiralling, evolving within the level, without purposeful interferences from the level above. In other words, it would be important to look further into where exactly in society, and how, the meta-discourse was pushed to change. This would provide a better answer to the still debated issue of how precisely the communist regimes of Eastern Europe were undone.

MANAGING BUDGETS

If 'economic' is understood in the broader and inclusive framework of 'behaviour as a mechanism, oriented toward the production and distribution of material objects' (Bateson 1987: 76), this chapter looks into how recipe exchange and collection helped women dealing with the specific economic circumstances in producing familial meals. It explores the application of scrapbooks in a market ridden by shortages, in households with only basic financial possibilities and in a society with a distinct understanding of the value of time.

FOOD RESOURCES

The shortages were the most prominent, notorious feature of the communist market. They meant a choice of foodstuffs, mostly limited to what was produced in the state, a permanent or very frequent shortage of more luxurious ingredients and regular disappearance of the basic ones for periods of time.

A systematic research of which products were in short supply in different periods of the communist rule in Bulgaria has not been done until now. However some sources give a general idea. An expert study from 1974 analysed the situation in one of the best-supplied stores in the capital. It established 'systematic' shortages of 42.6 per cent of the assortment expected by the regulations, which included raw and cured meat, fish, and fresh fruit, among other products. Another 29.3 per cent were reported to be available once in a while and included vegetables, other types of cured meat, chocolate products, spirits, and certain types of bread. Only 28.1 per cent of the assortment was delivered regularly, and these included the most common varieties of bread, milk, yogurt, sugar, certain desserts and canned fish (CSA 707-1-179 1974). However the study did not cover the frequent periods of crisis, when also many of the 'regularly delivered' products, such as oil, vinegar, yogurt, sugar, onion or even bread disappeared.

One of the direct consequences of this situation was that women usually had to cook with a very limited and unreliable palette of products. The five most used cookbooks seemed relatively adapted to the situation. Regarding required ingredients, all of them are generally sober and restrained in calling for foodstuffs that are extravagant for the communist market. Slightly more demanding was *Contemporary Domestic Cooking* (Cholcheva and Kalaydzhieva 1972), which, with its multiple references to foreign cuisines, seemed to have tried but not quite succeeded keeping within what was available. A number of the selected foreign recipes called for 'impossibles' like Brussels sprouts, asparagus, chestnuts, salted codfish or olive oil, as some examples.

Some of the books, and especially *Bulgarian National Cuisine* (Petrov et al. 1978), also called for a range of products – geese, capons, mutton, turkey, duck, snails and frogs, which might have been available to rural farmers in the periods, when they were allowed to keep private animals and gardens, but not to the urban population. It is curious that in an epoch when one went to the shop to buy 'meat' or 'minced meat', as this was the level of detail that the market allowed, most cookbooks featured extensive sections on cooking game meat. Complaining about the unfeasible recipes in Sotirov's (1959) book, Cathy Ivanova said 'Because, for instance, [the recipe requires] cream. Well, you look for it in the shop, and it is not available. So what do you do then? You just cook whatever you find'. This reverse logic rendered large parts of the available cookbooks quite unusable.

In comparison, the exchanged recipes were by default feasible – they circulated along with the cooked dishes themselves, which meant that they were dishes that were feasible to prepare. The narratives revealed also that they were sometimes filtered, and those featuring unavailable ingredients were discarded. Or they were adapted. In this way the scrapbooks were developed to be highly adjusted to the market. They played a crucial role in helping women to cope better within its limitations. Expressing the thoughts of many others, Kristin Razsolkova said that the prime goal of the recipe collection was to be able to make 'something out of nothing'. Pirogovskaya (2017: 345) observed precisely the same recurrent motive behind the Soviet recipe exchange practices, which suggests that the poverty of the communist market must have played an important role in the proliferation of scrapbooks. If there are nuances between the countries in the communist bloc, they might have been caused by the varying state of food procuration. Lakhtikova (2017: 121) associated scrapbooks and Soviet women's obsession with food with the chronic experience of hunger in their childhood, while actual hunger was never mentioned in the interviews with the Bulgarian women.

The narratives even provide an interesting insight into what a fluid and socially uneven matter the shortages in late communism were. Certainly not all the interviewed women experienced them in the same way or spoke of them in the same terms. Some were more hesitant to talk of shortages, compared to others, whether due to their personalities, or their general disappointment with the post-communist era, which drove them to be less critical of the past. But there was also a clear difference between the women's recollections on the grounds of their position in the hierarchy of the former communist society.

Vanya Pinteva, for instance, apart from recalling the lack of chocolate, said she did not remember shortages. Her work as a prosecutor in the centre of Sofia ensured her access to the good quality and cheap canteens of the Syndicates. She also lived in proximity to some of the best shops in town. She even recalled having access to a cheese shop, which sold Gruyère and Emmental – possibly the output of niche experiments of the Bulgarian cheese industry in the 1980s (Shkodrova 2014: 332). Violeta Kaloferova also said she did not have problems with the ingredients. She, too, was employed by a ministry in the centre of Sofia, which must have provided for her proximity to the best-supplied shops in the country. Keeping themselves within the reasonable range of products on the market, they said they lived without experiencing any great shortages in a punishing way.

This was an evaluation, quite different from that of women in a less privileged position, and even between those there were significant differences, depending on the area of their residence at the time.

The residents of more developed urban areas focused mainly on the absence of non-essential products. One of the most remembered is the craving for fresh exotic fruits, imported irregularly mostly from Cuba: lemons, oranges, mandarins, grapefruits and bananas. The latest may appear impossibly marginal from the point of view of contemporary consumption in Europe. Bananas, though, could be arguably defined as the very symbol of late communism shortages[1] – they appear as a coveted delicacy in an overwhelming number of published memories (as evident in Gospodinov 2006 and other publications across Eastern Europe). As this fruit was delivered mainly around New Year, many private stories are accounts of epic queues in the snow, freezing feet and hands, parents' love, children's sacrifice, New Year celebrations and even broken marriages. One of the authors in Gospodinov's book recalls how the behaviour of her husband in the queue convinced her that she had made a mistake marrying him and eventually led to her divorce.

In the narratives in this research the most often mentioned were the ingredients for pastry-making: chocolate, coconut flakes, cocoa powder. Essentials in pastry baking, such as vanilla, fresh cream, baking powder and gelatine were also cited as absent or difficult to find. But women in the cities also seem to have had more means to procure in alternative ways what they needed. Tsveta Tanovska said that an important source of household electronics and cooking ingredients were the visits to the GDR, which people from cities were able to make quite freely in the 1980s. Travelling there herself, she bought coconut flakes – an experience, which she said she 'will never forget' and that felt as if she was buying 'a diamond ring'. 'I even remember that in a shop in Berlin I saw two Bulgarians, who had filled up their shopping cart with rice. It said 'Coco's rice' on the boxes and I am positive they thought they were buying coconut flakes!' Bozhurka Velkova also remembered getting a supply of coconut flakes from abroad – from Macedonia. She recalled the shortage of gelatine, but added that if you wanted something, there were always ways to procure it by applying your *vruzki*.

Such opportunities to procure rare products were certainly rather exceptional and yet show the advantages of urban citizens in comparison to residents in smaller towns or rural areas. The cities were supposed to be more dependent on the state trade and the city shops were envisaged to be the best supplied. In the 1970s experts divided the country into three zones depending on the density of the population and Sofia had a priority, then followed all the other bigger towns, smaller towns and finally village shops, which were assigned the smallest assortment of goods (CSA 707-1-211, Shkodrova 2014). This left the villages dependent to a great extent on their own

---

[1] This was the case not only in Bulgaria, but in all communist states in the Soviet bloc. The craving for bananas in GDR, for example, is described in this article in Welt: https://www.welt.de/kultur/article5097869/Wie-die-DDR-zur-Bananenrepublik-wurde.html

production – the towns dreaming of what they considered the 'rich' supplies of the big cities, and the big cities still ensuring part of their diet by staying connected to the villages or via different forms of city farming.

Nedyalka Malcheva, who lived in the town of Preslav in north-east Bulgaria, said: 'I've seen my sister-in-law make small cakes in Sofia with slices of orange. Do you have any idea how much I have dreamed of seeing an orange in Preslav?!' She recalled that whenever vanilla or baking powder were delivered in the town shops, a queue formed. To make the delivery last for more people, salesmen set purchase limits. It was due to these shortages, that she found the cookbooks upsetting. 'They were not very good. They were upsetting people. Q: Upsetting people? A: Why yes! Not everyone could afford to eat what people in Sofia did!' She thought the cookbooks were meant to be read by Sofianites, and not by people in the countryside, where the shop-supplies were poorer. Just as Pirogovskaya observed about Soviet Russia, the discrepancies between the wealth on the cookbook pages and the empty shops was perceived indeed as 'wrenching' (Pirogovskaya 2017: 341).

Her words, which were supported by other narratives, seem to confirm the assertion of Možny (2003) that the source of frustration came more from the unequal access to luxury, than from the actual lack of it. Embodying the stratification in the society, it spread growing cynicism and provoked ridicule of the ideological proclamations of egalitarianism.

The disproportional effect of the deficits was also evident from the different focus of women's recollections when it came to deficits. Speaking of her life in the village where she still lives, Elena Salmadzhiyska was the only one who mentioned shortages of basic products. This hardly suggests that there were no shortages of basic products in cities, where even sugar, vinegar or oil were sometimes hard to find. Yet the single reference to the absence of basic products in the shop could well testify to the more painful, or extended experiences in the rural areas: 'There were many [shortages]. There was a time, when you couldn't find butter in the shop. (...) You couldn't find flour, the oil was sold one bottle per house, when they delivered from it in the shop ... Food stamps were introduced for the bread – I had to bake at home.'

To cope with the situation, women from small towns turned to their networks and sought local recipes. Salmadzhiyska collected cookery advice in her native village of Osikovo – motivated not by emotional attachments, but rather by the presumption that these recipes are based on what people grow or collect in their gardens and forests. Kalina Kechova explained in the same way her preference for recipes from the area of Smolyan, where she lived: they required ingredients that were easier to procure. Both mentioned the difficulty in finding foodstuffs that most cookbook recipes required: to their world the local cuisine was the mundane norm and the printed culinary advice still had to transform from 'esoteric to quotidian', to use the words of Goody (1977: 140) of pre-industrial societies. Pirogovskaya (2017: 336) argued that the scrapbooks of 1960s to 1980s Russia were typically Soviet, because they were based on the limited variety of food available through the Soviet chains of supply. Even if food shortages in Bulgaria hardly came close to those across the USSR, there is a clear parallel here. In the countryside, particularly with the nationalization of private land, traditional food chains were disrupted and forced to depend on centralized food production and trade.

Such trade though remained quite marginal in these same rural areas. Urban zones on the other hand had already grown dependent on commerce by the end of the 19th and the beginning of the 20th century. Facing the impotence of the communist food trade, they had to reconstruct procurement chains, based mostly on their own agricultural work – in native villages, in the gardens of newly purchased villas or at some point through state arrangements, allowing the exploitation of patches of land.

Apart from providing a body of advice, well adapted to the local market situation, the recipe exchange often came along with important information on the availability of rare ingredients, better quality commodities and the like. The process of exchange mobilized information networks, which involved friends, colleagues, acquaintances or even benevolent strangers, engaged in random chats in the tram, in a queue or at another public place. These information circuits were sarcastically dubbed 'Agency O.W.S.' (for 'One Woman Said'] and, as Elisaveta Shkodrova recalled, were very important in directing you where to buy particular products, if rare foodstuffs were released in the area, and in general provided many kinds of priceless tips.

One leading strategy to cope with the market's deficits was the yearly production of canned food, which occurred in most Bulgarian households over the summer. The jars, which in the autumn were lined up on the shelves of attics and cellars of almost every town apartment, were significantly more varied than what was available canned in the shops. Strawberries, raspberries, blackberries, quince, peaches, apricots, plums, black cherries, sour cherries, white cherries, pears were preserved in water and sugar or turned into jams. Peppers, eggplants, tomatoes, and carrots were processed in a variety of relishes. The pickles involved different sorts of peppers, cauliflower, carrots, garlic and onion, and cucumbers. Tomatoes, courgettes and okra were preserved in brine. Vats with sour cabbage were placed in cellars or on balconies. Vine leaves were conserved for the preparation of *sarmi*[2] in the winter. Some families also preserved cooked or cured meat.

In most narratives making home preserves was thought of as a means of survival, rather than a matter of luxury. Some of the interviewed spoke of themselves feeling 'forced' to do the work. Many mentioned the monotonous choice, the unreliable supplies and the dubious quality of canned food in the shops. Lilia Dencheva, for instance, said that only two types of preserved vegetables were found in the shops: tomatoes in jars and *lyutenitsa*[3]. She also mentioned green peas, immediately doubting her own words. 'There were just no preserved foods! You needed to make them yourself!' Frequently the intense activity of canning was justified in the narratives by the better taste of the home-made preserves. The scrapbooks, which were an important tool in the process, present clear evidence of the scale of this activity.

Recipes for preserves make up the second largest section in the scrapbooks: approximately 13 per cent of the examined collections. This proportion coincides with the situation which Sharpless established in the scrapbooks of deep rural Texas during the Great Depression, in a community cookbook from 1933 (Sharpless 2016: 199–200).

---

[2] Leaves – of vine or of cabbage – stuffed with rice, or a rice and meat filling.
[3] A vegetable relish, made of roasted peppers and other vegetables.

This category of recipes in the Bulgarian communist scrapbooks consisted of around 61 per cent of conserved vegetables, 25 per cent of drinks and 10 per cent of fruits – possibly because many types of fruits could be conserved using identical recipes. The recipes for vegetables showed much greater variation. On the one hand there were many basic recipes for vegetables in brine, specifying proportions of salt and water and details of the basic methods of pickling or sterilizing in jars. They confirmed that canning was practised by the households under communism to provide basic ingredients for winter cooking: peeled tomatoes and roasted peppers were a staple.

Some of the advice though was more complex. Almost all scrapbooks featured at least a few recipes for the laborious all-time favourites *lyutenitsa* and *kyopoolu*. These two relishes, the basis of which are roasted peppers in various combinations with aubergines, tomatoes, hot peppers, garlic and onion, parsley and more, were prepared in three stages. First peppers and aubergines were roasted, peeled and minced, then they were simmered for hours together, and eventually the relishes were poured into jars and sterilized. The method varied and there were shorter and longer versions, but they always involved long hours of work. Another explosion of variations was visible in the combinations of vegetables for pickles, including the often featured colourful *Tsarska turshia*. Endless blends of vegetables and spice were exchanged and noted in the scrapbooks.

Some scrapbooks stood out as particularly creative in this sense, asserting that preserves were made not only as an existential necessity, but as a treat. Tsveta Tanovska's scrapbook is one such example, featuring recipes that are imaginative and luxurious in the context: oranges and egg liquors, green walnut liquor, jellies, rare herbs and spice mixtures and spiced vinegars. Clearly basic necessities mixed with hedonistic pursuits and the roasted peppers, preserved with tablets of Aspirin[4], appeared alongside more refined and laborious preserves such as 'white walnut jam': a recipe calling for 90 to 100 hand-peeled walnuts, cooked in three changes of waters and flavoured with orange rinds (a recipe from Dani Tsacheva's scrapbook). This mixed content shows that women used scrapbooks to find advantage in a disadvantaged situation. While they were forced to provide for the basic needs of their family, they also used the opportunity to deliver luxurious food experiences, which were inaccessible to most in other ways.

FINANCIAL BUDGETS

When it comes to the levels of wealth, the narratives reveal a somewhat paradoxical situation: while from them there clearly transpires the general modesty of the financial possibilities of the Bulgarian population, they also show that this had a reduced effect on the quality of people's lives. Limited budgets and food prices had troubled the

---

[4] To make sure their preserves last through the winter, many Bulgarians practised conservation with chemical compounds such as salicylic and sorbic acids, and sodium benzoate. When salicylic acid was not found, it was substituted with tablets of Aspirin, which contained acetylsalicylic acid, was cheap and sold without medical prescription in the pharmacies. The practice continues today, judging by the many websites which offer entire sections of recipes for conservation with Aspirin.

women. But their accounts also suggested a lifestyle of relative comfort, in which money did not seem to have been a prime concern in their daily routine in the past. Moments of poverty, when the lack of financial means required austerity, were mentioned in only two of the accounts. Another four women described as not having had 'that much money', spoke of home-prepared food as 'cheaper' or said they sought for recipes that were cheaper to make. In any case it seems as if the shortage of food was more disturbing than the shortage of money.

One of the women who spoke of financial hardship, said that she tried to make everything cheaper because of the small salaries, which were hardly enough to raise two children, so that they had to be careful all year in order to be able to heat the house in the winter and 'all in all we were poor'. The other one said that during a period of time her family had to survive on a very tight budget. They both mentioned avoiding certain recipes in the printed cookbooks because of their excessive use of pricier ingredients, in particular butter and eggs. 'In that very famous book of Cholcheva, [there were recipes] calling for 300 g butter, 12 eggs – such things . . .', said one of them. 'Q: Did you find it wasteful? A: Yes! Besides, 300 g of butter is indeed a lot! Even if, as a graduate of a French school, I love butter!'

Her restricted budget had turned her scrapbook into a manual on how to cook better for less money. It had even pushed her to create new recipes. She recalled being unemployed and having at her disposal only two leva – the local equivalent of about one and a half US dollars at the time. This allowed her to buy four pork legs and, after long cooking and boning, and by adding butter and paprika powder, to produce a new dish. Friends visited that night and were so impressed that it quickly became her signature dish, mentioned with nostalgia in their private correspondence between the United States and Bulgaria in the following years.

But similar stories were rather exceptional in the narratives. The financial restrictions in the past were mostly presented in milder terms. Four women voiced the idea of being reasonably careful in their expenses and some of them specifically referred to scrapbooks as a helpful tool in these efforts. Two explicitly mentioned that they collected more affordable recipes. Others though said that they did not bother to think much about it. One of the interviewed recalled her mother-in-law often saying: 'Whatever you do, [products for] two leva always go in the baking dish!' The communist market did not offer many versions or qualities of the same ingredient at different prices. '[Price] was not a factor,' said another of the interviewed women – 'There was one type of yogurt, one type of milk, one type of sugar or flour. There was nothing to compare between. You'd just get what there is and make use of it, without considering it from such a perspective'.

If a few women stated that scrapbook recipes accommodated their need to be frugal, all of them said that the collections prevented them from wasting money by making mistakes. The quality of their contained recipes being tested and mostly tried out was seen as an insurance against waste. The scrapbooks were repeatedly described as a means to avoid failures: 'We didn't have that many products, to waste them . . . to try again and again . . .', stated one of the women.

But all these statements presented only one side of the economic significance of the scrapbooks. By opening the way to safe investments, they also became an instrument to practise (affordable) exuberance. In fact it is arguable which of these roles was seen as more important. Differently from the stories of frugality, those of exuberance were numerous in the narrators' accounts and some of them came even from those who otherwise spoke of the importance of economical cooking. One of the women recalled preparing boxes and boxes of sweets for a wedding – so many, that the people at the party could not believe she made them all on her own. Another one also spoke of orgiastic collective cooking in her youth in the absence of her parents. 'My parents travelled to the seaside, leaving us behind with eighty eggs. And on the second day my dad was calling back: 'So how many eggs are left?' He knew what we were up to, when they were away (…) We were getting together, of course, friends, partying … and cooking. So many sausages and hams! All kinds of things, but most of all we loved to bake! So much! Most of all we baked!'

Many testimonies of excess spoke of get-togethers, when people invested great resources in preparing food. After commenting on the exchanged recipes as 'a means of survival', one of them added: 'But of course there were recipes at the other extreme, lavish. Here, for instance this recipe for Josephinki – these Josephinki are a true challenge to prepare!' Another narrative evoking regular parties, which friends hosted in turns, revealed the regular domestic production of monumental quantities of cakes: one with twelve eggs was mentioned, and then another one with a width of about 70 cm, which took twelve hours to cook: with five separately baked base layers and one and a half litres of *crème patissière,* and so on.

Even the woman who said she wouldn't make a cake with 300 g of butter, added that she would never cook with margarine either: she would find a more modest recipe, but would use butter.

Thus, while reflecting the financial limitations of the households, scrapbooks also suggested that these limits were relative and often not of prime concern. They confirmed the argument of Steele that 'where there is no free market, there is no pricing mechanism, there is no economic calculation' (Steele 1981: 11). They also suggested that food exuberance was very well possible and accessible to most in late communism, even if within the framework of a generally modest material world. Considered from such a perspective, scrapbooks were one of the instruments of practising luxury, and also in many cases one of the family documents, which reflected the practising of luxury.

TIME

The evident excess involved not only money, but also time – another resource, the value of which the communist state had made stretchy. Time, spent on exchanging recipes, could be seen as 'reinterpretation' of the official time order, as a significant part of the process took place at work, where working hours were remade into hours to socialize: to share stories, gossip, food and recipes. Perhaps also the time, spent on excessive home cooking could be seen as such reinterpretation, considering the explicit efforts of the official ideology to regulate the use of private time on cooking and the state's attempts to claim private hours for state/party/ideology-related activities.

Some people took the state's attempts for time etatization (as per Verdery 1996) better than others. The narratives suggested that at least some of the women experienced the tension of time contestation in political terms. Tsveta Tanovska recalled being regularly summoned to meetings, organized by the local party unit precisely on the night when, according to the Orthodox tradition in Bulgaria, Easter eggs are painted. She saw this not as a coincidence, but as an attempt to keep people away from the religious celebrations – which of course it was, along with the deployment of militiamen around the churches on the night of the midnight Easter sermon. The eradication of old festivities and the imposition of new, communist ones was on the state agenda, pursued on all levels from militia to loyal grass-level organizations (CSA 417-4-91: 12).

In a similar vein, Dani Tsacheva spoke of 'them [a common abstract reference to the regime] arranging for the woman to have no time'. Her statement suggested that the choice of practising temporal reinterpretation or not was not only practical, but was prone to be loaded with political connotations, to be sometimes related to individuals' political affiliations and feelings. 'These, whose lives passed on [party] meetings, political pep talks ... those were running, those had no time. They thought that this is the new life ... To them the other thing was more important'.

In this statement, Dani Tsacheva spoke of those who have chosen to comply with the temporal allocations of the state. To her, they were 'the others'. Indeed, all those who avoided complying may not have thought of their choice as of destructive resistance, breaking up the system. But they often acted clearly aware of not complying. In the minds of at least some of the interviewed, complying was a behaviour, opposite to their own, its meaning being read in binomial opposition.

The ways, in which time was discussed in the narratives, supported the argument that the reinterpretation of temporality was more available to white-collar employees. The recollections also suggest that resorting to it eased some of the pressure, caused by the unfeasible social expectations towards women.

Those, whose lives remained tied to a rural lifestyle, such as Nedyalka Malcheva or Fatme Ali Inus, spoke of the deficit of time as insurmountable. Most of those living in urban areas, either ignored it as an issue, or thought of it as a matter of choice, priorities or effort. Fatme Ali Inus, for instance, rejected any possibility in the past of writing down a recipe on the grounds of lack of time: 'Q: Why did you never write down any recipes? A: Ha, as if there was any time for it! Q: You didn't have time for it? A [laughing]: Why, in the village the work is up to here! [pointing to her forehead with a typical gesture of being overwhelmed]'. Nedyalka Malcheva, who combined full-time work with running a small private farm, also spoke of similar unquestionable distribution of her time.

Ivanka Atipova, who spent part of her life in a rural area before moving to Sofia, articulated the temporal contrasts between the two lifestyles: 'I was born in a village and there people are very busy in the summer. Maybe they exchanged recipes in the winter – when they slaughtered their pigs, surely they did, but to start making pastries – I don't think they had time for such things ... I think recipes were more exchanged in the cities'.

If the urban zones were clearly different from the rural ones, there were also nuances within them. Certain differences seemed clear between white- and blue-collar lifestyles.

Bozhurka Velkova said that her mother, 'a simple working woman', sometimes took night shifts and tried to keep cooking as simple as possible. 'Her life was very different from that of an office worker, who sits all day long on a chair, writing, and who is not physically tired by the end of the day. Brains are not so important to perform your household chores, but you need physical energy to stand two hours at the stove to cook…'

Indeed, many of the women, who had worked in offices, did not even mention the issue of time. Dobrinka Boeva, who worked in the media, emphasized that she always found time for everything. Atanaska Terzieva, who worked as a bank clerk, also said that in her circles time for home cooking was never commented on as being an issue. In a similar vein, Elisaveta Shkodrova stated: 'You know how it goes: you either find time, or take from your time to sleep, or from another task, but you do what you've got to do'.

All this did not necessarily mean that white-collar workers were less overwhelmed. It indicates that they had a (slightly) greater choice as to how to spread their time budgets between their tasks. But the elasticity of their arrangements was limited. In spite of it, many found themselves overworked, lacking time to maintain their household well. Many office workers spoke emotionally about their burden, their experiences varying depending on their personalities and the support they have been obtaining in their families. Lilia Dencheva gave an emotional account of how she found her household obligations to be a toil. She said that taking care of food was extremely time consuming and she constantly felt overwhelmed: 'Why, all your time was spent on cooking! Not to mention walking around and looking for products to buy'.

She said that 'because you did everything alone, we didn't have time to make complicated things. Or risky…' Precisely in this sense, to many women scrapbooks were important timesaving instruments. They ensured easy and fast recipes, guaranteed that the dish would work out: they gave quicker access to the right culinary instructions. Lilia Dencheva, Ivanka Atipova and many others spoke of the importance of the recipes' reliability. As Lilia Dencheva said, 'there was no time to experiment – to get something wrong and to have to cook again!'

Besides, scrapbooks contained timesaving recipes, which many women deliberately sought. Several of the interviewed mentioned that making pastry during the weekday evenings was made more feasible with the collection of relatively easy and familiar recipes.

Scrapbooks also saved time as media: they were gathered in reinterpreted pockets of office hours and they were much faster to navigate, as their content was familiar. They also presented a concise selection of filtered, useful advice, which saved leafing through many pages in search of the right recipe. The first-hand experience with the dish allowed you to use your memory, instead of trying to understand descriptions. In many ways, they were shortcuts to the essential cookery advice, which made them a crucial instrument within the triple burden context.

In summary, scrapbooks were important management documents, which contain insights into how women worked with their time-, money- and food ingredients-budgets, the regulation of which was contested by the state. Scrapbooks saved time with the efficiency of their mediation; by containing a selection of time-sparing recipes;

by featuring advice adapted to the individual skills, skipping superfluous instructions, and by helping avoid failures. They supported a saving of financial and material resources. At the same time they reflected the expenditure of at times excessive resources on cooking: they helped to obtain affordable luxury by compensating the lack of material exuberance with greater quantities of efficiently invested time. They revealed that despite the double or even triple burden, of all available resources, time remained the one over which individuals had the greatest control.

SCRAPBOOKS AS SOCIAL CAPITAL

Kalina Ketchova was born in the mountain village of Stoykite in South Bulgaria: a few houses and a church, named after St Peter and St Paul, which every year are buried under snow between November and April. But in 1974, married and seeking employment, she migrated to Smolyan. Crammed between the mighty slopes of the Rodopi at a height of over 1000 metres, this town was created as an act of social engineering by the communist state. Several smaller settlements along the bed of river Cherna (Black) were united and now stretch for over 25 kilometres in the black shadows of the mountain. But Smolyan remains a small town with fewer than thirty thousand residents. Here Kalina Ketchova took jobs as a housekeeper in the forestry sector, and a school canteen, as a photo lab worker, a cook, a waitress, a cleaner. Finally she went on pension and in 2016, peaceful and fragile, I met her leading a quiet life in an apartment block in one of Smolyan's hilly neighbourhoods. It was a new building, accommodating only a few families: with sparkling clean stairways and inexpensive but shiny doors. She led me straight to her tiny living room, wrapped in the softness of carpets, blankets and thick tablecloths, and installed me in front of a glass of tea. But we were soon to move to the kitchen for there was the drawer, where laid evidence of her transition from a rural woman to a citizen: a pile of papers with recipes.

The distance between her native village and this place is less than 20 kilometres, but to her it felt like a new world. To match the new, more sophisticated environment, she needed to adapt her lifestyle. Her foodways were part of the process. She exchanged recipes both to learn and to prove herself worthy, equal. '[I needed] to learn, to know, to be able. To be different, skilled. Not to be so ... inane, maybe I should say. [My purpose was] to look less inane. And that is why we wrote them [the recipes] down, exchanged them, so that ... (...) To make them realise that I am also knowledgeable and skilful. And in this way I prove myself ... that I can learn from the others. To be different. Not from the *mahala*[1], but from the town.'

The words of Kalina Kechova, emotional and intense so many years later, reflect the dramatic ways in which the specific social divisions in communism were perceived by

---

[1] A neighbourhood or a hamlet, usually rural.

those who ended on the wrong side[2]. The use of the word *selyanin/selyanka* – Bulgarian for 'peasant', in communist times was exclusively pejorative (Vodenicharov 1999: 43). It epitomized the class division between peasantry and citizenry: the residents of the rural areas were often looked down on as uncultured, but also as non-achievers, incapable of coping with life. The restrictions on migration from villages to towns, which were in place through the decades of communist rule and were subjected to active trade in the networks of *vruzki*, only aggravated the problem.

To Kalina Kechova the process of recipe exchange was emancipatory. Her testimony suggests that she perceived urban food culture as superior to the rural one of her community and that she saw mastering it as an element of her adaptation and integration into the new environment.

It was partially a matter of building a new network: recipe exchange has been utilized in many contexts as a means of socialization, which forges networks of emotional and material support, and collective power among women, as suggested by the research of Counihan (2005), Theophano (2002), Pirogovskaya (2017), Lakhtikova et al. (2019). But it was also a matter of social standing: Kalina Kechova's narrative suggests that what she hoped for, was to elevate her social status. Her and many other interviews reveal that the exchange was instrumental to the women's efforts to improve their position within and outside their family circles.

The networks, created through recipe exchange, must have been a sort of safety net, which provided assistance in many difficult life situations, just as Theophano (2002) suggests. But the women refrained from using any dramatic terms: they did not speak of them as vital or as a source of help in situations of serious hardship. They saw them as a natural part of the social landscape, in which they simply merged. While some of them participated in the exchange with enthusiasm, to others it was an act of compliance with the environment rather than a deliberate choice. An instance of direct evidence for such a claim was that even women who were not interested in cooking and did not cook themselves, took part in the exchange. Sharing was just one of those things that were being practised by everyone and was the norm.

But even if sharing was a dominant discourse, which many women joined in a somewhat automated way, there is little doubt that it made them feel related to their community: extended family, colleagues, friends, role models. Moreover, the exchange was in the centre of a complex knot of ties, influences and powers, which helped women to navigate their social world and secure their place in it.

The two prevalent situations that demonstrate the social shifts experienced by women in communist Bulgaria were marrying and migrating. The first could sometimes involve a move between the muted remnants of old classes or between the layers, produced by the stratification in the communist societies. The accounts of the past imply that in both cases there were frictions between old and new foodways, and one

---

[2] The stratification was expressed in hierarchies, in which for example urban dwellers looked down on those living in rural areas; or people with closer connections to the establishment had a cynical attitude towards those who refused or were unable to secure such connections. The better educated also lacked respect for those with less education, one of the popular wisdoms being 'Study, so that you don't have to work!' Such expressions of superiority and inferiority were pronounced in the period.

way to soothe them was through recipe exchange. The second situation – migration – very often presented a transition from rural to urban, although intra-rural relocation also existed, as well as employment of people from the villages in the nearby towns.

BONDING IN THE FAMILY

The start of a new family came up in many narratives as an occurrence demanding adaptations of women's foodways. While this is, by default, a situation, in which the foodways of the new family are formed in an act of co-creation between everyone involved, the women often spoke of it as dominated by the family of the husband – just as marriage was often presented as joining the husband's family.

It seems that the challenges of a new environment, which was seen as more sophisticated in its culinary practices, motivated women more than the demands of their new roles as partners. In some stories it seemed as if the protection of personal dignity was a stronger motivation than the sense of duty. For example Bozhurka Velkova recalled her marriage at the age of twenty-one into a household where her mother-in-law was an outstanding housewife, in such terms. 'Q: Was there an element of competition? A: Oh, no, no. Not precisely competition, no, I wouldn't say that … Perhaps a tiny shade of competition. But she was an extremely sophisticated housewife and I wanted to be like her … In her house everything was shipshape and in general she was unique and I felt like an idiot. Because in fact I knew nothing …'

Emphasizing her appreciation of her mother-in-law, she spoke of her 'great desire' to learn, to become like her, to make herself fit for the new standards. Tsveta Tanovska spoke of a similar transformation, although less emotionally. 'When I joined the family of Dimitur … his aunt (…) and his mother cooked with a great deal of care… (…) Perhaps I wanted to join in the right position and this is why I so actively [collected recipes].'

To her collecting recipes and better cooking were clearly means to relate to the new social group, but also to take a better position in the internal domestic hierarchy. She has not preserved her earliest scrapbook, which might have brought further insights, but her later seven notebooks, each for a separate class of dishes: from soups to desserts, included items rare in the local context, and advanced recipes (Alcazar cake, taken from the German magazine Burda, French terrine, as some examples). Her ambition was to not simply acquire the widely shared skills, but surpass them. But seemingly not everyone was that ambitious and cases of timidity also came up in the narratives. Sofia Georgieva for example admitted that she found the new social environment after her marriage too demanding. 'I lived more with my mother-in-law than with my mother, who died early … with her I made *kozunak*.[3] But I never did this on my own. I had recipes, but simply had no courage to use them, because my mother-in-law prepared it [the kozunak] so well, and I was afraid of losing face.'

Many similar statements suggested that women responded emotionally to the contestations regarding food practices which took place in the families. To young

---

[3] A sweetish bread, similar to the brioche, which in Bulgaria is made traditionally for Easter.

brides, the women of the older generation in the households were both an authority, whose approval they aspired to, and competitors for the love of the husbands and children, who were equally targeted with the (often unconsciously) seductive instrument of home cooking.

Many narratives expectedly suggested that the women also strove to perform within standards that they thought would be up to the expectations, desires and needs of their husbands. The arrival of children in the family also had a clear impact on food practices. It often prompted women to develop a routine of daily home cooking. Just like the husbands, the children were seen as coming along with imperatives for specific diets, defined by their age: they were understood to need freshly cooked, warm, regular meals made of ingredients of a quality that was personally controlled by the women. Pleasing them and entertaining them was also a priority – as the narratives and the overwhelming number of dessert recipes in the scrapbooks, some with references to children's parties – suggest.

The use of cooking to consolidate families has been well mastered by women in many cultural frameworks, as is evident from the research of Theophano (2002) and Counihan (2005). Lakhtikova (2017: 120) described how her mother used her 'nurturing through invented rituals' to heal the family from the traumas which her stormy relation with the father caused to their children.

The Bulgarian narratives suggest that many women used this power of domestic cooking unconsciously, but there were also exceptions, in which the awareness of it was explicitly verbalized. The idea that special knowledge, special recipes or meals create bonds, sustain the sociality of the family and keep it together, was explicitly expressed by Lilia Dencheva. She stated that every woman wishes she could cook the tastiest food, because 'after all in this way you bring them [the children] home.' She recalled with satisfaction that when her daughter was small, she would not eat anyone else's food and would eat only at home. As Lupton warned in this regard, 'there is no such thing as a "pure" gift'. In her study of the symbolic and social meanings of food events, she argued that domestically prepared food is 'stamped both with the identity of the giver and that of the receiver' and that family meals produce familial identity (Lupton 1996: 48). Lilia Dencheva's words demonstrate that women, or at least some of them, were aware of this power of home cuisine and in some cases exploited it deliberately.

The power relations, encoded in home cooking, were very evident in these words and transpired from almost every one of the accounts. Considering the perceptions of the kibbutz women, who struggled for the right to feed their own children, Gvion noted that, 'unlike women in other Western societies, kibbutz women did not use their position to exercise power over their family members'. She argued that instead they supported their children developing their own tastes (Gvion 2015: 175). Gvion's observation probably reflects the perceptions of her narrators. But the increased attention to children's tastes does not change the essence of the mother–child relation over food as a power relation and the power of the mother to validate or not the child's choice or freedom of choice, where even a passive behaviour is a form of utilization. The mother is the giver, the child is the recipient, and as such is dependent on her approval and consent. Further, Gvion (2015: 182) herself argued that women embraced cooking as a means to build a relationship with their children and consolidate their family, which is in fact an application of social power.

In most recollections from communist Bulgaria, the supreme authority of the mother (or mother-in-law) on food matters seemed to be acknowledged and submitted to. The examples of Bozhurka Velkova, Tsveta Tanovska and Sofia Georgieva were already quoted. Lyubka Georgieva stated that she always thought of her mother as of a role model. Whenever her mother complimented her cooking, she said she perceived that as a tremendous recognition. 'I so much wished that at some point people would say that I have inherited her great cooking skills!'

Some narratives also suggested that once women gained authority, they could be quite protective of it. Atanaska Terzieva lived all her life with her mother, who only recently passed away. Her mother ruled in the kitchen and remained the only cook for decades after Atanaska had married and had children. Asked why she never considered taking ready-made food to ease the burden on her mother, she said: 'First of all, switching to canteen meals would have been an offence to her!' With the time passing and her mother ageing, she started taking over the cooking responsibilities. She said that she sometimes asked her mother if she approved of her dishes. 'It's edible', she'd reply!'

It seems typical of Bulgarian 20th century practices that while domestic cooking has retained a high value as family consolidator, the familial cuisine has remained a very fluid concept. Its transmission between the generations was rarely a straightforward handover of skills and recipes. The awareness of it, its degree of consolidation, varied between households and was hardly conceptualized as a privately owned know-how. Most narrators did not valorize it in abstract terms, and as a consequence did not think of preserving it beyond applying it in their own everyday lives. As a result it is a common feature that scrapbooks were only partially instrumental in conveying the knowledge of it.

Many of the interviewed spoke of having learned the routine of daily cooking from their closest relatives – in the traditional way, via demonstration and verbal explanations. As the everyday menu consisted of a relatively small range of stews, roasts, soups, starters, which were tolerant to modifications of ingredients and proportions and were frequently reproduced, the women often considered it unnecessary to write them down.

The few exceptions were related to sudden interruptions of the family routines. One such example was the case of Maya Mircheva, who lost her mother in her adolescence and, trying to recreate her cooking for herself and her father, was forced to collect recipes from aunts, who remembered her mother's cooking. Although she said she has not kept all those recipes, there are quite a lot of them in her scrapbook.

An accident also started Violeta Kaloferova's collection of familial recipes for everyday meals. When her mother-in-law, who habitually cooked for the entire family, suddenly had to spend ten months in hospital, she quickly found herself expanding her own collection. 'In the night she [Violeta Kaloferova's mother-in-law] would lay in some kind of a plaster cast bed. But in the day she could walk around and she was occupying herself with knitting. Every time we went to visit, she handed me a sheet with a recipe. Q: So this was the beginning of your scrapbook? A: This was the beginning of my cooking!'

Further into the conversation, speaking of her motivation to maintain her scrapbook, she said that she collected mainly the recipes of dishes she had tasted, or eaten at her mother's or at her mother-in-law's: 'That is what I wanted to remember. To memorize ... These were the things I wanted to write down – how to prepare them.'

Also exceptional were the statements of women, who said that with time they started thinking of handing over their cookery knowledge and recipes to their children. Only a few of them thought of their scrapbooks as a document or attributed value to their recipes that would transcend their lifetime. Asked about it, most of them agreed that their children might find this knowledge useful. However their reaction suggested that they had not seriously considered this idea.

NAVIGATING WIDER SOCIAL CIRCLES

Many researchers of cookery manuscripts mention, or even primarily focus on the use of recipe exchange as a way to socialize among women (Davis at al. 2014, Pennell 2004, Theophano 2002, Leonardi 1989, Counihan 1984). This most obvious aspect of the process within the context of 20th-century communism has been discussed quite exhaustively by Pirogovskaya (2017), who saw it as a means to create 'short- and long-term solidarities' and to perpetuate a sort of 'invisible community'.

It seems that the sharing of culinary advice has had similar social functions across a variety of cultural and temporal frameworks. What might be specific for the communist period, is that it was boosted by the practice of entertaining guests at home – as in late socialist Bulgaria the taste for social gatherings grew and to many the only opportunity to organize them remained at home. This widespread practice, little contested by the otherwise intrusive authorities, raised the value of good recipes, in particular of those that went beyond everyday cooking.

If modernization in late-19th-century Bulgaria shifted the focus from the biological to the social function of the meal in many households, it must have also created more need to diversify home cooking, i.e. to adapt the modest everyday menu, learned within the family through demonstration and aiming at satisfying hunger, to the rapidly evolving social practices, raising new requirements towards food. The early examples of recipe books from the 20th century suggest that inviting guests for a meal was practised as a social event at least in certain circles across the country. It developed in the upper social strata, which had access to education, leading to an advanced culture of personalized scrapbooks by the 1940s. Since the mid-1950s, leaving the austerity of the post-war years and of the harshest communist period, the society was quickly undergoing urbanization. People were abandoning their rural lifestyles in larger familial formats and replacing them with social contacts within their new, urban environment. The establishment of a milder version of totalitarianism and the development of a relatively comfortable lifestyle in the early 1960s renewed the quest for culinary pleasures and in late socialism affected very broad circles of society, especially in the 1970s and the 1980s.

At that time a specific communist restaurant culture had developed, in which regular meals were taken in popular public restaurants or professional clubs – a well-remembered and relatively colourful part of the cultural history of communist Bulgaria. This lifestyle though was accessible to the political establishment, the new upper classes and certain professional and intellectual groups of the urban population, which the state pampered to gain loyalty (Shkodrova 2014: 147). The average Bulgarian citizen was a lot more limited in his abilities to take his meals in restaurants. All the interviewed recalled going to a restaurant only as a special treat. Speaking of the 1960s and 1970s, only a couple of women said that their family went once a week, most said that they visited restaurants only for very special occasions, if at all.

One aspect of this was financial: the prices did not allow for everyday, or even weekly meals in restaurants. But it also transpires from the narratives that the food and the atmosphere of this part of the state nutrition network – more luxurious in theory – were rarely perceived as attractive. Public spaces were often seen as impersonal, lacking in character, unfriendly, and also as spaces of the 'collective' spirit pursued by the regime: spaces for official banquets really, rather than for private gatherings. 'Guests ... we never took them to a restaurant. Perhaps for some occasions ... very, very rarely. They [the restaurants] ... were taken over by those collective gatherings: banquets, anniversaries and so on,' said Dani Tsacheva of the communist lifestyle of the small-town middle classes. Tamara Ganeva recalled that in her town there were only two places – they were opened as restaurants, but soon turned into drinking bars and no one would use them for family-style get-togethers.

As a result 'people paid many visits to each other's houses': social entertainment in private homes was practised with frequency, varying from once a week to almost daily. These gatherings always occurred around food and naturally increased the opportunities to make use of the social powers of home cooking. The representative function of home-prepared food was noted by many of the narrators who mentioned dinners organized at home as rewarding moments when they could apply their acquired skills. Pointing at an entire menu, which she had composed for a party decades ago and still kept in her scrapbook, Elisaveta Shkodrova said: 'Home gastronomy was always appreciated during our gatherings, which was of course when you try to show off with more special things, more interesting dishes.'

Such occasions were seen as sublime opportunities for women to prove their skills and as points of formation and utilization of their influence. They contained a pronounced element of competition and strongly encouraged women to expand the limits of their culinary mastery.

Cooking skills came into the limelight not only because homes were the main, even only, places for social gatherings, but also because eating was one of the few available entertainments during such gatherings – and in general. 'In those times there was little entertainment – only one TV channel, and so on,' – recalled Elisaveta Shkodrova. Therefore, she said, a circle of friends from her and her husband's university years gathered each month. There were six families and each hosted the parties one after another. 'And the preparation was serious! You wouldn't want to lose face! For instance if my friend had made a salty cake, next time, when it is my turn, I would make some kind of a counterpoint to it – not exactly her dish, but slightly changed, developed, imagined further. And so it went on. In this way we just took care of our entertainment.'

Many women had their stories of intensive, frequent and challenging social gatherings, sometimes with a similar pattern of rotation between hosts. These examples, which according to the narratives and my own memories were common in late communist social life, were replicating practices from the luxurious life of the upper urban classes of the past. This lifestyle reproduction did not seem to have been always conscious. But those, who had somehow come to know about the entertainments of the past, spoke of the bygone practices as more sophisticated and luxurious and considered the communist-era ways inferior. '[My grandmother] would say: 'Kristinche, it's a shame! Three types of pastry and one cake is all that is left! If somebody comes to visit, we have nothing to offer!' For her it was absolutely insufficient!', recalled Kristin Razsolkova. She thought that the high housekeeping standards of the pre-communist past were no longer possible to achieve – under communism or afterwards.

Of course, this was only one aspect of the evolution and if social entertainment practices never levelled in style with those of the pre-war upper-middle class, they democratized: as a result of the modernization and despite its communist specifics they became accessible to more layers of society. Dinners with elaborate menus, involving complicated cooking or less conventional food seem to have been rarer in the provinces, but many residents of such areas recalled instead constant, and often less formal, spontaneous visits, during which women traded with home-made desserts and recipes.

KEEPING SECRETS OR SHARING?

Considering the central role of food in socializing practices, one might wonder why women did not keep their best skills and recipes secret. After all, preserving recipes within the family has not been unusual in history. Quoting one such example from the 17th century, Theophano (2002: 85–86) speculated that the wealthy owners of the concealed recipes probably valued food as entertainment and wanted to be able to surprise their guests with unexpected meals. She theorized that they might have wanted to define borders, close ranks. But the same, in particular the first, was clearly valid for the interviewed women, and yet they had not kept their recipes secret. Choosing between two possible actions: sharing or keeping this knowledge, they had made a uniform choice to share. Only one of the interviewed said that she did keep certain inventions and recipes to herself, not sharing them along with the bigger body of cookery advice, with which she participated in the recipe exchange. The subject of her proprietary feelings were her own inventions or serendipitous discoveries, which she found particularly valuable. Her reasoning to keep them to herself is eloquent of how the possession of special, different knowledge was seen as a source of power. She said that her main motivation was to be able to offer something unique to her guests: something, which no one else cooked: something 'good', which 'they would remember'. To create and keep a personal style, individuality in cooking, was clearly an important goal to her – as it was to many others of those interviewed. However no one else admitted having practised secrecy.

The social code of sharing was a strong one and as Pirogovskaya (2017: 352) also observed, refusing to share a recipe meant 'breaking an unwritten rule of communication and rejecting participation in social bonding'. It was read exactly like this, and as some narratives suggested, even the doubt of such refusal could be enough to frame negatively the possibly 'guilty' party. One of the interviewed women had a personal story, the very wording of which suggested that the family, suspected in withholding information from her, was already perceived as one of 'strangers'. 'One of my colleagues was an elderly doctor. (...) And his wife ... they were Jews. His wife had prepared [a cake] and he had brought me some of it. I tried it and I liked it very much. And I asked [to be given the recipe] ... One to two weeks passed, but I kept asking: "So where is the recipe?" ... And one day he tells me finally (...) "Come to our home and she will show you how to make it". And I went to their house, bought the products ... Went there, to be shown how to make the cake. Even then she did not give me the recipe! But when I returned home, with the prepared cake, I wrote down immediately all the steps of preparation'.

The narrative did not explicitly interpret the woman's possible reluctance to share the recipe as a protectiveness of her (different ethnic) identity, embodied in her special cooking skills and tastes. But such association was implied by the language used. The narrator articulated several times the 'otherness' of the woman, her different age, ethnicity and class: very old (versus her own youth then, which the interviewee mentioned); Jewish (versus Bulgarian); very refined (versus her own rural origin, and hard-working profile). The recipe is seen as part of clandestine family knowledge with somewhat mystical origins, buried in the unclear historical path of another ethnic group – 'it's said to be an old Jewish recipe', said the interviewee about it, concluding her account of the episode with the statement that the cake became the most favourite of all her family – a status, which it retains until the present day.

It seems that in general the interviewed women associated keeping recipes secret with a desire for supremacy. While outstanding cooking skills were appreciated, the attempts at claiming property rights on them were not seen as fair play. Ivanka Atipova for instance said: 'This is egoistic ... I knew such people. In fact there were people, who would omit certain ingredients deliberately, so that ... So as to be the only ones and to ... To be able to prepare this or that cake better than anyone else.' Tsveta Tanovska associated the described behaviour with a striving for 'uniqueness'. The interpretation of Dani Tsacheva was that those people who would always omit ingredients, when dictating recipes, were those 'who tend to harm others', and added, 'who does not want the others to cook a certain dish better than them'.

In fact most women acknowledged that the desire to cook better, to stand out, to shine with culinary skills was widespread in their circles. According to them cooking was one of the main fields where the desire for self-expression had found an outlet in those times. The narrators offered numerous illustrations of the mild competition taking place in this domain. One of them explained that in cooking for guests 'There was always a competition (...) To shine a little with something ... (...) that the others haven't made ... There was some kind of vanity ...' But in most narratives the competition was described as a friendly, mild ethos of benevolent rivalry, whose side effect was that everyone ate better.

Sharing did not exactly mean giving up on exploiting the social power of recipes. One possible reason given by most for not keeping them secret was that there was not much point in it. Working with a limited number of ingredients and technologies, women did not create extraordinary, complex dishes, and a housewife with experience was able to easily reproduce what she tried. The narratives contain several recollections confirming such abilities. This renders the situation quite different from the one among the seventeenth-century English nobility, where cooks prepared food, and not the masters, whose recipe collections 'signalled wealth, lineage and literacy' (Theophano 2002: 86).

Another possible reason was that recipes, substantially different from the bulk of circulating ones, were rare. Although many women added what they considered improvements or adjustments according to their and their family's tastes, their versions mostly differed insignificantly from each other.

There was also a third reason, which transpires from the interviews: that the exchange of recipes in a way was also an authority-exercising game. To be asked for a recipe to some extent already represented a recognition of your cooking expertise, acknowledgement of your authority. It seems that having unique skills was seen as less valuable than being able to influence the common discourse – which the women did via sharing their recipes. They repeatedly spoke of the satisfaction obtained in this process of exchange, of the acknowledgement, which they felt, should their advice be followed. Pepa Angelova for instance recalled that 'people were proud, that what they prepared was liked and eagerly exchanged', and that to be asked for a recipe was 'a recognition'. 'It is a matter of honour to a woman to be asked for a recipe. This makes her feel appreciated,' explained Tamara Ganeva. Pirogovskaya made a similar argument regarding the Soviet scrapbooks she studied (Pirogovskaya 2017: 345).

Another example of evidence that recipes were considered instrumental to social advance was the previously quoted case (see p.85), when an unsolicited offering of them was interpreted as an attempt to improve one's position in the workplace.

The situation of a person dictating and all her friends/colleagues hastily writing down is a momentary situation of subordination. And many women found these moments innocently (or less innocently?) rewarding. Elisaveta Shkodrova thought that sharing a recipe made a woman come across as a good housewife and also as a creative person, which was always appreciated.

Women also liked to see themselves as a source of commonly useful, important knowledge, in community service. Elena Salmadzhiyska said that when her recipes were copied again and again, on the copy machine in the village school, and then by hand, this made her happy, made her feel like a bearer of knowledge, important to her social group. 'The old women, who were giving me their recipes, were telling us that we needed to write them down, because this is how they will be transferred to the next generations and not forgotten. Probably they were also pleased. So am I, when I am asked for a recipe and advice'. If scrapbooks were not seen as a contribution to the knowledge of the following generations, the recipe exchange was.

In spite of the ingrained idea of serving social, even public interest, an element of power contest remained in the background. Neuhaus (2003: 95) argued that 'recipes are by their very nature prescriptive: they demand a certain set of actions, performed in a certain sequence, to produce a certain product'. Political scientist Finn (2011), who studied the intersection between food and politics, claimed even more radically that when marketed as perfect, recipes transform their intrinsic authority into autocracy and even tyranny. Direct aggressive assertiveness did not transpire from the recorded accounts, but a number of them suggested that the women believed in the supremacy of their own version of the recipe. One of them said: 'I made this recipe one way, other people made it differently ... But I like my version best ...'. She added that she found it nice when people approved of the changes she had made, i.e. her own contribution to the recipe.

Jack Goody (1977: 136) argued that written recipes with their 'very existence change the course and nature of teaching ... for the recipe now exists independently of the teacher, it has become depersonalised and acquired a more general, universal quality'. The exchanged recipes though, even if written, behaved differently – unlike the recipes, which circulated via cookbooks, press or other media in multiple copies, they never entirely 'depersonalised'. An exchanged recipe led an existence in proximity and relation to its 'author'. It remained associated with the trusted person, who shared it, and it could be at any time verified with her. No woman took credit for it in the sense that none claimed authorship. But in a way also each woman did take credit as the best authority to explain the recipe to the person she gave it to – the recipe just tended to change its 'authors'.

The recognition, obtained via exchange of recipes, often transcended women's skills in preparing one particular dish, one type of dish, or the women's cooking knowledge in general. It was frequently assigned to her general talents in running a household. Kristin Razsolkova highlighted this relation, saying that to be asked for a recipe not only indicated the good reputation of the giver, but in most cases positioned her as 'as a person well capable of making up a home (...) keeping the spirit of domesticity'.

Thus, considering the social advantages of sharing, it becomes less surprising that in the competitive arena of home cooking women preferred sharing: it made more sense and was more socially rewarding. It was the exchange, which made possible the building and practice of authority and influence within a mutually beneficial communication.

The research interviews leave little doubt that women used recipes for social advancement. Essentially, it was an act of producing and making use of the social capital, which, as Bourdieu (2003: 69) observed, was grounded in social groups, united by lasting and useful connections. But, however clear, the power contestation in the exchange and use of recipes remained an undercurrent in the narratives. To most women it was even an intolerable thought. They vehemently denied any involvement of authority issues.

Most women conceptualized the process mostly as a realization of a network for support, a set of connections, which in a way resembled an extended family, involving shared responsibilities and shared affection. The mutual support of which Theophano (2002) and Pirogovskaya (2017) wrote, was interpreted as a casual, entirely natural part of their existence. They spoke of the exchange as 'a way to communicate', 'to help each other', or as 'a sort of favour', an expression of 'people's goodness'. Some remembered its communality as contrasting with the individualistic lifestyle of present times. 'It was a form of communication, which I think is (...) fading away[4],' noted Kristin Razsolkova.

---

[4] Most of the narrators said they stopped collecting recipes in the 1990s. They explained this by family circumstances (the children having left home), loss of interest in cooking, and with the availability of many alternative sources.

In a way, it was a form of privately-organized collectiveness, alternative to the impersonal collectivism propagated by the ideology. At times seen in binomial opposition to the 'formal', it also sometimes merged with it and inspirited, domesticated and humanized it. Some of the interviewed gave emotional accounts of the spontaneity and warmth of the relations in the neighbourhood communities at the time. They described neighbours coming over in their slippers and dressing gowns, bringing over small plates of treats at any time, without invitations or warnings, just announcing their arrival with a ring on the doorbell and entering, without waiting for someone to open the door for them. 'Look what I made! ... Try it!' – and you can't wait to prepare it too ... (...) Yes, yes, it was fantastic!' exclaimed Pepa Mutafchieva, reminiscing over her childhood in the town of Svishtov. It is arguable if the parents always perceived these visits as happily as the children – I have clear recollections of the pursed lips of my own mother on similar occasions. But from the distance of time some women seemed to miss the neighbourhood conviviality under communism. Pepa Mutafchieva's nostalgic yearning was also offset by her disappointment with the increasingly individualistic life, which she experienced in Plovdiv, where she now lives: 'Now we just close our door.'

In urbanizing and modernizing communist Bulgaria, the described intimacy between neighbours, colleagues and friends was the urban replacement of the lost life within a broader family, practised previously in rural environments. Even if the official appeal to live in the spirit of a communist collective was generally ignored, the ethos of the period was one of collective living, quite distant from the idea of 'closing ranks' among 17th-century English nobility. The lifestyle of the society, which the communist regime produced, was one in which social groups share work and pleasure. It is possible that it had materialized as a result of the confluence of the communist ideology with evolving pre-modern patterns of social relations, in which people were exchanging culinary knowledge during related communal occupations. In fact remnants of the old practices of communal meals based around the meat from a large animal that had been slaughtered, which Rozin (2006: 36) noted to have been 'a major factor promoting food sharing/social eating', endured in Bulgaria. Elena Salmadzhiyska referred twice to such practices in different periods of her life. In the 1970s, when Bansko – now a somewhat overdeveloped skiing resort, was still a sleepy little place – she participated in social gatherings, which lasted for several days. Families came together to help each other with cattle slaughtering and with the preservation of the meat, consuming part of it on the spot. Just as Knezy (2003: 138) observed that large festive meals were of great importance in the transmission of cookery skills and innovations, these were gatherings where culinary knowledge was extensively exchanged: via observation and dictation. At her place of residence since the 1980s (a small southern village with a mild climate, Mikrevo), Salmadzhiyska was involved in another ritual of communal cooking. In her community women came together to roll out *yufka*: filo sheets, which are baked, dried and preserved to use through the year. In her present-day life this *yufka*-making is not essential, as the product is widely available in the stores. According to her account though the practice persists as an entertainment.

The narratives contained many references to different forms of joint cooking rituals: the preparation of home preserves, which often involved the entire community, or cooking vast quantities of food for important community events. Also on an individual level food was often prepared in large quantities with the sole purpose of being shared out. All the explanations implied a circular relationship, in which food necessities prompted the forging of social connections, for the maintenance of which food was used.

In many cases the exchange built a network, in which the social circles fed and validated the foodways of the individual women, while at the same time each woman participated in the formation of the common discourse of the group. On many levels it worked as a system, the elements of which interacted, and in the process of their interaction transformed each other.

AN EXCHANGE OF EXTREME FLUIDITY

One of the typical features of scrapbooks – the attribution of many recipes to the persons from whom they were obtained – has brought about the understanding that these documents thus reveal 'the number and prominence of one's kin and friends, demonstrating the breadth of a social network and one's standing in it' (Theophano 2002: 23–24). Communist-era scrapbooks also offered a map of the social contacts of their authors. But as Pirogovskaya (2017) suggested, also short-term, temporary alliances resulted in recipe exchange. Examples already quoted here further reveal that sometimes these connections were even unwanted, or disliked. This considered, could cookery scrapbooks still be a trustworthy source of women's social relations, and what do they tell us about them?

Some of the attributions positively expressed affection: the interviewed women spoke of emotional bonds to relatives prompting the notation of certain recipes. They also said that their culinary records developed emotional value with time. Tamara Ganeva stated that instead of copying the recipes which she received from friends into her book, she sometimes preferred to paste in the bits of paper: she thought that the handwriting conveys 'certain energy, something of the person'. Two other women stated that they wrote the attributions as a memory of the person, who gave them recipes. One gave the example that when she sees the name of her friend Albena next to the recipe for *banitsa*, 'immediately the sight, the taste, the aroma come to my mind! (...) This is no longer just a *banitsa*, or the *banitsa* of, say, Tsetska [the name of another friend]. These are different classes of *banitsa*!'

Many more narratives focused on the practical importance of the attributions, which were helpful to instantly recall a taste, a look, possibly even the recipe. The 'name tags' were also useful to distinguish between more variants of the same dish in the collection, or, for instance, many cakes with similar ingredients. Both cases were aiming at helping the navigation through the document. As Pirogovskaya (2017: 346) noted, the combination of recipe name and person name was the perfect 'trigger of cultural mnemonics', which women were able to recall decades after writing down the recipe. The narratives clearly suggested that the emotional often merged with the utilitarian in the scrapbooks, a perfectly customizable blend of (optional) sentimentality and convenience.

Another aspect of the extreme contextual and substantial fluidity of scrapbooks was the account in some of the interviews of starkly contrasting meanings, which recipe exchange gained within women's relations with their social groups. One of the women said that she traded culinary advice with her female colleagues, because that was about the only thing that she could find in common with them. 'They didn't read that many books. They were too busy raising children, running households, waiting in lines ...' While the immaterial culture, which appealed to her, seemed of no interest to her female colleagues, cooking was a topic of collective relevance. It was the biggest common denominator between her and her social group at work.

This statement contrasted with another narrative, which described the exchange of recipes as elevated into a particularly inspired, intellectual game. To some social circles imaginative cooking was an identity marker, a kind of unspoken argument with the meta-discourse that cooking is an occupation below the level of an intellectual. There, the status of cooking – as long as it was creative, exquisite, in one or another way outstanding – was elevated to entertainment, to a game and a spectacle, and it was more a gourmand attitude. 'A certain type of elite always existed, a limited society (...) People with greater interest in culture ... (...) They weren't just gluttonous, they participated in the cultural life of the town, a little bohemian most of them. (...) They were particularly appreciative of good food and good drink. And we were cooking a lot, a lot!'

These examples illustrated the ability of food and food practices to mediate many types of social communication and, moreover, to carry contrasting meanings. They show how flexibly women exploited the possibilities that food practices gave them on a social level.

In summary, discussed as a social practice, the recipe exchange in communist Bulgaria was an instrument to accumulate and exploit social capital (Bourdieu, 2003). The exchange allowed women to join a social group in and outside family, to secure a better place in social hierarchies, adapt to new cultural environments and social requirements. It facilitated their connection with their groups and, in defining their borders, confirming Fischler's argument of food being used to demarcate one's 'own group' (Fischler 1988: 280).

The narratives clearly indicated that exchanging culinary knowledge was also a process of levelling and updating, of integration of commonalities in the individual cuisine, while at the same time influencing the group discourses, the impact on which was perceived as power. The scrapbooks offer an excellent illustration of the dynamics of the negotiation between the individual and the social group and her agency in defining the group. The permanent exchange must have also meant permanent pressure to perform, and a constant encouragement of the competition between home cooks.

The widespread practice of sharing was popular on the one hand because it imitated, exploited and reinforced the models of sharing that were still current and which sprang from the traditional communal way of life . On the other hand, sharing recipes delivered more rewarding experiences, compared to the alternative option of maintaining exclusive rights over a piece of culinary information. The confluence of the two secured the very pronounced role of recipe exchange in the social life of women in late-communist Bulgaria.

The communication via recipe exchange and the social role of home cooking outside the family was further boosted towards excess by some specifics of the communist reality. The growing interest in social entertainment developed within a context where sufficient and appropriate public venues were lacking. As the narratives suggested, these circumstances pushed many women to entertain guests at home and private spaces became a particularly important arena of socializing. These circumstances called for mastery of the culinary arts beyond everyday food, and they created pressure to sustain and develop festive domestic cooking.

Thus recipe exchange was clearly instrumental to what Bateson called a 'sociological unity': 'the behaviour of the individuals, as oriented toward the integration and disintegration of the major unit, the Group as a whole' (Bateson 1987: 78). It was an important way of bonding, of the realization of belonging, which on the one hand was an alternative to the collectivism propagated by the communist ideology. While the communism advocated communal as an alternative to private, the form of sociality practised through the recipe exchange, in many ways reinstated the value of the individual. The interviewed women interpreted it as enabling them to personalize their cooking, gain private control over it.

This collectivist rationale behind the recipe exchange differed from, and in some cases was even seen as opposed to, the collectivism of communist ideology. It was less abstract, more negotiable, and more under the control of the practising individuals.

ENTERTAINING, INDULGING AND CREATING THE SELF

My mother reads poetry

(...) *Wash the apples, peel*
and remove the seeds, grate
in large strips, mix
with the sugar, the ground walnuts
and the cinnamon.
Take a pastry sheet,
grease it
and cover it with another sheet.
Spread some of the apple mix
over them and roll
them together. Repeat
with the other pastry sheets.
Grease them and bake
over medium heat, until
the top crust is red,
and the bottom pink.

When you bake it, it's a strudel,
but for now it's still a poem.

Georgi Gospodinov
Translated by Maria Vassileva

The daughter remembers the mother like this: galvanized, flying around the kitchen. As if on roller stakes, but barefoot. 'Always barefoot! ... And incessantly doing something! Non-stop!' The weekend baking has been prepared for days: new recipes were collected, the pantry was replenished and the child can't wait from excitement. And the mother? The mother is the person who in 1984 cooked 20 days in a row to prepare for her daughter's graduation day. The person, who, having fallen for the charms of certain tiny cookies, sent her husband to the blacksmith to order an iron cast and then day after day baked with it on a half-working communist iron plate, only to spend more days adding filling: to hundreds of cookies, because she thought they needed to be shared. Industrious and creative, she lived in a baking frenzy. To preserve her frequently overflowing produce and due to the lack of air-tight containers, she invented a new packaging technique: she soaked newspapers in water, wrung them out and sealed their ends over the dishes of pastries with an iron. This is how the daughter, Pepa Mutafchieva, remembers her late mother Kinche Angelova: 'It was so like a party to me!' Would the mother confirm her story?

The narratives revealed the many ways, in which women loved to cook – or at least had a love-hate relation with cooking. The memories of sweet moments of triumph sometimes interlaced with bitter recollections of work that was too much, too difficult, too unfairly shared. But there was always an element of passion. It was even more pronounced in the music of the narratives: speaking of cooking experiences, the words suddenly became brighter, the voices coloured with *joie de vivre*, the rhythm of the speech quickened and the mind, all at once, delivered minute details, as if electrified by the opportunity to take a walk down memory lane.

But what was remembered with joy? Was it the work, that was sensually enjoyable or entertaining, or was it the gratification of pleasing a child, or a friend? Was it the happiness of the palate afterwards, or the satisfaction of meeting or surpassing your own or others' expectations? Or was it the sudden realization that back then you were making your own history? Or was it, banally, the distance in time that sweetened the reminiscences, transforming them in daydreaming?

The difficulty in telling which it is lies not in the 'defects' of memory: for when speaking of a present moment, of our motivation to perform one or another of our daily routines, our feelings about it seem just as entangled. Still some strands stand out, identified in negotiation with circumstances and social discourses, or expressed unconsciously in our speech, an upsurge of feelings in our bodies.

Opinion polls may not be perfect for capturing people's passions, but they are good in quantifying the popularity of discourses. According to the representative poll conducted for this research, the overwhelming majority of women recalled cooking in the period of communism with pleasure. Around 76 per cent of the female participants in the survey remember having cooked eagerly, 16 per cent recall they did it more out of obligation and 5 per cent said they did not cook. This fact alone suggests that the kitchen is remembered by most women as a space where they felt content. Besides, as scrapbooks convincingly show, they were not only arenas of chores, but also of entertainment. As Giard (De Certeau et al. 1996: 151) observed in the kitchens of France, cooking, with its high degree of ritualisation' and 'strong affective investment', is 'for many women of all ages a place of happiness, pleasure, and discovery.'

Scrapbooks in communist Bulgaria were instrumental to the pleasures of cooking by default – even though to claim that they were meant by their creators to be a tool for 'entertainment cooking' would be an exaggeration. Many women started their collections as beginners in the kitchen and they perceived their recipes as essential to their basic household obligations. But as the mechanics of recipe collection followed the pattern 'someone cooked at home, brought it to share, I liked it and asked for the recipe' with the regularity of a technical protocol, they led naturally to the prevalence

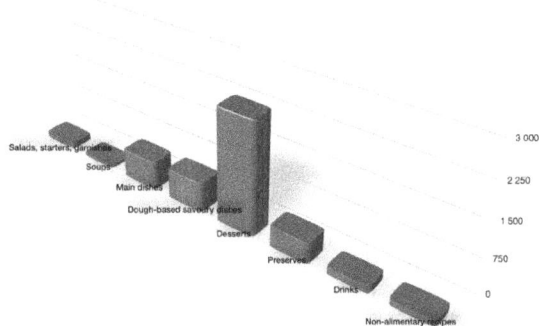

Figure 12 *Proportion of recipes for the main categories of dishes in the collections examined for this research.*

of recipes for treats and snacks: salty or sweet food, created most of all to entertain the palate.

The structure of the scrapbooks manifests their relation to women's free time and to their and their families' entertainment, rather than to the routine of daily life. On average, recipes for desserts or for dough-based dishes, which were associated with homely comfort and festivity, made up 66 per cent in the narrators' scrapbooks. In eight of the scrapbooks they made above 70 per cent and in two of them they reached 85 per cent.

These proportions conform to those observed in other cultures and periods. Writing on community-created cookbooks in the United States in the 1930s, Sharpless (2016: 199) noted that 'many cookbooks contain a plethora of recipes for sweets'. She rightfully pointed out that the reason for this was the greater complexity of recipes for cakes, and the importance of their exact proportions – a reasoning, which was confirmed by the interviewees in Bulgaria. But in the case of communist Bulgaria the pattern of trading recipes also played a very important role. As the exchange very often took place in the workplace, the recipes were limited to dishes which were easy to bring and share. It is also possible that there was a certain cultural predisposition – an argument which Sharpless dismissed regarding American cooks. Desserts were an affordable small luxury in communism, and one of the few that were under the control of most women. The sweet, argued Bulgarian philosopher Raycho Pozharliev (2014: 312), a permanent quality of the dessert in Bulgaria, is seen 'not as a necessity, but as an exception, a kind of whim.' In a society in which there was little access to luxury, desserts were one of the few accessible indulgences. Their preparation and consumption was also seen as comforting – just as in many other societies – and the interviews suggested that the women had a well-established habit of turning to it as a source of family comfort.

In any case special-occasion dishes were meant to add variety and to give pleasure – generally the more hedonistic part of the family cuisine made up the bulk of the collected recipes. Differently from the routine set of meals, the recipes in the scrapbooks were not cooked on a daily basis and were much more varied. They were often recipes of more complicated dishes or of pastry, with longer lists of ingredients and stricter requirements of proportions, which made them more difficult to memorize. The practice of exchange, the social code of it, turned scrapbooks into kind of entertainment manuals, guides through the pleasures of food, and a family record of enjoyable experiences. They were, to use the words of Supski (2013: 14), recipes, 'associated with happy times'.

But this perfunctory feature is only one of the ways in which scrapbooks manifested themselves as instruments of positive emotions and entertainment. They were a source for and a reflection of the desire to entertain, of the enjoyment gained from creating and of the satisfaction from forging personal identities. They were the discrete record of how the sensual pleasures of eating, enjoying tastes, met the satisfaction from different types of social (self-) validation.

IMPROVISING VERSUS COMPLYING

Humans experience constant tension between their desire to explore new foods and the distrust which they feel for them, argued Fischler (1988: 278). This 'Omnivore's Paradox', as he called it, is often used in food studies to explain behavioural contradictions when it comes to food choices and practices. This 'oscillation between the poles of neophobia and neophilia', of which Fischler wrote, could be found in people's varying approaches to recipes. Improvising on the basis of a recipe, or strictly complying with it are two substantially different approaches, which commonly coexist in the individual's foodways. Selecting between them is usually a matter of purpose and circumstances: preferences of the person who will consume the food, the cook's own mood and taste, diets, ingredients, equipment, to name just a few. Still, as this research suggests, usually the individual chooses one of them to identify himself with.

In this self-definition the interviewed women could be divided into three groups: nine of them chose to describe themselves as eager improvisers, nine said they always complied with a recipe and one claimed that she practised both. This self-evaluation though was not confirmed by the narratives. Four of the women who said they were strict compilers, described later how they amended, or even invented recipes. All the women said that they didn't know anyone who invented recipes, as complying with the advice was an overwhelmingly dominating practice. Seven of them though turned out to have created dishes themselves.

Even when following recipes, the narratives suggested that it was a realization of a choice, an active attitude, rather than a 'blind obedience', of which Finn (2011: 516) wrote, investigating the 'tyranny' of the recipe. He related this attitude to an 'inability to reflect and examine what constitutes the good life'. But the passion with which women spoke of acquiring cooking skills, and their motivation – the desire to recreate a known and loved taste, – seemed to be just as much a quest for the good life, as for those, who preferred to improvise. It seemed as if their definition of 'good life' was simply different. To several of the 'strict compliers' it consisted in reconstructing familial tastes.

The appreciation of familiar cuisines alone though could not be held accountable for the attitude of compliance, for it was shared also by some, who expressed a liking for improvisation. What looked like more 'conservative' behaviour might have been boosted by the chronic market shortages, which made the exact following of many recipes challenging and therefore desirable.

In any case, while abundance, new products and free time are often associated with creativity in the kitchen, the narratives illustrate the opposite phenomenon of 'famine gastronomy' (Capatti 1989, Montanari 1994, Ferguson 2005). They suggest that the general spirit of unification and greyness, of deficits and pressure for the collective, with which communism is remembered, also provided a strong impetus for women to improvise, alter and seek variations in food. The lack of inspiring cookbooks and the deficits forced the women to be extra ingenious to put together a meal, which both feeds and entertains the palate.

Speaking of enslaved Puertorriqueñas, given nothing to eat by their masters but plantains, and using collective skills and ingenuity to transform them into delicious meals for their families, Ore (2011) interpreted their behaviour as 'acts of resistance', commonly manifested under systems of oppression. While the use of the term 'resistance' might be overstating the meanings invested by slave cooks in preparation of meals, the example certainly illustrates well the 'creativity of poverty' – in any case a poverty much milder in late communist Bulgaria than among the slaves of Puerto Rico.

A closer look at the narratives offers abundant evidence of how the process of innovation worked, with both the deficit of ingredients and of information motivating creativity. Tamara Ganeva for instance said: 'whenever I had a certain product, which I wanted to prepare but I didn't feel like cooking any of the dishes for which I had recipes, or if, say, I lacked a certain ingredient ... So I improvised with what I had. My mother very much enjoyed creating recipes in this manner. While my aunt in Sofia loved to improvise in pastry-making.'

Saying that she changed recipes for lack of certain ingredients, Elisaveta Shkodrova pointed out that this practice brought her only a few failures, but many unexpected successes. She recalled how once, having barely half of the necessary quantity of filo pastry, she decided to add cake dough to the planned sweet *banitsa*. This resulted in a kind of a hybrid dessert – an invention, matching in spirit the contemporary croissant-donut symbiosis *cronut*. This recipe, which delighted her sons, husband and guests, is written in her scrapbook and to her it is not just cookery instruction, but an (unwritten, inexplicit) memory of her little triumph, her moment of happiness and self-satisfaction. This example gives an insight into the private way, inaccessible to strangers, in which scrapbooks are read by their owners.

The absence of ingredients, which prompted improvisation and adaptation of recipes, is certainly a process which occurs in every household around the world, and it was receiving an additional boost from the regular deficits of a broad range of products. The shadow of poverty is also distinguishable in this sort of indigenousness, as a previously quoted example of soup made with pork legs suggested (see p.127).

Yet the narratives and the scrapbooks show that the creation of recipes was, most often and above all, not work in need, but a pursuit of pleasure in cooking. Accounting for their practices of innovation, the interviewed women mostly referred to their occupations during weekends and holidays, in particular to pastry-making, and they spoke of it as of entertainment. Recalling her improvisational activities, Ivanka Atipova described how she invented a chessboard-styled dessert, discovering only later that it already existed. 'In half of the dough I added cocoa powder, then rolled out one white and one brown sheet of dough, cut stripes and made the cookies in a way that when you cut the dough, they are like a chessboard, it was very interesting! I have discovered it myself!' Further, she spoke at several instances of the pleasures of improvisation.

Many narratives included such recollections of pleasurable experiments – intended, or serendipitous. In comparison, memories of struggling with daily cooking came up rarely. Nedyalka Malcheva for instance told of her sudden improvisation over a dish well-known from her childhood, when she, already an experienced housewife, saw a pitcher of milk on her table and spontaneously decided to use it. The dish, which she then improvised, became one of the favourites of her family. She also recalled sitting in front of the stove and roasting peppers, when suddenly she got an idea how to prepare them into a completely new dish.

Dobrinka Boeva also remembered how she improvised to prepare food to the taste of a distinguished visitor, producing a dish that was remarkable in her and her guest's opinion. The details that she remembered, and the mouth-watering language which she used to tell the story, suggested she found the experience genuinely memorable: the chicken nuggets were fried 'gently', the pasta was in 'such little figurines, which I cooked nicely', then came 'a touch' of butter ... 'And it turned out gorgeous!'

Experimenting with an ingredient available in the house, was at least as frequent a reason for innovation as a lack of one – several times the need to use some foodstuffs, or curiosity as to how they would combine was mentioned as leading to experiments and discoveries. The women also associated their tendency to improvise with their confidence in their cooking skills. 'I always assume that I can improve a recipe, instead of just copying it,' repeated one of them, an observation that many made.

Curiosity often blended with self-entertainment. According to Kristin Razsolkova, women were curious about cooking skills not 'as a matter of social code', but because they 'sincerely liked' to discover 'another interesting and nice thing' to prepare. The conversations offered many indications that creativity in the kitchen was experienced as a joy. The weekend baking was an entertainment, to which Pepa Mutafchieva and her mother seem to have been whole-heartedly dedicated: 'I loved it so much!', she exclaimed. Many women used repeatedly the word 'interesting' to describe their activities and repudiated my suggestions that the work must have been overwhelming. 'No, never, on the contrary: I found it interesting to prepare new things', said Ivanka Atipova. Mara Tseneva, who was a professional cook, stated that home cooking was to her a ... hobby. 'It is indeed my profession, but I did like to cook. And I still do.'

Cultural food studies have repeatedly observed the co-existence in domestic food practices of toil and pleasure (Warde and Martens 2000: 221; Short 2006: 12). As Julier (2004: 19) argued, the divide between the two is not clear cut in everyday experiences. It is questionable if this entanglement of emotions is possible to defragment to some sort of basic elements, as it seems that they are two sides of the same thing and function like communicating vessels. But if on a discursive level the fluidity seems to be innate, it might be possible to refine the grain of further investigations in food practices: by distinguishing between everyday cooking and festive cooking. Many arguments, related to the differences in investments and expected rewards can be put forward: in any cultural framework, people spend on festive and leisure cooking more efforts, planning, time and money. They dedicate to it more creativity, and better or more special ingredients. Against this investment, excessive in comparison to everyday cooking, they hope also to obtain greater rewards, reaching a greater circle of people and creating a more lasting social effect. This research was not done with the idea of explicitly distinguishing between everyday and festive cooking – in fact, this idea derives from it. But it seems as if a significant part of the memories, and in particular those which had to do with the pleasures of creativity, were mostly related to festive and leisure cooking – not least because this is what the women's scrapbooks mostly reflected.

The accounts of cooking experiments were made in emotional and sensual language, saturated with reminiscences of tastes and aromas. Cooking was called an 'itch', giving pleasure, contentment and satisfaction; adding colour and character; and giving way to fantasy and imagination. Kristin Razsolkova compared the process to a 'creative lab', which produced 'thousands of variations'. 'It is simply incredible!' she exclaimed. 'The differences could be tiny – there could be just a pinch of anise added, or the butter replaced, but there is always something changed ...'. An insight into this process could be gained through a closer look at the variations in the recipe for *Agnesi* – a very popular dessert in the '70s. The recipe is featured in thirteen of the scrapbooks, sometimes in more than one version, and in *Zhenata dnes*. These sources reveal that however minor the deviations of each variant were, they concerned practically every aspect of the cooking instructions: from proportions of the main ingredients to aromas and decoration. While exchanging the recipe, the women have adapted it on each level at least a little, so that its existence has become as if constantly flickering its 'body and wings'.

From the narrations it transpired that many women tended to underestimate their own creative input. Sometimes they denied having made any additions or inventions, very soon accounting for precisely such additions or inventions. They obviously enjoyed their cooking and baking, but did not think highly of it, or did not conceptualize it as very valuable outside of their household. Perhaps the main reason was that they saw their additions as adaptations to their own taste, which made their value to others questionable. The other explanation could have been the view of this culinary knowledge as 'creative commons', as shared – the same explanation as that which prevented them from keeping recipes for themselves. At most they thought of it as good advice in cooking, which they could offer to friends and relatives, and this is how they, in a way, fed back into the network of the recipe exchange, which in its turn was feeding them.

This mechanism of culinary knowledge exchange, in which recipes were obtained mostly orally, to be written down, and again passed on orally, offered freedom in more than one ways. On the one hand it was the type of freedom that a written recipe gives to a scientist, 'where exact measures may be a prelude to discovery and invention' (Goody 1977: 140). On the other hand, the sort of recipe exchange, which left so much space for customization to the recipient, neutralized what Finn (2011) thought to be the dictatorship of 'perfect' recipes – their demand for blind obedience. The women found the recipe they had collected themselves more liberating than constraining.

In fact the interviewed women seemed to have found one of the greatest merits of home cooking to be precisely the **freedom** it gave them. This freedom had more than one face. It was interpreted, as already mentioned, as liberation from the outside world, as **privacy and safety.** The perception of the kitchen as a space, exempt from regulations, or at least from control – a space if not of ideological, then of practical autonomy – transpired repeatedly in the scrapbooks and the narratives.

The safety, which women experienced in relation to their private kitchens and recipe collections, is well illustrated by the use of scrapbooks as hideouts for political satire and political defiance in the already quoted examples. The domain of domestic food was a safe space of freedom, allowing for alternative thinking. It is not unusual in history that cookbooks become to women 'more than a place to record recipes (…) also sites to discuss political issues' (Inness 2006). This was also valid for communist Bulgaria in many ways. Tamara Ganeva's instinct to hide the evidence of her political dissent was not unique: political satire often ended up in the scrapbooks, as this and Nenov's research (2013) suggest. The pages of Kristin Razsolkova's cookbook, for example, preserved a satirical version of a popular song from the 1970s, addressing a socialist prime minister in the early 1990s.

> 'Plenums, congresses, nightlife,
> elections after elections go by in this tone,
> give up, comrade, your state post,
> for all that is left of us is skin and bones.'

The women spoke of the domain of food as their own, as opposed to the foreign, outside world. They perceived the recipes, exchanged within the social circles, as

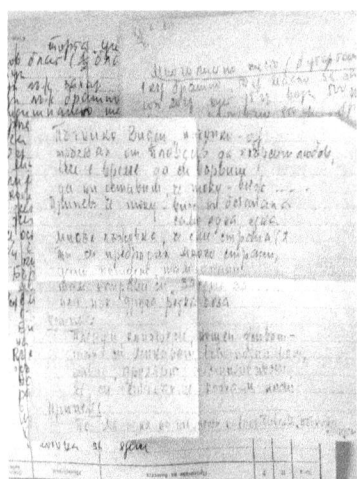

Figure 13 *A page of political satire, kept between the pages of Kristin Razsolkova's scrapbook (left) and pages from Tamara Ganeva's cookbook with the manifesto of the dissident Ecoglasnost (right). The rest of the pages were torn out under circumstances which Tamara Ganeva does not remember.*

personalized, personal possessions, i.e. their 'own', and in this sense opposite to the cookbooks, which were seen as 'somehow from outside'. Cooking gave them space for 'something different'.

THE SATISFACTION OF BUILDING IDENTITY

They had different names for their shared drive to search 'for something different, something better,' as Cathy Ivanova puts it. She called it a 'need', Dani Tsacheva named it 'a striving', Ivanka Atipova defined it as an 'interest', Kalina Kechova called it 'an opportunity'. They often spoke of it as of a search for 'variation' – not from the point of view of nutrients, but of tastes and for something not yet savoured, which was assumed to give pleasure (Lilia Dencheva).

The cookbooks of the state publishing houses were not instrumental in this drive towards cooking 'something different', except that they served as a baseline to set up the 'matrix', as Kristin Razsolkova named it. A few mentioned them as a source of inspiration and most described them as 'standard', 'traditional', 'mainstream' and 'quite in the tradition of canteen food', also 'vexingly boring'. Lilia Dencheva (who owned *The Housewife's Book*, Cholcheva and Ruseva eds, 1956) emotionally exclaimed: 'and besides they were ... somehow... why, so common! (...) Very common! Boringly common!'

As Fischler argued, the inclination for 'something different' is rooted in human biological nature (Fischler, 1988: 278). But it also has a cultural side to it and it is strongly related to the perception of identity. To narrators, to be different was to seek visibility and a clearer profile in their social group, to give enjoyment, but also to offer it in a way in which no one else does, which would create lasting memories (and eventually probably lasting feelings of affection, the pursuit of which remained unspoken). A good example how the connection was made is offered in the narrative of Bozhurka Velkova. 'In times of holidays I prepare several things [dishes], which are mine ... I mean, with which I am well familiar, and which are favourites of mine and of which a few people know: my circle of people, who visit us often ... Somebody is coming, "will you make this?" – "yes" – and I make it... Right, several things, not so many, but things that you can't find elsewhere, that not everyone makes ...'

The narratives suggest that to be different, in times when both the choice of consumer goods is limited and uniformity is imposed by ideology restrictions, was thought to be difficult. For this reason it was particularly valued. Having only their own free time at their disposal and under their private control, women often found the key to wellbeing, leisure and entertainment lay all in their own hard work. Investing excessive (according to the narrators' current estimation) amounts of time, energy and thought in celebrations and other events in their social circles was a usual practice – some important examples have already been quoted. Lyubka Georgieva said that she gave a month of her life to make the birthday of her daughter 'different'.

Memorable signature dishes seem to have given the satisfaction of uniqueness, of a particular profile, upon which friendships and relationships were built. The desired element of surprise (which would ensure the memorability of the experience) recurred in the narratives. Dani Tsacheva spoke of women's friendly competition to stand out as the most imaginative, the most creative, to come up with unexpected new ways of cooking even a familiar dish. Many implicitly interpreted home cooking as a statement, a declaration of character, of what Fischler called the 'cook's concern for uniqueness'. Developing Rozin's idea of common 'flavour principles', existing in larger social groups, such as nations, Fischler highlighted that there were also culinary 'dialects', but most of all that within these broad culinary 'nations', individual cooks always strive 'to mark the irreducible maternal singularity' of their work (Fischler, 1988: 266).

Mostly starting their recipe collections without any other purpose than to reproduce a dish to their liking, many women gradually realized they have been constructing a record of their own private foodways, a piece of their family history. As Davis et al. (2014: 81) highlighted, the amendments and annotations, the handwritten marginalia, the very use of scrapbooks makes them materialize, and symbolizes cooking knowledge and heritage that is shared within families.

Once the women understood their scrapbooks as capturing familial foodways and history, they quickly started interpreting them as heritage: an individuality, worthy to be handed over. Not all had developed such attitudes to their recipe collections, but Tamara Ganeva and Cathy Ivanova with their efforts to produce copies for their children, or Vanya Pinteva, who wrote a dedication to her grand-daughter on the head page: 'To Raya – the recipes of grandmother Vanya and great-grandmother Gergana, who both loved to cook tasty dishes' clearly had. Kristin Razsolkova said that whenever she moves, changes houses, 'this scrapbook is one of the first objects to take'.

A great many of the interviewed made statements, confirming that they saw their cooking as an activity which forged family traditions. Lyubka Georgieva explicitly said that she was trying 'to plant' in her children the 'necessity to prepare certain dishes for certain celebrations as a tradition, which is being transferred in the family. I would really, really like to make them do it'.

This striving to forge familial foodways with a distinguished profile was clearly related to the women's ideas of character and identity. Building an identity means constructing a self in a complex process of negotiation with yourself and the social environment. Building a cuisine with identity similarly means bringing into being a sophisticated construct, shaped at the point where the biological specifics of a palate meet an individual's character, as well as the material and immaterial context. The personal cuisine – that range of ingredients, techniques and recipes, the selection of which occurs where physiological preferences meet the 'soup' of the social strata – is an intriguing, rich indicator of social belonging. As a solidified expression of identity and taste, it bears all the complexities of these notions.

The long discussion in food studies over the formation of taste has resulted in a fine-grained understanding of it as physiological and subjective, but to a great extent socially 'kneaded' and determined (De Maret and Geyzen 2015, Milne 2013). As Scholliers wrote (2001: 4), 'diet and identity are not "given" or just "out there" ready to grab, but both are interpreted, adapted or rejected according to one's needs, means and intentions.' This complicated negotiation process is practically a quest for what seems to be a very central and rewarding element of the individual foodways or the construction and expression of identity, and most of the narrators gave indications of pursuing it in a dedicated way and finding satisfaction in it. Warde argued against the importance of food choices as self-determining. According to him food is one of the many ways, and a marginal one, to express identity (Warde 1997: 199–200). But the effort and passion which the narrators put into obtaining and adapting recipes, selecting and defining, and creating their cuisine suggests that at least in this cultural context food was to many quite an important indicator of identity – one, that could hardly be called marginal.

The process of recipe exchange and creation of scrapbooks captures particularly well the negotiation which took place in identity construction. The elements of selection, reworking, adding personal comments and touches, corrections and adaptations of the recipes, are all steps in the process of domestication of a recipe, in which biographies and characters are forged and come to the surface. The scrapbooks were an instrument, which helped women to stream part of the broader pool of familiar tastes into what was perceived as domestic, as home.

SEEING BINOMIALLY

The narratives of this identity construction often brought up negotiations with the ideological discourses that have taken place during the communist period. The private food practices and the identity, which they expressed, were often – consciously or not – seen in opposition to whatever was perceived to be the official ideology, and most of all the uniformity and constraints that it implied.

For example many women recalled their desire to escape the 'equalization', which they explicitly related to the communist period. The idea was succinctly expressed by Kristin Razsolkova who, talking with affection about the food culture, lost under communism, spoke appreciatively of the spirit of cooking before 1944 in Bulgaria. The cuisine 'was not made uniform, it was . . . It contained the desire to charm, to attract . . . To express something . . . And not to just feed someone and be done with it.'

The very fact that the communist cookery books were seen as a rigid and tedious 'matrix', which pushed women to seek the delights of gastronomy elsewhere, was a manifestation of a certain juxtaposition between the 'official' and the informal, which endorsed the scrapbooks as a primary instrument in the quest for 'something different'. 'This exchange [of recipes] grants opportunities to be creative, to try different things . . .,' said one of the women. The communication within the social network offered secure alternative knowledge. It granted those who wanted to walk the extra mile a chance to do so and build upon it.

The narratives suggest that within this safe haven women often saw possibilities for self- expression. Building up skills, individual style, identifying and defining the border of what they would construct to be the family cuisine, seems to have been one of the most satisfying household activities, and sometimes well beyond. Lakhtikova (2017: 118) observed that simply by starting her scrapbook, and even without actually using the collected recipes, her grandmother cultivated a self-image of 'a contemporary, fashionable woman, a socialite, who could master the art of entertaining'.

In his groundbreaking essay 'Food, Self and Identity', Fischler argued that cookery 'serves to tame the wild, threatening forces that inhabit nature and the universe' and this supports the process of incorporation of food, its transition from 'outside' to 'inside' (Fischler 1988: 264). Within this argument, the recipe could be seen as a phase in the process of taming the wild: a set of instructions on how to process it which encodes the idea of the final – identifiable and acceptable – shape of food. It is an act of intellectual incorporation, preceding the bodily one. In this regard the scrapbooks were one step further in the domestication of food, compared to the cookbooks: they were a next stage, a product of the personal taming and acceptance of the 'wild'.

As opposed to the 'strangeness' of the relatively unmanageable volume of information in a general cookery manual, these private collections of recipes carried the comfort of domesticity, which was the comfort of the familiar, of the tamed. To their authors this culinary advice – tasted, tried, associated with friends, with socializing within circles of intimacy – meant not only convenience, but comfort.

The domain of home cooking, so contested between contradictory variations of the ideological discourses and traditional practices, was certainly not safeguarded individually: it was secured on the one hand by the cracks in the unity and consistency of the ideological meta-discourse, but most of all by the social circles, which by intensively exchanging recipes for culinary delights were constantly reclaiming the right for pleasure.

However within this collective safeguarding there was a place left to construct individuality, express it and validate it socially. One of the dominant themes, when the narratives meandered towards the satisfaction gained from domestic cooking, was the possibility of personalizing the domestically prepared food, of imprinting personal individualities on it.

ELEVATING THE STATUS OF HOME COOKING: FROM CHORE TO ENTERTAINMENT

The recipe exchange had at least two immediate positive consequences on the private lives of women in communist Bulgaria. On the one hand it worked to increase the pleasure of eating: the process of selection, adaptation and often step-by-step improvement of recipes delivered more joy to the palate and increased women's satisfaction from their work, protecting them from failures and helping them forge better meals from the modest palette of ingredients.

On the other hand the practice worked to elevate the status of cooking experience. It allowed domestic cooks to see it as an entertainment, as an intellectual self-realization, in which they manifested creativity, knowledge, efficiency, intellectual capacity.

The narratives delivered plentiful evidence of how women sought to transform cooking into more than just a chore. With the help of their scrapbooks, they had elevated it to the status of a mind game, of creative, intellectual entertainment – even if they practised it each on a different level. Two particularly striking examples were given of cases when food was inspired by literature. Tamara Ganeva spoke of her acquaintances, an old 'bourgeois' family of Sofianites, who were voracious readers and occasionally sent recipes, which were somehow related to the books they devoured. Kristin Razsolkova said that she herself tried to cook after reading different works of fiction – Isabel Allende's novels or Laura Esquivel's *Like Water for Chocolate*, although the experiments which she recalled dated from after 1989.

In summary, the many recollections of creativity and mastery in the kitchen clearly highlight why and how home cooking remained a desirable activity, the positive sides of which outbalanced the toil. Its transformation into an entertainment, into a field of freedom for identity construction and realization, was crucial to ease the tension between the pressure of the old and persistent patriarchal model over women to cook, and their understanding of themselves as modern, free-willed individuals – creators, rather than slaves or servants of their families and of circumstances.

In this process the exchange of recipes was instrumental not only because it provided access to essential skills, recipes or information, but also because it validated women's achievements and was part of the arena of the realization of their success. The scrapbooks on the other hand provided a record of this realization. Often completely unintended, they gradually turned into records of women's pursuits of individuality and expression, as much as chronicles of feasts, family celebrations or social contacts – in other words they reflected a significant proportion of the modest pleasures which the grey communist reality had to offer.

PART FOUR

WHAT MADE SCRAPBOOKS INDISPENSABLE

'What interests the historian of everyday life', pondered Paul Leuilliot, 'is the invisible.' 'It's not that invisible', De Certeau (1998: 3) corrected him. Everyday life is that wide open gate between the tangible and the intangible (so Leuilliot and De Certeau were both right), and studying its history could mean to focus on one of the two, or, as in this case, continuously examine the flow between them: the material and its immaterial meanings.

Scrapbooks, after all, are material objects, consisting of paper, letters, marks, stains, doodles, drawings, colours, shapes, the significance of which, though, 'lies in the dark, to be discovered, and there it is that we call upon our imagination and memory of all we know and seek the hidden universe' in them, to use the beautiful words of Tymieniecka (2002: 6). Although scrapbooks' call to venture into Husserlianian contemplations is as good as irresistible, I will limit myself to pointing out two aspects of their 'invisibility'.

In the first place, scrapbooks are in certain ways invisible as objects. Things as ubiquitous as those related to domestic cooking, are often made unseen by their mundanity: like a word that is repeated until its meaning has become opaque. They tend to remain undistinguished by the hurried eye and mind, deemed unworthy of consideration in the shadow of high-brow issues.

Also the significance of the scrapbooks' material form remains eternally elusive. Being a private document, their content is less considerate of social conventions, – and hence their meanings are more difficult to identify. The memories, which they encode, are only accessible to their users, and so are some of the notes, which only make sense, supplemented with the skills, logic and experience of their creator. What hierarchies and meanings can be deciphered? What kind of hints have their continuous transformations and renegotiations left on the pages of an old notebook, a clutch of wallpaper or on the back of a letter envelope? How could they be read, reconstructed from these enigmatic documents?

This research unfolded four different aspects of the meanings that recipe exchange and scrapbooks held for women who ran households in late communist Bulgaria. **In summary,** from a structural point of view, it examined how women negotiated their foodways within the existing context of often conflicting discourses. It established that home cooking remained a key element of the idea of womanhood. This idea was not simply inherited, but retained in a negotiation with conflicting discourses and circumstances: while ideology, full employment and growing availability of affordable canteen food discouraged home cooking, the patriarchal social model and the faults of the communist modernization boosted it. Whenever women felt they were being impeded in cooking for their families, they began seeing this activity not only as a duty, but as a right, a privilege. The discourses, which disparaged domestic cooking, were perceived as a contestation of power and were always attributed to the 'others', whatever the definition of this category was in each particular case.

Relatively high prices, reproduced patriarchal order, lack of trust in quality, logistical hurdles, private taste, and the pleasure of cooking were all reasons not to use ready-made food, even when it was available. Canteens were perceived as a mostly accessible but undesirable source of cooked food, as a fallback way to feed the family. The scrapbooks on the other hand were used as an instrument to produce food which, besides nutrients, meant also social glue and fulfilment.

From an economic angle, this research offered an insight into how recipe exchange enhanced home cooking within the specific economic circumstances. A close look into how the narrators chose their sources of culinary information suggested that the scrapbooks were instruments to purposefully shape home cuisine in preferred directions. They were cultural, emotional and practical tools to cope with food necessities, using the limited range of products available. On the one hand they served as shortcuts in the women's daily cooking routine and helped them live through shortages. On the other they were also instrumental in giving the women access to affordable exuberance within the framework of a materially frugal world. Considered from such a perspective, the scrapbooks were both an instrument for and a record of the practice of affordable indulgence.

The recipe exchange and cooking were also seen as an instrument for social growth. They were used as social capital: they served to join social groups, consolidate families, secure a better place in social hierarchies, adapt to new cultural environments. The widespread practice of sharing was popular on the one hand because it functioned along the lines of the living understanding of communal life. On the other hand, sharing recipes was more rewarding than keeping them private. The combination of the two factors provided for the very pronounced, enhanced role of recipe exchange in late communist Bulgaria.

From an affective point of view, scrapbooks were instrumental in enhancing the bodily pleasures of eating, in entertaining the palate. They were also essential to women in transforming the toil of cooking into pleasure, self-expression and (self-) entertainment. With time they turned into a precious material trail, left in the meandering process of identity construction, beloved life-time calendars, in which even the imperfections were treasured, not unlike 'an old ragged teddy bear or doll' (Davis et al. 2014: 80).

The narrators found satisfaction and pleasure in home cooking, and especially in that part of it, where they were able to construct and reconfirm an identity of their own. They found the experience pleasurable on many levels, seeking, improving and proving their skills and enjoying the process itself, whenever they were able to turn it into an entertainment. They also found important and pleasurable the social bonding which surrounded it: the collection of recipes, as well as the sharing of culinary skills and knowledge, of recipes and self-prepared dishes. They found deep satisfaction in the recognition of the results.

The rich cluster of meanings, which home cooking had for them, was able to deliver a great variety of emotional rewards. Turning home cooking into an entertainment, into a field of identity construction and realization, was crucial to ease the tension between the gender roles, which the narrators were assigned by the old and persistent patriarchal model and by the circumstances, and their understanding of themselves as modern, free-willed women.

Bringing the different aspects together to gain insight into the social practice delivers a complex map, which could probably be outlined in many ways. I opted to visualize it via a diagram in the visual style of the scrapbooks.

In the centre of this analytical construction is the individual narrator. She is surrounded by her immediate social circle. The outer circle reflects more distant social layers, which were able to influence her directly or via the inner circle.

Figure 14 *The diagram reflects some of the ways in which the individual narrators remember interacting with their inner and outer social circles, while negotiating and shaping their foodways.*

The analysed material suggests that these three units interacted in a variety of ways to form the foodways of the individual. The diagram is naturally also a simplification and serves merely to highlight in a snapshot part of what was observed in the narratives.

The individual in the centre has her own needs, expressed in the narratives as being relevant to her practice of home cooking and recipe exchange: for example a need to position herself well socially, to gain recognition and authority, to be remembered, to stand out, to care for (feed) others and herself well, to be efficient, to express love, to bond, to consolidate the family, to excel, to learn, to create, to indulge, to preserve sentimentally and practically a valuable heritage, to be entertained, to be free, and eventually, among many other things, to express herself and be herself.

The inner social circle consists of people, perceived as 'own': family, friends, colleagues and role models. They interact directly with the individual, satisfy some of her needs, mentioned above, in exchange for her investment in home cooking and recipe exchange. For example by providing the favourite food for her family, the woman gains love, loyalty and trust from its members. By entertaining friends and cooking memorable meals for them, she receives back love and recognition. In the process of this exchange she creates and practices her identity. The unspoken social arrangement, assigning her the gender role, is expressed in expectations, which in turn are perceived (consciously or not) as pressure to invest further in the activity.

The outer circle is emotionally more distant from the individual: these could be the larger working collective, the different social institutions outside family, one of which is the state. The interactions with this layer are usually not direct, but mediated (by intermediators of the state-validated discourses). They can also involve the individual in various large social formats (meetings of the collective, manifestations etc.). The emotional bond is more distant and the potential for pressure, although still existent, is smaller. The influence is less direct, or the ability to pressurize depends on the extent to which the inner circle is prone to serve as its medium. Were the inner circle to accept the ideology, discouraging home cooking, it would have enhanced its influence and amplified the pressure of the state. But the narratives suggest that in communist Bulgaria, or at least in the social environment of the interviewed women, this was not the case. The early and enduring ideological pressure, discouraging women from cooking at home, remained in the outer strata. The inner circle was not receptive to it, and instead of boosting the message, it softened, even neutralized it. Even if the notion reached the narrators, it did not affect them enough to create in them any tension against outer pressure.

The outer strata, though, did affect the narrators profoundly: not by the means of ideology, but by defining the economic model, which changed the framework and the structure of the society. As a result all women of active age in the individual's inner circle, including herself, worked full-time. Here the generational memory of the inner strata played a role, creating tension between the individual and her obligations in the new framework. The notion of a previous social order, in which a woman had more time at her disposal to excel in her gender role, was opposing the modern model of a working woman with very limited hours, but similar responsibilities in the household.

COOKBOOKS VERSUS SCRAPBOOKS?

The diagram offers a possibility to visualize also the difference in the position of cookbooks and scrapbooks in the narrators' social interactions. The analysed material suggests that the communist cookbooks, with their more or less outspoken compliance with the ideology and their anonymous, 'restaurant-like' recipes, were perceived to belong to that outer stratum. The attitude to the magazine recipes seems to have been more ambivalent, since they sometimes were included as clipping in the scrapbooks (quite rarely among the narrators). The poll also shows that magazines had marginal importance compared to the scrapbooks and cookbooks as a written source. The scrapbooks, on the other hand, belonged to the inner space. They were produced mostly in interaction between the individual and her inner social circle and were increasingly individualized, customized, internalized, becoming a sort of emanation of the narrator's self-perception. This is both a reason and an explanation of why the women often gave priority to their scrapbooks, compared to cookbooks.

In fact, here is a good place to consider the possibility of a binary opposition between cookbooks and scrapbooks, which some of the narratives suggested. In Bulgaria, just like in Russia (Pirogovskaya 2017: 336), the two were experienced as distinctively different, and in both places women distinguished between the scrapbooks as 'own' and the cookbooks as 'theirs', i.e. representative of discourses, that were at least in a certain sense official, having passed through the scrutiny of state censorship. But on the other hand part of the contrast between scrapbooks and cookbooks originated from their radical differences as media: this research showed one of them featuring information coming from outside, and the other, information already processed, customized; food, that was already domesticated. These important contrasts, while clearly distinguishing scrapbooks from cookbooks, also suggest that the two are not entirely comparable. They are, instead, complementary. But while this could be very well the case in a context in which there are more cookbooks and the trust in them is greater, the complementarity was subdued in relation to the communist cookbooks, which were both scarce and a product of aggressive ideologies.

The narratives certainly suggest that the answer why women held on so much to their domestic cooking practices and recipe exchange is a complex one. One peek at the very core of it through the basics of psychology is helpful. As Katz (1960: 163) wrote, 'at the psychological level the reasons for holding or for changing attitudes are found in the functions they perform for the individual, specifically the functions of adjustment, ego defence, value expression, and knowledge'. Back at the centre of the diagram the needs, which the narrators mentioned being addressed by home cooking and recipe exchange, may indeed sound diverse. But in fact each of them could be identified as part of the three innate psychological needs, motivating humans: the need of competence, of autonomy and of relatedness (as defined by Deci and Ryan 2000: 27).

The striving to learn, to excel, to expand or preserve knowledge – which often stood behind the exchange of culinary experience and the desire to experiment, to explore – clearly built up the women's self-confidence in their **competence**. The process of recipe exchange not only enhanced this competence, but also displayed it, transformed it into a social gain. Continuously challenged by peers throughout the process of the exchange, the women felt pushed to develop their skills.

On the other hand, the exchange constructed bonds and ensured **relatedness** of the individuals within their group. So did the construction and preservation of the familial cuisine. Cooking and sharing food with the family and in the inner social circle was a realization of bonding via help and care, via outlining the borders of the group, in the sense defined by Bourdieu (2003: 70).

Finally, home cooking clearly also addressed the need for **autonomy**, providing a private space for creativity and individuality, for self-expression. This autonomy had a double value in the social framework, which was both patriarchal, i.e. favouring the masculine, and also collective, thus limiting the possibilities of actual autonomy in the public sphere.

Unlike many other fields, the authority of women in the kitchen was unchallenged within the family. One insight into the comfort which they found in this situation, is offered by their reluctance to ask for more involvement from their partners. An illustration of this is a research from 1970 (Ilieva 1970), enquiring where Bulgarian women themselves see the possible solutions for lessening their household work. Among married women, 70.7 per cent found it best for their working hours to be reduced. Only 3.2 per cent considered as advisable the increased involvement of their partners. Perhaps one could even reasonably ask if the variation of circumstances and discourses kept women in the kitchen more than it kept the men away from the kitchen.

Thus, in addition to being an economically sensible way for the narrators and their closest group to survive and sustain themselves on a daily basis, home cooking delivered a powerful combination of incentives. The knot of meanings which it provided, was unchallenged within the specific context, where the domains of professional activities and state-regulated socialization models did not address well any of these needs. The prescriptive nature of the state system limited heavily the individual autonomy, and the acknowledgement of competence through recognition of individual achievements was exceptionally rare, as the credit was given to the collective. Even when their professional competences were acknowledged, the benefits remained of marginal importance to other family members – while relatedness with partner and children remained a priority to the ones with professional circles.[1] In this hierarchy communist Bulgaria did

---

[1] Part of these observations was published in my 2019 article 'Home Cooking from a "Slavery" to a "Right". The Impact of State Socialist Feminism on Domestic Cooking Practices in Bulgaria' in *Food & History* Journal (Shkodrova 2019).

not differ from Western societies, where in the late 20th century, family relationships and love constituted 'central human fulfilment' (Taylor 1989: 293).

Thus home cooking provided a rare opportunity, in which the needs of autonomy, competence and relatedness were all answered at the same time, on the basis of interaction with and shared with the closest inner social circle.

One kind of motivation, that seems to be left out of an analytical construct, based on Deci and Ryan (2000), is the bodily pleasure. The pursuit of taste, however it is shaped, is also a pursuit for sensual satisfaction. But the issue of bodily pleasures was not discussed enough in the narratives and there is not enough material to explore it. Hence the source material does not challenge the psychological motivation theory enough. The fact that the women did not raise their own sensual pleasure from home cooking as an issue of importance, does not mean that it did not play a role (they named it as a motivation not to use canteen food, for example). It indicates rather that the dominant discourses assign it a minor role: in other words, that we are not used to accommodate enough the bodily aspects of our lives in our reasoning about our motivation and experiences. Not challenging these discourses could be considered a limitation of this research.

The complex relationship between women and home cooking, the elaborate map of meanings, which the interviewed invested as discussed above, could not be considered specific to the communist countries, or to Bulgaria in particular. Similar meanings can be found in most patriarchal or even post-patriarchal societies and many examples of this were given earlier. My research though, suggested that the recipe exchange in communist Bulgaria was perhaps excessive compared to other places in the Western world.

This could be explained with some specifics of the context. Although planned to be based on public catering, communist everyday life in reality boosted home meals – both the routine familial ones, and those for entertainment. While on the one hand people were pushed to change their lifestyle by urbanization and modernization, and while they achieved by the 1970s a certain economic stability, the state system was unable to fully and simultaneously build the infrastructure of production and services, which this lifestyle required. This situation confined modern families to old patterns of food supply.

The pressure/incentives to reform the patriarchal relations within the family were also not adequate to the ideological claims. The new, urban lifestyles had to be served through old practices. Apart from family survival, there was the issue of social entertainment. Home cooking played a particularly important role in the far-reaching arena of social relations. Urban lifestyle, which involved socializing in quite broad and multiple circles, was in place, and at the same time the main available arena for this socializing remained the private households. This provided for disproportional focus on domestic food preparation.

To reduce the pressure, which circumstances and discourses put on them, women took control of the process of home cooking. In other words, feeling unable to avoid it, they found ways to take the most out of it. Refusing to feel slaves in the process, many of them tried to transform it into pleasure, in a key, powerful social instrument. The networks of recipe exchange validated this elevated status of home cooking as entertainment.

COMMUNIST FOODWAYS AS AN ACT OF RESISTANCE

I started this research to find out to what extent (if any) resistance could be identified behind women's passionate recipe exchange under communism. The collected material suggested that at least some of the interviewed did see elements of their foodways as a micro-resistance and perceived some of their food-related activities as opposing the meta-discourse. They had even developed certain practices that only made sense as opposing the dominant state ideology and arrangements.

The research also unexpectedly identified micro-resistance, based on opposition not to the political ideas of the communist regime, but to the consequences of its modernization project, which resulted in the mass employment of women. Some of the interviewed resented the loss of the old lifestyle, which they perceived as superior, and saw as a privileged situation in which women had more time for the household.

From the point of view of some recent theories on how to conceptualize daily life under communism, these findings are controversial. Discussing similar expressions of non-compliance with the order intended by the communist regime – namely daily acts of escapism – Yurchak (2005: 156) argued that they 'should not be seen as spaces of authenticity and freedom that were clandestinely "carved out" from the spatial and temporal regimes imposed by the state.' He argued that instead of being exceptions, such acts were 'paradigmatic manifestations of how these regimes functioned during late socialism. The forms of existence of even the most esoteric milieus discussed earlier illustrate the principles that were central to the functioning of the late Soviet system, not being in opposition to it.'

While Yurchak is right to point out that binomial models of thinking are not nuanced enough to describe everyday life under communism, in this particular case his theory reaches the opposite extreme. Neither the frequency of such acts of alternative use of space and time – of taking freedom and expressing individuality where it was not expected by the ideology to be – nor the actual tolerance of the regimes towards them disqualifies them as acts of (micro-)defiance. Such frequently appearing acts can be interpreted as paradigmatic of how the communist regime functioned, but also how it malfunctioned. Essentially Yurchak's argument builds on the fact that for a period of time such practices were in a way internalized by the regime in the sense that they ventilated the pressure and helped it go on. Or that they were counted on to cover the gaps in the communist economy, for example. It is a matter of choice of seeing the period of late communism as a free-standing historical arrangement, or as a phase in the undoing of the state communist project. In any case though, the everyday actions in questions – acts of micro-resistance – were unavoidable from the point of view of the state, rather than purposefully created or sustained. More importantly, they were understood as non-compliant by their doers. In this research many interviewed testified how the sheer contradiction to what they thought to be the ideological meta-discourse was motivating some of their actions (for example collecting Western recipes, which were practically unusable).

Foucault asserted that 'Where there is power, there is resistance', pointing out that 'yet, or rather consequently, this resistance is never in a position of exteriority in relation to power' (1978: 95). Resistance is part of normality of any social order, and more explicitly so of the oppressive ones. Being part of normality though does not disqualify it in any way from being resistance, to be conceptualized as in opposition to what is perceived as meant, expected, demanded.

As Crewe (2007: 257) wrote on life in prison, '[t]he extensive space between open rebellion and absolute consent represents the normal reality of prison life, in which order prevails, but often tenuously and uneasily, based on a combination of forces.' Making a classification of the different types of response behaviour, he argued that 'The way these components are balanced and combined within an institution delimits the distinctive forms of compliance and resistance that result.'

Indeed, it is not the persistence of the acts, their rate of successful realization, but the conceptual background of their genesis that distinguishes them as (micro-) resistance or not. And as the collected narratives clearly suggested, the idea of pursuing practices, related to home cooking, as alternative to what was imposed, suggested, meant by the system, did exist among some of the narrators. Some narratives implied that not only practical, but also political notions were implicated in the negotiation of individual foodways, related to the use of time, the hierarchy of culinary information sources, the perception of freedom and stimulation of creativity in the kitchen. None of these acts was planned as subversive, but they were often understood as incompliance. In some examples, those who complied – in the sense used by Verdery (1996) – with the temporal allocations by the state, were also sometimes identified in the narratives as 'the others', 'the exception'. In other words, it is difficult to deny that the communist cooks, these silent, invisible heroes of our everyday life, were also (at least tacitly!) rebellious.

References

Primary Sources

'*202 рецепти за ястия от риба*' (202 Recipes for Fish Dishes). (1974), Sofia: Reklama.

'*250 изпитани рецепти*' (250 Tried and Tested Recipes). (1938), Burgas: Zhensko prosvetno druzhestvo 'Samosuznanie'.

Alexandrova, N. (1962), 'В отговор на читателско писмо' (In reponse to a reader's letter), *Zhenata dnes*, 8: 23.

Alexievich, S. (2013), *Secondhand Time*, London: Fitzcarraldo Editions.

Atanasov, G. and I. Masharov (1981), '*Млечна промишленост в България в миналото и днес*' (Dairy Industry in Bulgaria in the Past and Today), Sofia: Zemizdat.

Bakurdzhiev, N. and E. Konov, K. Penchev, H. Hadzhinikolov and S. Chortanova (1968), '*Безалкохолните и алкохолните питиета и сервирането им*' (Soft and Alcoholic Drinks and their Presentation), Sofia: Zemizdat.

BCP (Bulgarian Communist Party), (1954), *VI Конгрес на БКП* (VI Congress of BCP. Stenographic protocols), Sofia: Izdatelstvo na BKP.

BCP (Bulgarian Communist Party), (1973), *X Конгрес на БКП* (X Congress of the Bulgarian Communist Party: Elevating the Role of Women in the Construction of Developed Socialist Society), Sofia: Izdatelstvo na BKP.

Bulev, V. (1951), '*Технология на приготвянето на храната в къщи*" [Technology of domestic preparation of food], Sofia: Nauka i izkustvo.

Cholcheva, P. (1947), '*1000 изпитани рецепти за готвене*' (1,000 Tried and Tested Cooking Recipes), Sofia: Knigoizdatelstvo Hristo Cholchev.

Cholcheva, P. (1952), '*1000 изпитани рецепти за готвене*' (1,000 Tried and Tested Cooking Recipes), Sofia: Nauka i izkustvo.

Cholcheva, P. (1964), '*Съвременна готварска книга*' (Contemporary Cookbook), Sofia: State Military Publishing House.

Cholcheva, P. and A. Ruseva, eds. (1956), '*Книга за домакинята*' (The Housewife's Book), Sofia: Otechestven Front.

Cholcheva, P. and T. Kalaydzhieva (1969, 1972), '*Съвременна домашна кухня*' (Contemporary Domestic Cooking), Sofia: Technika.

Cholcheva, P., V. Angelova and M. Kalenderova (1967, 1970, 1977), '*Книга за всеки ден и всеки дом: Домакинска енциклопедия*' (Book for Every Day, for Every Home), Sofia: Technika.

Chortanova, S. (1976), '*Ястия от месни полуфабрикати и колбаси*' (Dishes with Semi-Prepared and Cured Meats), Sofia: Technika.

Chortanova, S. and N. Dzhelevov (1977), '*Нашата и световната кухня и рационалното хранене*' (Our Cuisine, World Cuisine and Rational Nutrition), Sofia: Meditsina I Fizkultura.

CSA (Central State Archive), (1957, 1968), *417-4-42*, 'Комитет на Българските жени. Масово-организационна дейност' (Committee of Bulgarian Women. Mass Organisational Activities), Sofia.

CSA (Central State Archive), (1969), *707-1-136*, 'Състояние и тенденции за развитие на потребителското търсене на кулинарни изделия' [State and trends in the development of consumers' demand of culinary produce]. Sofia: Center for market studies at the Ministry of domestic trade.

CSA (Central State Archive), (1972), *707-1-211*, 'Динамични норамтиви за задоволяване с хранителни и нехранителни стоки на единица население в различните функционални категории населени места до 1990 г.' (Dynamic Normatives for Supplies of Food and Non-Food Products Per Unit of Population in the Different Functional Categories of Populated Zones Until 1990), Coordination Group at the Ministry of Interior Trade and Services, Sofia.

CSA (Central State Archive), (1964–1972), *417-4-91*, 'Комитет на българските жени. Доклади, планове, информации, преценки и други по проведените курсове за повишаване на битовата култура в семейството' (Committee of Bulgarian Women), Sofia.

CSA (Central State Archive), (1973), *417-4-36*, 'Комитет на българските жени. Масово-организационна дейност' (Committee of the Bulgarian Women. Mass Organisational Activities), Sofia.

CSA (Central State Archive), (1974), *707-1-179*. 'Определяне на асортимента и структурата на стоковите запаси по типове супермаркети' (Assortment and structure of goods supplies, according to types of supermarkets), Sofia.

CSA (Central State Archive), (1976), *417-5-440*: Комитет на българските жени. Стенографски протокол от курса за обмяна на опит по политически и социално-битови въпроси с предстедателки на градските съвети на жените, състоял се на 1-17 декември 1976 г. (Committee of Bulgarian Women), Sofia.

Detrez, R. (2015) *Historical Dictionary of Bulgaria*. 3rd ed. Lanham: Scarecrow, 2006. Print. Historical Dictionaries of Europe 46.

Dimcheva, I. (1983), '*Какво да сготвим набързо*' (What To Cook in No Time), Sofia: Technika.

Dimitrov, N. (1971), 'Полуготово и недовършено' (Half-prepared and Unfinished), *Anteni*, 22 October 1971.

Dimova, E. (1964), 'Нова година удома' (New Year at Home), *Zhenata dnes*, December 1964, Issue 12.

Dinkova, M. (1971), 'Жената днес и утре' (Women Today and Tomorrow), *Zhenata dnes* May 1971, Issue 5.

Dinkova, M. (1980), '*Социален потрет на българската жена* ' (Social Portrait of the Bulgarian Woman), Sofia: Profizdat.

'*Domashna gotvarska kniga*' (Domestic Cookbook), (1895), Sofia: Bulgarski Almanah.

Duhteva, P. and D. Gerova (1973), '*Българката. Опит за портрет* " (The Bulgarian Woman. An Attempt at a Portrait), Sofia: Partizdat.

Enderlein, H. (1968), '*Домашно приготвяне на сладкиши*' (We Bake it Ourselves), Sofia: Technika.

Engels, F. (1975), '*Произход на семейството, частната собственост и държавата* ' (The Origin of the Family, Private Property, and the State), Sofia: Partizdat.

Fialova. Y. (1984), '*Кухнята на гастронома*' (The Gastronomer's Cuisine), Sofia: Meditsina i fizkultura.

Georgieva, I. and D. Moskova (1981), *'Жената в съвременното българско село '* (Women in the Contemporary Bulgarian Village), Sofia: BAN.

Gospodinov, G., ed. (2006), *'Аз живях социализма*' (I Lived Socialism), Plovdiv: Zhanet 45.

Hadzhinikolov, H. (1954), Abuse and Waste in Trade – a Social Evil, '*Социалистическа търговия*' *(Socialist Trade)* 4: 11–19.

Hadzhinikolov, H. (1970), 'Проблеми на централизацията и концентрацията на производството на общественото хранене в България' (Problems of the centralisation and concentration of production in public catering in Bulgaria). Institute for scientific Research in Trade and Public Catering. CSA (Central State Archive) *707-1-30*, Sofia.

Hadzhinikolov, H. (1983), '*Работническото столово хранене*' (Worker's Nutrition in Cantinas), Sofia: Profizdat.

Hristova, S. (1937), '*Календар по готварство*' (Cooking Calender). Sofia: Royal Court Printing House.

Hubenov, Y. (1968), '*Коктейли и други смесени напитки*' (Cocktails and Other Mixed Drinks). Sofia: Technika.

Ignatova, L. (1971), 'За да ни стига времето' (To Have Enough Time), *Zhenata dnes*, March 1971 (3): 18.

Ilieva, N. (1970), '*Икономически и социални проблеми на трудовата заетост на жените*' (Economic and Social Problems of Women's Employment), Sofia: Nauka i izkustvo.

Ilieva, N. (1983), '*Кулинарен спектър*' (Culinary Spectrum) Sofia: Zemizdat.

Ivanov, V. (2006), 'Храната, УБО и леля Димитринка' (The Food, UBO and Aunty Dimitrinka), in Gospodinov, G., ed., '*Аз живях социализма*' (I Lived Socialism), 325–326, Plovdiv: Zhanet 45.

Kanturski, G. (1968), '*Полезни съвети за домакинята*' (Useful Advice for the Housewife), Varna: Durzhavno izdatelstvo.

Kassurova, B. and S. Dimchevska (1933), '*Готварска книга*' (Cookbook), Sofia: Knipegraf.

Koleva, M. (1958), 'Спестени часове' (Hours Saved), *Zhenata dnes* 2: 8–9.

Kondova, S. and I. Dimcheva (1984), '*Какво да сготвя, когато мама я няма*' (What To Cook When Mum Isn't Home), Sofia: Technika.

Konstantinova, A. (1958), '*Нашата кухня*' (Our Kitchen), *Zhenata dnes*, 5: 16.

Kovachev, P. (2013), '240 000 активни борци се радват на привилегии през 1980' (240 000 Active Fighters Enjoyed Privileges in 1980). *24 Chasa. Available online:* https://www.24chasa.bg/Article/2290544 *(accessed 16 July 2019).*

Kovacheva, A., ed. (1966), '*Книга за домакинята*' (The Housewife's Book), 6th edition, Sofia: Otechestven front.

Lenin, V. I. (1966), *The Emancipation of Women; From the Writings of V.I.Lenin*. New York: International Publishers.

Lesichkov, Ts. (1970), Report from 19 September 1970 by Tseko Lesichkov, director of Reklama. *CSA (Central State Archive) 739-2-8:* 87.

Lyutov, A., C. Alexieva, R. Gocheva, N. Ilieva, K. Cholakova, L. Peeva, eds. (1977), '*Жената – труд и бит*' (The Woman – Labour and Lifestyle), Sofia: BAN.

Maleev, I. and N. Stanchev (1948), '*Храна и кухня: Ръководство за семейни и обществени столове*' (Food and cuisine: Manual for domestic kitchens and public canteens), Sofia: Lekopizdat.

Marinov, M. (1959), '*Домашно консервиране на месо и риба*' (Home Preservation of Meat and Fish), Sofia: Profizdat.

Metodieva, E. (1984), 'В тила на кулинарния магазин' (In the Back of the Culinary Shop), *Zhenata dnes*, 5: 23.

Mircheva, S. (1983), 'Опашката' (The Queue), *Sofia*, 1: 23.

Naydenov, I, and S. Chortanova (1955, 1967, 1971), *'Наша кухня'* (Our Cuisine), Sofia: Nauka i izkustvo.

Naydenov, I, and S. Chortanova (1953), *'Ръководство по обществено хранене'* (Public Catering Guide), Sofia: Nauka i izkustvo.

Obedineni domakinski spisania (1947), ('United Household Magazines'), 3.

Paneva, K. (1958), 'Ценна помощ за нашите трудещи се домакини' (Precious Help to Our Working Housewives), *Zhenata dnes*, 5: 17.

Petrov, A., M. Shatarov and D. Krustev (1983), *'Хранителната промишленост в България. Минало, настояще, бъдеще'* (Food Industry in Bulgaria. Past, Present and Future), Sofia: Technika.

Petrov, L., N. Dzhelepov at al. (1978), *'Българска национална кухня'* (Bulgarian National Cuisine), Sofia: Zemizdat.

Peykova, T. (1932), *'Любимите ядената на киноартистите'* (Favourite Dishes of the Movie Stars), Sofia: Ikonomia i domakinstdomashnvo.

Popova, D. (1984), 'Семейно на ресторант' (With the Family at a Restaurant), *Zhenata dnes*, 4: 18.

Saraliev, P. (1984), *'Готварска книга за мъже'* (A Cookbook for Men), Sofia: Zemizdat.

Shishkov, Georgi, and Stoil Vuchkov. (1959), 'Български национални ястия' (Bulgarian National Dishes), Sofia: Profizdat.

Slaveykov, P. (1870), *'Готварска книга или наставления за всякакви гостби според както ги правят в Цариград'* (Cookbook, or Instructions on Various Dishes, as They Are Prepared in Istanbul), Istanbul: Macedonia.

Smolnitska, S. (1983), *'Сладкарско изкуство'* (The Art of Pastry-Making), Sofia: Technika.

Smrikarov, D. J. (1874), *'Додатъци на Златния извор'* (Additions to the Golden Source), Belgrade: Knigopecatnica na Nikola Stefanovic.

Sotirov, N. (1959), *'Съвременна кухня'* (Contemorary Cuisine), Sofia: Technica.

Spasovska, L. (1974), 'Диктаторът Кухня' (The Dictator, Called Kitchen), *Zhenata dnes*, 9: 24.

Stoyanova, Y. (1978), 'Как да посрещнем гости' (How to Entertain Guests), *Zhenata dnes*, 4: 18.

Trifonova, L.D. (1954), *'Детска кухня'* (Cooking for Children), Sofia: Nauka i izkustvo.

Tsoncheva (1941), 'Грижи за българския дом' (Caring for the Bulgarian Home), *Mir*, 19 June 1941: 3.

Vassilev, T. (1966), 'Образът на съвременната жена' (The Image of The Contemporary Woman), *Zhenata dnes*, 1: 18.

Voynov, K. (1957), 'Фабрика за витамини' (A Factory for Vitamins), *Zhenata dnes*, 12: 5.

Vulcheva, R. (1981), "Потребителски стоки' (Consumer Goods), *Zhenata dnes*, 5:23

We Cook Well (1984) *'Ние готвим добре'*, transl. from German Wir kochen gut, Doseva Y., tr., Sofia: Meditsina i fizkultura.

Wheldon, R.H. (1914), *'Бъдещата храна'* (The Food of the Future), tr. A.N.A., Svishtov: Vuzrazhdane.

Yearly Statistics Book (1989, 1993), *'Статистически годишник'*, Sofia: Statistichesko izdatelstvo.

Zareva, D. (1988), *'Сезонна кухня'* (Seasonal Cuisine). Sofia: Medicina i fizkultura.

Zhenata dnes (1959), 'Какво ново ще предложи на купувачите лската и хранителна промишленост' (What novelties will the food industry and light industry offer to the consumer?), unsigned, *Zhenata dnes*, 4: 17.

Zhenata dnes (1967), 'Какво да приготвим за гостите' (What to prepare for our guests), unsigned, *Zhenata dnes*, 12: 19.

Zhenata dnes October (1969), 'The dining corner', unsigned, *Zhenata dnes*, October 1969, 10: 19.

Secondary Sources

Abrams, L. (2010), *Oral History Theory*, London: Routledge.
Albala, K. (2012), 'Cookbooks as Historical Documents', in Pilcher, J. M., ed., *The Oxford Handbook of Food History*, Oxford: Oxford University Press.
Appadurai, A. (1988), 'How to Make a National Cuisine: Cookbooks in Contemporary India', *Comparative Studies in Society and History* 30 (1) 3.
Ashcroft, B. (2001), *Post-Colonial Transformations*, London: Routledge.
Auslander, L. (1996), 'The Gendering of Consumer Practices in Nineteenth-Century France', in V. De Grazia (ed), *The Sex of Things*, 79–112, Berkeley, Los Angeles and London: University of California Press.
Avakian, V. A. (1997), *Through the Kitchen Window: Women Writers Explore the Intimate Meanings of Food and Cooking*, Boston: Beacon Press.
Avakian, V. A. and B. Haber, eds. (2005), *From Betty Crocker to Feminist Food Studies*, Amherst and Boston: University of Massachusetts Press.
Baločkaite, R. (2011), 'Pleasures of late socialism in Soviet Lithuania: Strategies of resistance and dissent', *Journal of Baltic Studies*, 42(3): 409–425.
Bateson, G. (1987), *Steps to an Ecology of Mind*, London: Jason Aronson Inc.
Bisschop, C. (2014a), 'Een verhaal van mensen en structuren. Interviewen over rurale organisaties' (A story about people and structures. Interviews on rural organisations), *Belgisch Tijdschrift voor filologie en geschiedenis*, 2014 (92): 671–688.
Bisschop, C. (2014b), *Leren luisteren. Een handleiding voor mondelinge 'geschiedenis van alledag'* (Learning to Listen. A Manual for Oral 'History of Everyday Life'), Centrum Agrarische Geschiedenis, Leuven: Colofon.
Bleyen, J. and L. Van Molle (2012), *Wat Is Mondelinge Geschiedenis?* (What is Oral History?), Leuven: ACCO.
Bourdieu, P. (2003), 'Социалният капитал' (The Social Capital), *Sociologicheski problemi* 1: 69–71.
Bower, A. L. (1997), 'Our Sisters' Recipes: Exploring 'Community' in a Community Cookbook', *Journal of Popular Culture*, 31(3): 137–151.
Boym, S. (1994), *Common Places*, Cambridge: Harvard University Press.
Boym, S. (2001), *The Future of Nostalgia*, New York: Basic Books.
Bren, P. (2010a), 'Women on the Verge of Desire: Women, Work, and Consumption in Socialist Czechoslovakia', in Crowley, D. and S. E. Reid, eds., *Pleasures in Socialism: Leisure and Luxury in the Eastern Bloc*, 177–95, Evanston: Northwestern University Press.
Bren, P. (2010b), *The Greengrocer and his TV. The Culture of Communism after the 1968 Prague Spring*, Ithaca: Cornell University Press.
Bren, P. and M. Neuburger, eds (2012), *Communism Unwrapped*, Oxford: Oxford University Press.
Brunnbauer, U. (2008), 'Making Bulgarians socialist: The Fatherland Front in communist Bulgaria, 1944–1989.' *East European Politics & Societies*, 22 (1): 44–79.
Buchli, V. (2000), *An Archeology of Socialism*, London: Bloomsbury Academic.
Buck-Morss, S. (2002), *Dreamworld and Catastrophe: The Passing of Mass Utopia in East and West*, Cambridge: MIT Press.

Bulgaria XX Vek Almanach (Bulgaria 20th Century: Almanac), (1999), Sofia: Trud.
Bundzhulov, A. (2003), 'Какво възниква на мястото на? Изкуствени стави и мрежи при социализма' (What comes in the place of...? 'Artificial joints' and networks under socialism), *Sociologicheski problemi*, 1-2: 87-105.
Buntman, F. L. (2003), *Robben Island and Prisoner Resistance to Apartheid*, Cambridge: Cambridge University Press.
Burt, R. S. (1982), *Toward a Structural Theory of Action*, New York: Academic Press.
Capatti, A. (1989), *Le Goût du nouveau: Origines de la modernité alimentaire* (The Taste of the New: Origins of Modern Food), Paris: Albin Michel.
Castillo, G. (2009), 'The American "Fat Kitchen" in Europe: Postwar Domestic Modernity and Marshall Plan Strategies for Enchantment', in Oldenziel, R. and K. Zachmann (eds), *Cold War Kitchen. Americanization, Technology, and European Users*, Boston: MIT Press.
Charles, N. and M. Kerr (1988), *Women, Food, and Families*, Manchester: Manchester University Press.
Charmaz, K. (2009), 'Shifting the Grounds. Constructivist Grounded Theory Methods', in Morse, J.M., P.N. Stern, J. Corbin, B. Bowers, A.R. Clarke and K. Charmaz eds, *Developing Grounded Theory. The Second Generation*, 127-54, Walnut Creek: Left Coast Press.
Clarke, A. E. (2009), 'From Grounded Theory to Situational Analysis', in Morse, J.M., P.N. Stern, J. Corbin, B. Bowers, A.R. Clarke and K. Charmaz eds, *Developing Grounded Theory. The Second Generation*, 194-233, Walnut Creek: Left Coast Press.
Corrin, C. (1992), *Superwomen and the double burden: women's experience of change in Central and Eastern Europe and the former Soviet Union*, London: Scarlet Press.
Counihan, C. (1984), 'Bread as World: Food Habits and Social Relations in Modernizing Sardinia', *Anthropological Quarterly*, 57 (2): 47-59.
Counihan, C. (1999), *The Anthropology of Food and Body: Gender, Meaning, and Power*, New York/London: Routledge.
Counihan, C. (2005), 'The Border as Barrier and Bridge: Food, Gender and Ethnicity in the San Luis Valley of Colorado', in Avakian, V.A. and B. Haber (eds), *From Betty Crocker to Feminist Food Studies*, Amherst and Boston: University of Massachusetts Press.
Cowan, R. S. (1987), 'Less Work for Mother?', *American Heritage* 38, no. 7 (October 1987).
Creed, G. (1998), *Domesticating Revolution. From Socialist Reform to Ambivalent Transition in a Bulgarian Village*, Pennsylvania: Penn State University Press.
Crewe, B. (2007), 'Power, Adaptation and Resistance in a Late-Modern Men's Prison', *British Journal of Criminology* 47 (2): 256-75.
Crowley, D. and S. E. Reid (2010), *Pleasures in Socialism*, Illinois: Northwestern University Press.
Dantec-Lowry, L. (2008), 'Reading Women's Lives in Cookbooks and Other Culinary Writings: A Critical Essay. *Revue Française D'études Américaines*', 116(2) 99-122.
Davis, H., B. Nansen, F. Vetere, T. Robertson, M. Brereton, J. Durick, and K. Vaisutis. (2014), 'Homemade Cookbooks: A Recipe for Sharing', 73-82, Proceedings of the 2014 Conference on Designing Interactive Systems. New York: Association for Computing MachineryVancouver, BC, Canada
De Certeau, M., L. Giard, and P. Mayol (1998), *The Practice of Everyday Life*. Vol. 2. Minneapolis: University of Minnesota Press.
De Grazia, V. (1996), 'Nationalising women', in De Grazia, ed., *The Sex of Things. Gender and Consumption in Historical Perspective*, 337-358, Berkeley, Los Angeles and London: University of California Press.

De Jaegher, H. (2016), 'A Dialogue on Interactive Brain Hypothesis', *Enso Seminar Series*, available online at https://youtu.be/h218JtQks4s (accessed 13 August 2016).

De Jaegher, H. and E. Di Paolo (2007), 'Participatory Sense-Making: An Enactive Approach to Social Cognition', *Phenomenology and the Cognitive Sciences*, 6 (4): 485–507.

De Maret, O., and A. Geyzen (2015), 'Tastes of Homes: Exploring Food and Place in Twentieth-Century Europe', *Food and Foodways*, 23 (1–2): 1–13.

Deci, E. L. and R. M. Ryan (2000), 'The "What" and "Why" of Goal Pursuits: Human Needs and the Self-Determination of Behaviour', *Psychological Inquiry*, 11(4): 227–68.

Detchev, S. (2010), 'Bulgarian, but not precisely Shopska. Over one of the culinary symbols', *Bulgarski Folklor*, 1: 125–140.

Detchev, S. (2019), 'From Istanbul to Sarajevo via Belgrade—A Bulgarian Cookbook of 1874', in Jianu, A. and V. Barbu (eds), *Earthly Delights*, 376–401, Leiden: Brill.

Deyanov, D. (2003), 'Society of networks and socioanalysis of the gift (Pierre Bourdieu and IVO MOŽNÝ)', *Sociologicheski problemi*, 1–2: 72–86.

Deyanov, D. (2006), 'The Economy of Shortage and the Network Revolution (Rethinking 1989)', *Sociologicheski problemi*, Special issue: 372–387.

Deyanova, L. (2003), 'The diary of Georgi Dimitrov and the places of memory', *Sociologicheski problemi*, 1–2: 196–207.

Deyanova, L. (2005), '1948. Символна еуфория, символен терор' (1948. Euphoria of symbols, terror of symbols), *Kultura i kritika*, 4, Varna: liternet, available online https://liternet.bg/publish14/l_deianova/1948.htmp (accessed 8 September 2020)

Dichev, I. (2005), '*Пространства на желанието, желание за пространство*' ('Spaces of Desire, Desire for Space'), Sofia: Iztok-Zapad.

Dillnbergerova, S. (2003), 'Industry, Business and Mass Media as Determining Factors in Nutrition in Slovakia', in Petranova L. and D.J. Oddy, eds, *The Diffusion of Food Culture in Europe from the Late Eighteen Century to the Present Day*, 277–81, Prague: Academia.

Dimova, M. (2005), 'Жената днес – 60 години суета' (Zhenata dnes – 60 Years of Vanity), Sega Daily, October 2005, republished online by *Zhenata dnes*. Available online: https://www.jenatadnes.com/mesta-neshta/quot-zhenata-dnes-quot-60-godini-sueta/ (accessed 16 July 2019).

Douglas, M. and B. Isherwood (1979), *The World of Goods: Towards an Anthropology of Consumption*, New York: Routledge.

Douglas, M. (1997), 'Deciphering a Meal', in Counihan C. and P. Van Esterik (eds), *Food and Culture - The Reader*, 36–54, New York: Routledge.

Dutta, M. (2008), *Communicating Health*, Cambridge: Polity Press.

Dutta-Bergman, M. (2004), 'The unheard voices of Santalis: Communicating about health from the margins of India', *Communication Theory*, 14: 237–63.

Eamon, W. (1994), *Science and the Secrets of Nature: Books of Secrets in Medieval and Early Modern Culture*, Princeton: Princeton University Press.

Einhorn, B. (1993), *Cinderella goes to market*, London: Verso.

Elenkov, I. (2008), *'Културният фронт'* (The Cultrual Front), Sofia: The Institute for Studies of the Recent Past.

Elenkov, I. (2011), 'Ideological Messages for Everyday Life of the 1960s through the Perspective and Memory of Little Things', *Sociologicheski problemi*, 3–4: 136–147.

Elenkov, I. (2015), 'The Union of Bulgarian Artists and the Image of Everyday Life in the First Half of the 1950s', *Sociologicheski problemi*, 1–2: 58–74.

Ferguson, P. (2004), *Accounting for Taste : The Triumph of French Cuisine*, Chicago: University of Chicago Press.

Ferguson, P. (2005), 'Eating Orders: Markets, Menus, and Meals', *The Journal of Modern History*, 77(3): 679–700.
Finn, J. E. (2011), 'The Perfect Recipe: Taste and Tyranny, Cooks and Citizens', *Food, Culture and Society*, 14(4): 503–524.
Fischler, C. (1988), 'Food, self and identity', *Social Science Information*, 27(2): 275–292.
Fleites-Lear, M. (2012), 'Mirrors in the Kitchen, The New Cuban Woman Cooks Revolutionarily', *Food, Culture and Society* 15 (2): 241–60.
Foucault, M. (1978), *The History of Sexuality*, Vol. 1: An Introduction, trans. Robert Hurley, New York: Pantheon.
Franc, M. (2003), *Řasy, nebo knedlíky?* (Seaweeds or dumplings?), Prague: Scriptorium.
Fukuyama, F. (1997), *'Доверие'* (Trust), Sofia: Riva.
Gavrilova, R. (1999),*'Колелото на живота'* (The Circle of Life), Sofia: Sofia University 'St. Kliment Ohridski Press.
Gavrilova, R. (2016), *'Семейната сцена'* (The Familial Stage), Sofia: Sofia University 'St. Kliment Ohridski Press.
Geist, E. (2012), 'Cooking Bolshevik: Anastas Mikoian and the Making of the Book about Delicious and Healthy Food', *The Russian Review*, 71 (2): 295–313.
Gell, A. (1992), *The Anthropology of Time*, Oxford: Berg.
Geyzen, A. (2018), *De Smaak Van Thuis* (The Taste of Home), Leuven: Leuven UP.
Ghodsee, K. (2014), 'Pressuring the Politburo: The Committee of the Bulgarian Women's Movement and State Socialist Feminism', *Slavic Review*, 73 (3): 538–62.
Giddens, A. (1984), *The Constitution of Society: Outline of the Theory of Structuration*, Berkeley: University of California Press.
Glushchenko, I. (2010),*'Общепит: Микоян и советская кухня'* (Obchstepit: Mikonyan and the Soviet Cuisine), Moskva: GU Visshaya Shkola Ekonomiki.
Goody, J. (1977), *The Domestication of the Savage Mind*, Cambridge: Cambridge University Press.
Grigorova, I. (2013), 'Introduction of Renault Automobile Production in Bulgaria – Successes and Failures', *Istoricheski pregled*, 1–2: 182–99.
Gronow, J. (2003), *Caviar with Champagne : Common Luxury and the Ideals of the Good Life in Stalin's Russia*, Oxford: Berg.
Gronow, J. and S. Zhuravlev (2011), 'The Book of Tasty and Healthy Food. The Establishment of the Soviet Haute Cuisine', in Strong, J. (ed), *Educated Tastes*, Lincoln: University of Nebraska Press.
Guentcheva, R. (2009), 'Mobile Objects: Corecom and the Selling of Western Goods in Socialist Bulgaria', *Etudes Balkaniques* 1: 3–28.
Gvion, L. (2015), 'The Changing Significance of Cooking and Meals for Kibbutz Women', *Food and Foodways*, 23(3): 163–185.
Halbwachs, M. (1976), *Les cadres sociaux de la mémoire (The Social Franewokrs of Memories)*, Berlin, New York: De Gruyter Mouton.
Haynes, D.E. and G. Prakash (1992), *Contesting Power: Resistance and Everyday Social Relations in South Asia*, Oakland: University of California Press.
Hristov, H. (2015), *'Империята на задграничните фирми: създаване, дейност и източване на дружествата с българско участие зад граница 1961–2007'* (The Empire of International Companies: creation, activity and depleting of trade companies with Bulgarian participation abroad 1961–2004), Sofia: Ciela.
Hristov, T. (2015),'Икономика на дефицита / арбитражна икономика' ('Shortage Economy' / Arbitrage Economy'), *Sociologicheski problemi*, 1–2: 92–110.

Inness, S. (2006), *Secret Ingredients: Race, Gender, and Class at the Dinner Table*, London: Palgrave.
Ivanov, M. (2011), 'Социалистическото благоденствие и консенсусът на лицемерието', ('Socialist Welfare State and the Consensus of Hypocrisy'), *Sociologicheski problemi*, 1–2: 235–256.
Julier, A. (2004), 'Entangled in our meals', *Food, Culture & Society*, 7(1): 13–21.
Jung, Y. (2009), 'From Canned Food to Canny Consumers', in Caldwell, M. (ed), *Food and Everyday Life in the Post Socialist World*, 29–55, Bloomington: Indiana University Press.
Katz, D. (1960), 'The Functional Approach to the Study of Attitudes', *Public Opinion Quarterly*, 24 (2): 163.
Keating, M. (2018), 'Power of Discourse: Cookbooks in the People's Republic of Poland', conference paper at the *Dublin Gastronomy Symposium*, 29–30 May 2018, available online https://www.semanticscholar.org/paper/Power-of-Discourse%3A-Cookbooks-in-the-People%27s-of-Keating/3b6111ff8570bc3f4238252294cfff9293165c2c?p2df.
Khare, R.S. (1976), *The Hindu Hearth and Home*, New Delhi: Vikas.
Kiradzhiev, S. (2010), '*София каквато беше, 1944–1989*' (Sofia as It Was, 1944–1989), Sofia: Gutenberg.
Kirshenblatt-Gimblett, B. (1997), 'The moral sublime: The Temple Emanuel Fair and Its Cookbook, Denver 1888', in Bower, ed., *Recipes for Reading*, 136–153, Amherst: University of Massachusetts Press.
Klumbyte, N. and G. Sharafutdinova, eds. (2013), *Soviet Society in the Era of Late Socialism, 1964–1985*, Lanham: Lexington Books.
Knezy, J. (2003), 'Innovations in Food Culture among the Rural Communities of Hungary, 1920–1970', in Petranova and Oddy (eds), *The Diffusion of Food Culture in Europe from the Late Eighteen Century to the Present Day*, 135–51, Prague: Academia.
Kniga o vkusnoi i zdorovoi pishche (The Book of Tasty and Healthy Food) (1939), Moscow: Pishchepromizdat.
Kotseva, T. and I. Todorova (1994), '*Българката – традиционни представи и променящи се реалности*' (The Bulgarian Woman: Traditional Ideas and Changing Realities), Pernik: Krakra.
Kurtz, C. (2014), *Working with Stories in Your Community or Organization: Participatory Narrative Inquiry*, Mountain View: Creative Commons.
Kundera, M. (1983), *The Book of Laughter and Forgetting*, London: Penguin Books.
Lagerspetz, O. (1998), *Trust: The Tacit Demand*, Dordrecht: Kluwer Academic Publishers.
Lakhtikova, A. (2017), 'Emancipation and Domesticity: Decoding Personal Manuscript Cookbooks from the Soviet Union', *Gastronomica*, 17 (4): 111–26.
Lakhtikova, A., A. Brintlinger, and I. Glushchenko, eds. (2019), *Seasoned Socialism: Gender and Food in Late Soviet Everyday Life*, Bloomington: Indiana University Press.
Lakhtikova, A. (2019), 'Professional Women Cooking: Soviet Manuscript Cookbooks, Social Networks, and Identity Building', in Lakhtikova A., A. Brintlinger, I. Glushchenko, (eds), *Seasoned Socialism. Gender & Food in Late Soviet Everyday Life*, Bloomington: Indiana University Press.
Lebow, K. (2013), *Unfinished Utopia: Nowa Huta, Stalinism, and Polish Society, 1949–56*, Ithaca: Cornell University Press.
Ledeneva, A. (1998), *Russia's Economy of Favors: Blat, Networking and Informal Exchange*, Cambridge: Cambridge University Press.
Legerski, E. M., and M. Cornwall (2010), 'Working-Class Job Loss, Gender, and the Negotiation of Household Labor', *Gender and Society*, 24(4): 447–474.

Leuilliot, P. (1977), Preface to G. Thuillier, *Pour une histoire du quotidien au XIXe siècle en Nivernais*. (For a history of everyday life in the 19th century in Nivernais), Paris and The Hague: Mouton-EHESS.
Leonardi, S. (1989), 'Recipes for Reading : Summer Pasta, Lobster à la Riseholme, and Key Lime Pie', *PMLA*, *104*(3): 340–347.
Lévi-Strauss, C. (1962), *The Savage Mind*, Chicago: University of Chicago Press.
Lévi-Strauss, C. (1969), *The Elementary Structures of Kinship*, Boston: Beacon (first ed. 1949).
Lilkov, V. and H. Hristov (2017), *'Бивши хора по класификациите на Държавна сигурност'* ('Former people', as classified by the State Security Services, Sofia: Ciela.
Lomnitz, L. A. (1988), 'Informational Exchange Networks in Formal Systems: A Theoretical Model', *American Anthropologist*, 90 (1): 42–55.
Lupton, D. (1996), *Food, the Body, and the Self*, London: Sage Publications.
Malinova, L. and R. Chernokozheva, eds. (2015), 'Вестник За Жената" (1921–1944). Ракурси Към Женското', Conference procedures from the Conference Vestnik za zhenata (1921–1944), held at the National library, Sofia, on 27 November 2015.
Markov, G. (1980), *'Задочни репортажи за България'* (In Absentia Reports about Bulgaria), Zurich: Georgi Markov Fund. Available online: https://chitanka.info/text/2898-zadochni-reportazhi-za-bylgarija (accessed 16 July 2019).
Massey, G., K. Hahn and D. Sekulić (1995), 'Women, Men, and the 'Second Shift' in Socialist Yugoslavia', *Gender and Society*, 9(3): 359–379.
McEvoy, K. (2000), *Paramilitary Imprisonment in Northern Ireland*, Oxford: Clarendon Press.
McKie, L. and R. Wood (1992), 'People's Sources of Recipes: Some Implications for an Understanding of Food-Related Behaviour', *British Food Journal*, 2: 12–19.
Meigs, A. (1997), 'Food as a cultural construction' Counihan C. and P. Van Esterik (eds), *Food and Culture – The Reader*, 95–106, New York: Routledge.
Miller, D. (1987), *Material Culture and Mass Consumption*, London: Blackwell.
Milne, R. (2013), 'Taste', in Jackson, P. (ed), *Food Words: Essays in Culinary Culture*, 214–221, London: Bloomsbury.
Mineva, M. (2003), 'Разкази и образи на социалистическото потребление' (Narratives and Images of Socialist Consumption (study of the visual construction of consumption culture in the 1960s in Bulgaria)), *Sociologicheski problemi*, 1–2: 143–165.
Miroiu, M. (2007), 'Communism Was a State Patriarchy, Not State Feminism', *Aspasia* 1 (1): 197–201.
Montanari, M. (1994), *The Culture of Food*, Oxford: Blackwell.
Možny, I. (2003), *'Защо така лесно . . . Някои семейни основания за нежната революция'* (Why so easy . . . A few family reasons for the Prague spring), Sofia: Iztok/Zapad.
Nenov, N. (2001), 'Рефлексии на народната култура във взаимоотношенията „град-село"' ('Reflections of folk culture in the relations between city and village'), in Goev, A. (ed), *'Народна култура на балканджиите'* (*The Folk Culture of Balkandzhii*), vol. 2, 49–52, Gabrovo: Architekturen complex Etura.
Nenov, N. (2006), 'Fearing the industrial city in biographies of migrants', *Annals of the Regional Historical Museum in Rousse*, v.10, Rousse: Historical Museum.
Nenov, N. (2013), 'Еротиконът на птицекомбината. Vita sexualis на социализма' ('The Eroticon of the Poultry Farm. Vita Sexualis of Communism'), *Yearly Edition of the Association for Anthropology, Ethnology and Folklore Ongle*, 145–167, Sofia: Ongal.
Neuhaus, J. (2003), *Manly Meals and Mom's Home Cooking: Cookbooks and Gender in Modern America*, Baltimore: Johns Hopkins University Press.

Nikolova, N. (1991), 'Политанатомия на модерния човек' ('Political Anatomy of the Modern Man'), *Kritika I Humanizum*, 3: 91–108.

Nikolova, N. (2011), 'Частно пространство при социализма?' (Private Space under Socialism?), *Sociologicheski problemi*, 3–4: 148–64.

Nikolova, N. (2015), 'Санитарната култура: тоалетни предизвикателства' ('Sanitary Culture: Toilet Challenges'), *Sociologicheski problemi*, 1–2: 191–206.

Nikolova, M. and K. Ghodsee (2015), 'Socialist Wallpaper: The Culture of Everyday Life and the Committee of the Bulgarian Women's Movement, 1968–1990', *Social Politics: International Studies in Gender, State & Society*, 22 (3)): 319–40.

Nilgen, N. (2020) 'Recipe for Compromise? The Negotiation of East German Foodways' In Shkodrova, A., P. Scholliers and Y. Segers, eds. *Food in 20th Century Communist Europe, Food&History*.

Notaker, H. (2008), 'Cookery and ideology in the Third Reich', *Food and History*, 6(1): 67–82.

Notaker, H. (2012), 'Printed Cookbooks: Food History, Book History, and Literature', *Food and History* 10(2): 131–59.

Nuss, S. A. (1980), 'The position of women in socialist and capitalist countries: A comparative study', *International Journal of Sociology of the Family*, 10: 1–13.

Oldenziel, R. and K. Zachmann, eds. (2009), *Cold War Kitchen. Americanization, Technology, and European Users*, Boston: The MIT Press.

Ore, T. E. (2011), 'Something from Nothing: Women, Space, and Resistance', *Gender and Society*, 25(6): 689–695.

Parys, N. (2013), 'Cooking up a culinary identity for Belgium', *Appetite*, 71: 218–231.

Pennell, S. (2004), 'Perfecting Practice? Women, Manuscript Recipes and Knowledge in Early Modern England', in Burke, V.E. and J. Gibson (eds), *Early Modern Women's Manuscript Writing: Selected Papers from the Trinity/Trent Colloquium*, Abingdon-on-Thames: Routledge.

Pesheva, R. (1962), "*Буржоазни остатъци в отношението към жената*' ('Bourgeois Remnants in Attitudes Towards Women'), Biblioteka za zhenata, Sofia: OF.

Petranova, L. (2003), 'Language, Patriotism and Cuisine: The Formation of the Czech National Culture in Central Europe', in Petranova and Oddy (eds), *The Diffusion of Food Culture in Europe from the Late Eighteen Century to the Present Day*, 167–79, Prague: Academia.

Petrov, A., M. Shatarov and D. Krustev (1983), „*Хранителната промишленост в България. Минало, настояще, бъдеще*' (The Food Industry of Bulgaria. Past, Presetn and Future), Sofia: Technica.

Petrova, D. (1993), 'The Winding Road to Emancipation in Bulgaria', in Funk, N. and M. Mueller (eds), *Gender, Politics and Post-Communism*, 22–29, New York: Routledge.

Pirogovskaya, M. (2017), 'Taste of Trust: Documenting Solidarity in Soviet Private Cookbooks, 1950–1980s', *Journal of Modern European History* 15 (3): 330–49.

Popova, G. (*330–49*), '*Тялото в оксимороните на социализма*' (The Body in the Oxymorons of Socialism), Sofia: Faber.

Portelli, A. (1997), *The Battle of Valle Guilia: Oral History and The Art of Dialogue*, Madison: University of Wisconsin Press.

Pozharliev, R. (2014), 'Сол и пипер' (Salt and Pepper), *Sociologicheski problemi*, 1–2: 311–325.

Reid, S. E. (2002), 'Cold War in the Kitchen : Gender and the De-Stalinization of Consumer Taste in the Soviet Union under Khrushchev', *Association for Slavic, East European, and Eurasian Studies Stable*, 61 (2): 211–52.

Régnier, F. (2003), 'Spicing Up the Imagination: Culinary Exoticism in France and Germany, 1930-1990'. *Food and Foodways*, 11 (4): 189-214.

Revel, J.-F. (1982) *Culture and Cuisine: A Journey through the history of food*, trans. H. R. Lane, Garden City: Doubleday.

Risman, B. J. (2004), 'Gender as a Social Structure: Theory Wrestling with Activism', *Gender and Society*, 18(4): 429-450.

Rozin, P. (2006), 'The Integration of biological, social, cultural and psychological influences on food choice', in Shepherd and Raats (eds), *The Psychology of Food Choice*, Guildford: University of Surrey.

Roth, K. (1997), 'Между модернизация и традиционализъм. Всекидневната култура на селото в Югоизточна Европа' ('Between modernisation and traditionalism. Everyday life in South-East Europe'), *Bulgarski folklor*, 3-4: 26-38.

Rubin, A. T. (2014), 'Resistance or friction: Understanding the significance of prisoners' secondary adjustments, *Theoretical Criminology*, 19(1):23-42, DOI: 10.1177/1362480614543320.

Sacks, M. P. (1977), *Unchanging times: A comparison of everyday life of Soviet working man and women between 1923 and 1966*, Belgrade: Printing Office of the SFRY.

Scarboro, C. (2012), *The Late Socialist Good Life in Bulgaria*, Lanham: Lexington Books.

Schachtel, E. (1982), 'On Memory and Childhood Amnesia', in U. Neisse (ed), *Memory Observed*, 189-200, San Francisco: W.H. Freeman.

Scholliers, P. (2001), *Food, Drink and Identity: Cooking, Eating and Drinking in Europe since the Middle Ages*, Oxford: Berg.

Scholliers, P. (2013), 'Food Recommendations in Domestic Education, Belgium 1890-1940', *Paedagogica Historica*, (6): 1-19.

Schudson, M. (1995), 'Dynamics of Distortion in Collective Memory', in Schacter, D. (ed) *Memory Distortion. How Minds, Brains and Societies Reconstruct the Past*, 346-64, London: Harvard University Press.

Scott, Erik R. (2012), 'Edible Ethnicity How Georgian Cuisine Conquered the Soviet Table', *Kritika: Explorations in Russian and Eurasian History*, 13(4): 831-58.

Scrinis, G. (2008), 'On the Ideology of Nutritionism', *Gastronomica*, 8 (1): 39-48.

Shkodrova, A. (2014), *'Соц гурме'* (Communist Gourmet), Plovdiv: Zhanet 45.

Shkodrova, A. (2018a), 'From Duty to Pleasure in the Cookbooks of Communist Bulgaria: Attitudes to Food in the Culinary Literature for Domestic Cooking Released by the State-Run Publishers between 1949 and 1989', *Food, Culture & Society*, 21 (4): 468-87.

Shkodrova, A. (2018b), 'Revisiting Coca-Cola's 'Accidental' Entry into Communist Europe', *Gastronomica*, 18 (2): 59-72.

Shkodrova, A. (2018c), 'Investigating the History of Meanings of a Dish. An Enactivist Approach to the Life of the Russian Salad in 20th Century Bulgaria', *Volkskunde*, 3: 343-64.

Shkodrova, A. (2019), 'Home Cooking from a "Slavery" to a "Right". The Impact of State Socialist Feminism on Domestic Cooking Practices in Bulgaria', *Food & History*, 16 (1): 117-139.

Sharpless, R. (2016), 'Cookbooks as Resources for Rural Research', *Agricultural History*, Spring 90: 195-209.

Short, F. (2006), *Kitchen Secrets: The Meaning of Cooking in Everyday Life*, Oxford: Berg.

Smith, S. and J. Watson (2010), *Reading Autobiography: A Guide for Interpreting Life Narratives*, Minnesota: University of Minnesota Press.

Smollett, E. W. (1989), 'The Economy of Jars: Kindred Relationships in Bulgaria - An Exploration', *Ethnologia Europaea*, 19: 125-140.

Stanoeva, E. (2015), 'The Organization of Socialist Trade in Bulgaria', *Sociologicheski Problemi*, 1-2: 111-33.
Stoykova, E. (2005), 'Ролево конструиране на образа на жената' (Construction of the women's role), in *Yearbook of Sofia University St Kliment Ohridski, Faculty of Filosophy*, 101-118, Sofia: Sofia University.
Sullivan, O. (2004), 'Changing Gender Practices within the Household: A Theoretical Perspective', *Gender and Society*, 18 (2): 207-22.
Supski, S. (2013), 'Aunty Sylvie's Sponge: Foodmaking, Cookbooks and Nostalgia', *Cultural Studies Review*, 19: 28-49
Szilágyi, M. (1997), 'Halételek, mint férfiételek' (Fish Dishes, Cooked by Men Away at Work), Romsics, I. and E. Kisbán (eds), *Á táplálkozáskultúra változatai a 18-20 században*, 167-182, Papers from the conference in Kalocsa, 24-26 October 1995.
Taylor C. (1989), *Sources of the Self: The Making of the Modern Identity*. Cambridge: Harvard University Press.
Tchalakov, I. (2003), 'Socialism as a society of networks and the problem of economic development', *Sociologicheski Problemi*, 1-2: 106-130.
The Concise Oxford Dictionary of Politics. 3rd edition (2009), Available online: http://www.oxfordreference.com/view/10.1093/acref/9780199207800.001.0001/acref-9780199207800 (accessed on 26 February 2017).
The Kitchen Sisters (2014), 'How Russia's Shared Kitchens Helped Shape Soviet Politics'. Transcript with photos. NY: NPR, 20 May 2014. Available online: https://www.npr.org/sections/thesalt/2014/05/20/314054405/how-russias-shared-kitchens-helped-shape-soviet-politics?t=1563306942935 (accessed 16 July 2019).
Theophano, J. (2002), *Eat My Words. Reading Women's Lives Through The Cookbooks They Wrote*, London: Palgrave Macmillan.
Tominc, A. (2015), 'Cooking on Slovene National Television during socialism: an overview of cooking programmes from 1960 to 1990', in *Druzboslovne Razprave*, *XXXI* (79): 27-44.
Tomlinson, A., ed. (1990), *Consumption, Identity and Style*, London: Routledge.
Tymieniecka, A.-T. (2002), *'The Visible and the Invisible in the Interplay between Philosophy, Literature and Reality'*, Analecta Husserliana: The Yearbook of Phenomenological Research 75, Dordrecht: Kluwer.
Utehin, I. (2001), '*Очерки коммунального быта*' (Studies of the Communal Lifestyle), Moscow: OGI, Available online: http://www.fedy-diary.ru/?page_id=4177 (accessed 17 July 2019).
Valentine, G. (1999), 'Eating in: home, consumption and identity', *Sociological Review*, 47(3): 491-524.
Vanhecke, N., and M. Eckert (2016), 'DEBAT. Doen vrouwen het zichzelf aan?' (Do women do this to themselves?), *De Standaard*, 2 June 2016. Available online: https://www.standaard.be/cnt/dmf20160601_02319289 (accessed 17 July 2019).
Velcheva, D. (2006), 'Сборник с готварски книги' (Collection of Cookbooks), in *Yearly Books of Sociology Department Students*, 49-65, Sofia: Sofia Univerity St. Kliment Ohridski Press
Verdery, K. (1996), *What Was Socialism and What Comes Next*, Princeton: Princeton University Press.
Virtual Museum of the Professional Highschool for Argicultural Farming 'Queen Yoanna' in Pazardzhik. Available online: http://www.pgss-pz.com/pgss/museum.php (accessed on 11 November 2016).
Vodenicharov, P. (1999), *Language, Sex and Power*, Blagoevgrad: BOASO.

Vogel, L. (2013), *Marxism and the Oppression of Women: Toward a Unitary Theory*, Leiden: BRILL.

Von Bremzen, A. (2013), *Mastering the Art of Soviet Cooking*, New York: Black Swan.

Warde, A. (1997), *Consumption, Food and Taste. Culinary Antinomies and Commodity Culture*, London: Sage Publications.

Warde, A. and L. Martens (2000), *Eating Out: Social Differentiation, Consumption and Pleasure*, Cambridge: Cambridge University Press.

Weiner, A. (1976), *Women of Value and Men of Renown*, Austin: University of Texas Press.

Weiskopf-Ball, E. (2013), 'Experiencing Reality through Cookbooks: How Cookbooks Shape and Reveal Our Identities', *M/C Journal*, 16 (3). Available online: http://journal.media-culture.org.au/index.php/mcjournal/article/view/650 (accessed on 20 December 2019).

Wheaton, B. (1998), 'Finding Real Life in Cookbooks: The Adventures of a Culinary Historian', *Humanities Research Group Working Paper 7*, Available online: http://hrgpapers.uwindsor.ca/ojs/leddy/index.php/ HRG/article/view/22/27> (accessed on 7 November 2016).

Young, M. (1971), *Fighting with Food*, Cambridge: Cambridge University Press.

Yılmaz, S., B. V.d. Putte, and P. A. J. Stevens (2017), 'Work–Family Conflict: Comparing the Experiences of Turkish and Native Belgian Women', *Community, Work & Family*, 3 August 2017: 1–18.

Yurchak, A. (2006), *Everything Was Forever, Until It Was No More*, Princeton: Princeton University Press.

Zlotnick, S. (1996), 'Domesticating Imperialism: Curry and Cookbooks in Victorian England', *Frontiers: A Journal of Women Studies* 16, 2/3: 51.

Znepolski, I. ed. (2011), '*НРБ от началото до края*' (People's Republic of Bulgaria From Beginning to End), Sofia: Ciela.

Index

agency under communism 8, 11–12, 146

Bateson, Gregory 12, 65, 89, 106, 112, 121, 147
binomial conceptualisation of communism 12–13, 114, 117, 129, 144, 159, 171
bourgeois heritage 11, 27, 29, 37, 48, 50, 93, 106, 109–12
Bulgarian cuisine 19, 62
Bulgarian Communist Party (BCP) 7, 19–20, 26, 36, 41–4, 50–1, 64, 107, 112, 115, 128–9

canning in Bulgaria
    industrial 26, 103, 125
    domestic 5, 27, 69, 72, 99, 125–6, 144
canteens, canteen food 21, 24–5, 37, 41, 63, 78, 91, 102–6, 122, 133, 137, 157, 164, 169
Cholchev, Hristo 20–1
Cholcheva, Penka 10, 21, 30, 33, 62, 75, 77, 78, 81, 94, 127
class (social) and food under communism 28, 40, 42, 92, 95–6, 107, 111, 134, 139–41, 146
Clementis, Vladimír 19
collectivism 28, 36, 116, 144, 147
commensality 35, 37, 114, 139, 144, 147
Committee of Bulgarian Women (CBW) 50–51
communist modernisation 19, 24, 27–9, 31–2, 34, 36, 39, 97, 102, 114, 117, 140, 164, 169, 171
connections (vruzki) 21, 25, 42, 44, 70, 134, 143, 145
consumption 11–12, 27–35, 38, 48, 64, 91, 105, 118, 123
cookbooks
    Soviet 9, 11
    Bulgarian, dating from before 1944 17, 19, 22–23, 39, 41, 47–8, 63
    Bulgarian, from the communist period 6, 21, 23, 32, 34–5, 38, 48, 50, 60–3, 70–1, 73, 75, 77–8, 80–3, 86
    manuscripts, early modern 10, 53
cooking classes 5, 17–18, 51–2
CORECOM (Comptoir de represntation et de commerce) 107–108
creativity in cooking 126, 142, 146, 150–1, 153–5, 157–9, 172
culinary shops 25, 122–3
Czechoslovakia 29, 32, 48–9, 110

diet 22, 32, 38, 47, 61, 62, 74, 86, 87, 105, 124, 136, 152, 158
domestication of recipes/food 85, 159–60

education for girls 17, 47
equipment *see* kitchen appliances
establishment (political), *see* classes (social)
everyday cooking and festive cooking 55, 98, 138, 154, 155

family life and foodways 135–7, 169
Fatherland's Front, FF (Otechestven front) 50–1
feminism, state-feminism 20, 28, 35, 38–42, 92, 102, 105, 165, 166
frugality 27, 30, 127–8, 138, 164

gender roles in the household 7, 37, 38–9, 41–2, 65, 92–3, 97–102, *see also* feminism, state-feminism
"generic cookbook" illusion 60, 70

home cooking 3, 65, 93–6, 101, 115–16, 166, 169
housewife (ideal) 9, 29, 35, 61, 115, 116, *see also* feminism, communist and gender roles in the kitchen

ideology in cookbooks 9, 22–3, 41, 50, 60, 62, 83, 111, 114–15, 167
industrialisation of food and cooking 2, 24–7, 31–2, 48, 122
innovation 31, 48, 49, 86, 127, 144, 153–5, 157–9

Khrushchev, Nikita 3, 10, 27, 31
kitchen (the physical space)
    communist 3. 6–7. 33, 69, 112–14
    Frankfurt 69
kitchen appliances 23, 31–2, 46, 47, 62–4, 75, 109, 152
the Kitchen debate 31
KOMSOMOL 3
Kundera, Milan 19

literacy 17, 59
luxury
    under Stalin 11
    in Eastern Europe 28–29
    in communist Bulgaria 47, 75, 111, 114, 115, 118, 124–5, 128, 131, 151

minorities 51–2, 57
money 43
Movement for New Socialist Material and Cultural Life 50

national socialism and state socialism 2, 9, 22, 41
nutrition, nutritionism 9, 22–3, 30, 34, 37, 48, 51, 61–2, 83, 110

oral history 54–7

participative sense-making 56
peer pressure 96, 115, 168
perestroika 2, 61, 65
pleasure in cooking 34, 50, 110, 138, 150, 152–5, 157–60
public kitchens 25

recipe exchange (highlights) 65, 85, 125, 141–3
    the technology of. 4–5, 34, 49, 78, 83, 151
    trust in the process of 83–5

resistance 52, 83, 171–2
    in everyday life, theory of 12, 45, 117–18
    through food 3, 7, 52, 153, 171–2
restaurants under communism 24–5, 95–6, 104–6, 114, 138–9, 167

scrapbooks
    Bulgarian 1, 5–6, 10, 53, 58–9, 66, 71, 80–3, 167–8
    Soviet 10–11, 83, 85, 122, 124, 167
    the structure of 72–4
shortages 21, 26, 32, 42–3, 46, 48, 65, 106, 121–4, 127, 153, 164
social ecology 65
social networks and recipe exchange 23, 54, 84, 138, 143, 145, 159
social power in/through food 49, 84–4, 96–7, 105, 136–7, 139–40, 142–3, 166, 168
Soviet Union 3, 9, 39–40, 52, 85, 111–12
State Security (Durzhavna sigurnost) 2, 7, 19

taste 2, 5, 19, 24, 51, 85, 87, 97, 102–103, 125, 145, 152, 154, 155, 158, 164, 169
time 42–5, 128–30
trade with foodstuffs 49
trust 10–11, 27, 56, 70–1, 76, 83–7, 97, 101, 103, 104, 110, 143, 152, 164, 166, 167

urban foodways 25–6, 36, 39, 47–9, 53–4, 58, 61, 69, 75, 94, 98–9, 123–4, 129, 133–5, 144, 169

Vysotski, Vladimir 3

the "West" 3, 12, 20–1, 28–9, 59, 61–2, 106–9, 172
The Woman Today, see *Zhenata dnes*.
women's magazines 17, 20, 50, 63–4, 97, see also *Zhenata dnes*.
women's societies 18

Zhelev, Zhelyu 2
Zhenata dnes 2, 20, 21, 24, 29–35, 37–8, 40–1, 46, 50, 63, 64, 92, 98, 104, 155
Zhivkov, Todor 19, 28, 41, 64, 95

www.ingramcontent.com/pod-product-compliance
Lightning Source LLC
Chambersburg PA
CBHW070639300426
44111CB00013B/2173